JAPANESE MODELS OF CONFLICT RESOLUTION

Japanese Studies
General Editor: Yoshio Sugimoto

JAPANESE MODELS OF CONFLICT RESOLUTION

Edited by
S. N. Eisenstadt and Eyal Ben-Ari

KEGAN PAUL INTERNATIONAL
London and New York

2119 4828 ✓

First published in 1990 by
Kegan Paul International Limited
PO Box 256, London WC1B 3SW, England

Distributed by
John Wiley & Sons Ltd
Southern Cross Trading Estate
1 Oldlands Way, Bognor Regis,
West Sussex, PO22 9SA, England

Routledge, Chapman & Hall Inc
29 West 35th Street
New York, NY 10001, USA

The Canterbury Press Pty Ltd
Unit 2, 71 Rushdale Street
Scoresby, Victoria 3179, Australia

© Kegan Paul International 1990

The publishers gratefully acknowledge the assistance of the Japan Foundation in
the publication of this volume.

Set in Times 10/12 pt.
by Columns of Reading

Printed in Great Britain by TJ Press Ltd

ISBN 0 7103 0342 4

British Library Cataloguing in Publication Data
Japanese models of conflict resolution.– (Japanese studies).
  1. Japan. Social conflict. Resolution
  I. Eisenstadt, S. N. (Shmuel Noah), *1923*– II. Ben – Ari, E. (Eyal), *1953*–
  III. Series
  303.6′0952

ISBN 0–7103–0342–4

US Library of Congress Cataloging in Publication Data
Applied for

Contents

Contents

Acknowledgements

This volume – and most of the essays presented within it – originated in an international seminar on 'Japanese Models of Conflict Resolution', held at the beginning of 1987. This seminar, which formed part of an ongoing programme on comparative civilizations at the Harry S. Truman Institute for the Advancement of Peace, also benefitted from the sponsorship of the Department of Sociology and Social Anthropology and the Department of East Asian Studies at the Hebrew University. We would like to take this opportunity to thank the staff of the Truman Institute for their help, and especially the Institute's chairman, Professor Ben-Ami Shillony, for his constant encouragement and support.

S. N. Eisenstadt and Eyal Ben-Ari (*Editors*)

The Contributors

MICHAEL ASHKENAZI
Michael Ashkenazi is a lecturer at the Department of Behavioral Sciences at Ben-Gurion University of the Negev, Israel. He has published several papers on Japanese religion, Japanese management practices, and Ethiopian immigrants to Israel. He has recently co-edited *Ethiopian Jews and Israel* (Transaction Books, 1987) and is currently co-writing a book (with Professor Alex Weingrod) which summarizes five years of work on the Ethiopian immigrant community in Israel.

HARUMI BEFU
Harumi Befu is a professor at the Department of Anthropology at Stanford University. He has published extensively on various aspects of Japanese society and culture. Some of his recent publications have appeared as articles in *Social Analysis*, *Rice University Studies* and *Senri Ethnological Studies* and as chapters in *Nihonjin no Zoto* (edited by M. Ito and Y. Kurita, Minerva, 1984) and *The Challenge of Japan's Internationalization* (edited by H. Mannari and H. Befu, Kodansha, 1983).

EYAL BEN-ARI
Eyal Ben-Ari is a lecturer at the Department of Sociology and Social Anthropology and a research fellow at the Harry S. Truman Institute at the Hebrew University of Jerusalem. He has written a number of articles about urban communities in Japan (published in *Administration and Society*, *Cambridge Anthropology* and *International Journal of Sociology of the Family*), and co-edited (with Brian Moeran and James Valentine) *Unwrapping Japan* (Manchester University Press).

The Contributors

SHMUEL N. EISENSTADT
Shmuel N. Eisenstadt is Rose Isaacs Professor of Sociology at the Department of Sociology and Social Anthropology at the Hebrew University of Jerusalem. Among the many books he has written are *Israeli Society* (Basic Books, 1967), *From Generation to Generation* (The Free Press, 1971), *Revolutions and the Transformation of Societies* (The Free Press, 1978) and (with A. Shahar) *Society, Culture and Urbanization* (Sage, 1987). Among the books he has recently edited are *Patterns of Modernity* (Francis Pinter, 1987), (with M. Abitbol and N. Chazan) *The Early State in African Perspective* (Brill, 1988) and (with I. Silber) *Knowledge and Society* (JAI Press, 1988).

EHUD HARARI
Ehud Harari is Associate Professor at the Departments of Political Science and East Asian Studies at the Hebrew University of Jerusalem and chairman of the Department of East Asian Studies. He has written *The Politics of Labor Legislation in Japan* (University of California Press, 1973) and *Policy Concertation in Japan* (Verlag Ute Schiller, 1986), as well as numerous chapters and articles on advisory bodies in the Japanese policy processes, industrial relations and labour policy and politics in Japan, and organizational problems in multinational corporations.

CHALMERS JOHNSON
Chalmers Johnson is Rohr Professor of Pacific International Relations in The Graduate School of International Relations and Pacific Studies at the San Diego campus of the University of California. He is the former Walter and Elise Haas Professor of Asian Studies at the University of California, Berkeley, and former chairman of Berkeley's Center for Chinese Studies and its Department of Political Science. He has written extensively on the subjects of East Asian political economy, revolution and social movements, including such books as *Peasant Nationalism and Communist Power*, *An Instance of Treason*, *Revolutionary Change*, *Conspiracy at Matsukawa*, *Autopsy of People's War*, *Japan's Public Policy Companies*, and *MITI and the Japanese Miracle*. He is a fellow of the American Academy of Arts and Sciences and a member of the Council on Foreign Relations.

MICHAEL SHALEV

Michael Shalev is a senior lecturer in the Departments of Political Science and Sociology and Social Anthropology at the Hebrew University of Jerusalem. He has published a number of articles dealing with the comparative analysis of labour movements and their consequences for public policy in the Western nations. A collection of essays by Shalev entitled *Labour and the Political Economy in Israel* is forthcoming from Oxford University Press.

BEN-AMI SHILLONY

Ben-Ami Shillony is a professor in the Department of East Asian Studies and chairman of the Harry S. Truman Research Institute for the Advancement of Peace of the Hebrew University of Jerusalem. His major publications include *Revolt in Japan* (Princeton University Press, 1973) and *Politics and Culture in Wartime Japan* (Oxford University Press, 1981). He has also published several books in Japanese.

Part One
INTRODUCTION

1 Contrasts and Comparisons in the Analysis of Conflict Management in Japan: An Introduction

E. Ben-Ari

This book forms part of the growing literature on aspects of conflict and conflict management in Japanese society (Koschmann, 1978; Moeran, 1984; Hendry, 1987, pp. 185–200). The explicit aim which has guided the volume's creation, however, has been to add a comparative perspective to this expanding stream of scholarly studies. In recent years a host of excellent works centring on conflict in Japan has appeared: for example, Najita and Koschmann's (1982) compilation of historical studies, Sugimoto's (1978) documentation of post-war strife, Mouer and Sugimoto's (1986) discussion about conflict in theories of Japanese society, or Krauss, Rohlen and Steinhoff's (1984) attempts to apply systematically existing theories of conflict to the Japanese case. This book, however, attempts to extend in another direction the growing social scientific recognition of the tensions and disaccords found in Japanese society.

In order to explore this direction, we arranged an international workshop which took place at the Harry S. Truman Research Institute for the Advancement of Peace in 1987. On the basis of papers presented at this workshop, we have assembled in this volume contributions which represent attempts to examine the theoretical usefulness of juxtaposing the Japanese case – or cases found within Japan – with other societies or social units. Along these lines, we have assembled studies rooted in a variety of disciplines – sociology, political science, economics, history, and anthropology – and utilizing an assortment of comparative, and contrastive, strategies.

S.N. Eisenstadt's 'Patterns of conflict and conflict resolution in Japan: some comparative indications' (Chapter 2) applies to the Japanese case two of the major analytical tools used in

3

comparative macro-sociology: a very wide-ranging consideration of historical examples, along with a powerful theoretical analysis of the chain of social causality which links these examples together. Thus, Eisenstadt not only relates different Japanese eras, institutions and relationships to each other (for example, feudalism, the Meiji Restoration, urban developments or post-industrial strife), he also goes on to show how the application of the comparative civilizational theory he has been developing in the last decades (Eisenstadt, 1967; 1986) in the Japanese context may illuminate a basic set of patterns which underlies these institutions and historical developments.

In this way, Eisenstadt shows not only how Japanese society as a whole can be taken as a unit of analysis and comparison, but also how the interweaving of certain structural and cultural dimensions of social action has influenced patterns of conflict (and its resolution) in Japan. He demonstrates how certain ideals of group harmony or of rights of benevolence (rooted as they are in basic Japanese conceptions of self, society and nature) have *not*, by means of some metaphysical mechanics of influence, guaranteed automatic compliance or lack of discord. Rather, he shows – in concrete historical cases – how these ideals have shaped the way in which social élites have behaved and been appraised, and through that how these ideals have shaped the more concrete patterns of conflict management in Japan.

Chalmers Johnson's 'The Japanese economy: a different kind of capitalism' (Chapter 3) commences from the following assumption: that in analysing Japan, there is a need to go beyond a reliance on some 'mystical' elements such as Japanese 'culture' or 'characteristics' towards a comparative analysis of economic and political institutions. Johnson's analysis, which uses concepts taken from what is essentially a theory of political economy, relies on what Scocpol and Somers (1980, p. 178) have characterized as a sort of contrast-of-contexts approach. Johnson makes use of the Japanese–American contrast in order to bring out the unique features of each case and to show how these features affect the workings of a whole set of capitalistic institutional arrangements. He is interested, however, not only in describing these individual institutions – such as the financial system, enterprise groups and lineages, deliberations councils, or labour relations – but also in showing how they function as part of one integrated system.

As he sees it, the social sciences have taken too long to recognize that, although Japan is an advanced capitalist society, its institutions of capitalism have been built up through industrial policies which differ fundamentally from those found in America. In other words, Japanese capitalism can be explained by the same economic or political theories as those that pertain to the West, but these theories are realized through different organizational arrangements. Accordingly, it is the special, complex patterning of these institutions which determines the existence and development of tensions and frictions. For instance, Johnson shows how the high degree of institutional innovation found in Japan has led to a relative lack of conflict, how the undoctrinaire borrowing of institutional arrangements channels conflict to matters of interest rather than principle, and the ways in which the legitimacy of administrative guidance or the prevalence of non-legalistic orientations shapes the outcomes of clashes and struggles.

Michael Shalev's 'Class conflict, corporatism and comparison: a Japanese enigma' (Chapter 4) examines a problem which stands between the economic and the political spheres, and which has commanded scholarly attention for more than a decade (Pempel and Tsunekawa, 1979). In Shalev's own words:

> Why is it that a society in which the labour movement has been almost continuously excluded from political power and where labour unions are weak, politicized and competitively divided, the political economy nevertheless generates outcomes characteristic of Sweden, Norway and Austria, countries in which class conflict is managed by 'corporatist' arrangements which emerged against a backdrop of political dominance by strong labour movements?

Among these outcomes, Shalev cites longterm full employment, a relatively equal distribution of income, and successful attempts (in the wake of the economic shocks of the early 1970s) at stabilization on the basis of sacrifices made by organized labour.

Utilizing a method akin to what Campbell and Stanley (1963) termed 'quasi-experiments', Shalev carefully moves back and forth between explanatory hypotheses about and comparisons of a number of national contexts, or order both to test the limits of state corporatist theory and to illuminate the Japanese case. On the basis of his analysis, Shalev argues that state corporatist theory does not, despite a number of previous attempts to do so, fit the case of Japan. Thus, for example, attempts that have been made to apply concepts derived from this theory – like talking about micro, company-based welfare corporatism (Dore, 1973) – have usually changed the original meaning of these concepts to such an extent as to seriously weaken their explanatory power. At the same time Shalev goes back to the 'Japanese enigma' and suggests that it may be accounted for in terms of alternative causalities. In other words, he indicates how the similar political and economic outcomes found in Japan and in a number of Western European countries may be explained through the workings of parallel but different causal chains.

Eyal Ben-Ari's contribution 'Ritual strikes, ceremonial slow-downs: some thoughts on the management of conflict in large Japanese enterprises' (Chapter 5) tackles a more limited set of phenomena than those analysed by Johnson and Shalev. The focus of this study are the strikes which are 'staged' periodically by the unions of the large enterprises. These protest actions are apparently held in order to stress the basic conflict between labour and management, but actually figure as an integral part of the process by which union–management cooperation is effected. Ben-Ari addresses two issues in respect of these staged strikes: their internal social dynamics, and their relations to the cultural reality and the social-structural constraints of the large firms.

Ben-Ari's thesis is that these actions should be seen as what Gluckman (1963) has termed 'rituals of rebellion': i.e. special rites which emphasize conflicts in certain ranges of relationships, yet which establish cohesion within the wider social order over a longer period of time. Wielding concepts developed in symbolic anthropology (Bateson, 1972; Turner, 1985), he expands this initial formulation to account not only for the type and levels of communications transmitted during these occasions, but also for their character as cultural performances: liminal constructs which are set apart from everyday relations, but which also allow the people participating in them to comment upon, explore and define the ties that bind them together.

Ben-Ami Shillony in his 'Victors without vanquished: a Japanese model of conflict resolution' (Chapter 6) is interested in elucidating how a certain code or ideal of behaviour is expressed consistently throughout Japanese history. Shillony's contention is that the ideal solution to clashes or hostilities in Japanese thought has not been a total victory for one side and a humiliating defeat for the other. Rather, the ideal has been one of an accommodation by which both winner and loser could co-exist without too much loss of face. Shillony, however, does not stop at an elucidation of the logic of this ideal and its expression in concrete historical instances. In ways similar to Ishida's (1961) earlier analysis, he illuminates how this model of conflict resolution is rooted in a set of basic religious and cultural orientations of the Japanese people.

Ehud Harari's contribution 'Resolving and managing policy conflict: advisory bodies' (Chapter 7) focuses on a relatively little studied yet theoretically important set of phenomena: the over 400 public advisory bodies that have been established in Japan. As Harari well points out, these organizations are of special significance for the study of conflict in Japan because of their unique structural characteristics. Public advisory bodies (of the statutory and non-statutory varieties) stand between such un-structured mechanisms for conflict management as informal talks on the one hand, and structured institutions explicitly formed for this aim, like the courts or Diet committees, on the other.

Harari begins his analysis by showing how special advisory bodies figure in all of the stages of policy conflict and in a variety of different roles: i.e. as mediators and conciliators, or as catalyzers and legitimators within the conflict process. He then goes on to compare the operation of these organizations in Japan with their performance in Western countries where no norm of consensus exists. This is done in order to highlight what aspects of such bodies are related to their organizational peculiarities and what aspects are related to the cultural background against which they function. Harari concludes with a careful specification of the variables – i.e. the conditions and processes – through which public advisory bodies may contribute 'positively' to the manage-ment or resolution of conflict and, no less importantly, how they may figure 'negatively' in the intensification of strife.

Harumi Befu's first contribution 'Conflict and non-Weberian bureaucracy in Japan' (Chapter 8) brings us back to the kind of problems raised by Eisenstadt in Chapter 2. Befu's aim is twofold: to revise Weber's seemingly universal theory of

7

bureaucracy and, through this revision, to contribute to a general theory of civilizations. He does this first by constructing (on the basis of a systematic application of exchange theory) an ideal type of Japanese bureaucracy; and then by contrasting this type with Weber's well-known formulations about what now appears to be an essentially Western bureaucracy (Gerth and Mills, 1958, pp. 59–60). In line with Weber's methodological approach, Befu is interested less in discussing concrete cases than in arranging certain elements of reality into logically precise conceptions – the ideal types – which can then be used in relation to any particular problem.

Befu's central contention is that, in contrast to Western theoretical expectations, generalized exchange and balanced exchange are compatible (i.e. can co-exist) within the framework of Japanese bureaucracy. He then goes on to explain how conflict in Japan is played out through two *analytically separate* aspects of this kind of bureaucratic organization: group orientation and binary (patron–client) commitment. In this way Befu exemplifies through the detailed analysis of a set of Japanese phenomena, Krauss, Rohlen and Steinhoff's (1984) caution in the introduction to their volume: that culture should be seen as part of the conflict process and not just as a policeman preventing conflict from happening.

The piece by Michael Ashkenazi, 'Religious conflict in a Japanese town: or is it?' (Chapter 9), is guided by a central question: what mechanisms (i.e. social relations and processes) work to defuse, limit or contain religious clashes in Japan? In answering this question Ashkenazi takes up Beidelman's (1970, pp. 510–1) older and Parkin's (1987) more recent arguments about the utility of intra-societal or intra-regional comparisons. Thus, by carefully juxtaposing a number of cases taken from a specific area where he did fieldwork, Ashkenazi describes and analyses these mechanisms of conflict management.

As the title to his contribution suggests, Ashkenazi's conclusion is that religious conflict in Japan usually functions as 'clothing' for other types of friction: for instance, inter-communal contentions over political, economic or status interests. Moreover, he usefully outlines a number of social arrangements which further limit religious conflict – and which bear import for conflict management in Japan in general: for instance, the ability to separate and to live with contradictory beliefs in the public and the private spheres (see also Ishida, 1984); the existence of cross-cutting ties which act to defuse struggles; or the avoidance of clear-cut winners and losers.

Harumi Befu's second chapter, 'Four models of Japanese society and their relevance to conflict' (Chapter 10), offers a fruitful approach by which to conclude the volume. In this piece Befu juxtaposes four models of Japanese society and then draws out the implications of each of these for understanding various aspects of conflict. He begins his analaysis by focusing on the group – sometimes termed consensus or harmony – model which for many years has been at the centre of controversies surrounding the social scientific analysis of Japanese society. He then goes on to elaborate and to give an empirical ex-emplification of three other models: stratification, exchange, and symbolic interaction. In focusing on these models – one developed in relation to Japan and three which have been elaborated elsewhere – Befu seeks to go beyond the formulations of such people as Krauss, Rohlen and Steinhoff (1984) who have applied models specifically devoted to the analysis of conflict to Japan. Befu, in contrast, applies a number of wider theories whose analytical power lies precisely in relating general social and cultural characteristics – and not necessarily those directly related to conflict – to the way tensions and struggles are structured and managed.

Befu ends his analysis on a note that is of significance to the social sciences as a whole. As he puts it, the four models he has outlined should not be seen as competing but rather as complementary: each fits its own 'niche' and is needed in order to explain different phenomena. Or, as Moeran (forthcoming), has recently put it, the rejection of theoretical absolutism – as, for example, in the propagation of a single model of Japanese society – recognizes that any characterization of Japan will inevitably be partial, requiring supplementation from other angles.

References

Bateson, G. (1972), *Steps to an Ecology of Mind*. New York, Ballentine.
Beidelman, T.O. (1970), 'Some sociological implications of culture' in

J.C. McKinney and E. Tiriyakian (eds.), *Theoretical Sociology*. New York, Appleton, pp. 499–527.

Campbell, D.T. and J.C. Stanley (1963), *Experimental and Quasi-Experimental Designs for Research*. Chicago, Rand McNally.

Dore, R. (1973), *British Factory, Japanese Factory*. London, George Allen.

Eisenstadt, S.N. (1967), *The Decline of Empires*. Englewood-Cliffs, Prentice-Hall.

Eisenstadt, S.N. (ed.) (1986), *The Origins and Diversity of Axial-Age Civilizations*. Albany, SUNY Press.

Gerth, H.H. and C.W. Mills (1958), *From Max Weber: Essays in Sociology*. New York, Oxford University Press.

Gluckman, M. (1963), *Order and Rebellion in Tribal Africa*. London, Coles and West.

Hendry, J. (1987), *Understanding Japanese Society*. London, Croom Helm.

Ishida, E. (1961), 'A culture of love and hate', *Japan Quarterly*, 8, pp. 394–402.

Ishida, T. (1984), 'Conflict and its accommodation: *Omote-ura* and *uchi-soto* relations' in E.S. Krauss *et al.* (eds.), *Conflict in Japan*. Honolulu, University of Hawaii Press, pp. 16–37.

Koschmann, J.V. (ed.) (1978), *Authority and the Individual in Japan: Citizen Protest in Historical Perspective*. Tokyo, University of Tokyo Press.

Krauss, E.S., T.P. Rohlen and P.G. Steinhoff (eds.) (1984), *Conflict in Japan*. Honolulu, University of Hawaii Press.

Moeran, B. (forthcoming), 'Introduction – Rapt discourses: Anthropology, Japanism and Japan' in E. Ben-Ari, B. Moeran and J. Valentine (eds.), *Unwrapping Japan*. Manchester, Manchester University Press.

Moeran, B. (1984), 'Individual, group and *seishin*: Japan's internal cultural debate', *Man*, 19(2), pp. 252–66.

Mouer, R.M. and Y. Sugimoto (1986), *Images of Japanese Society*. London, Kegan Paul International.

Najita, T. and J.V. Koschmann (eds.) (1982), *Conflict in Modern Japanese History*. Princeton, Princeton University Press.

Parkin, D. (1987), 'Comparison as the search for continuity' in L. Holy (ed.), *Comparative Anthropology*. Oxford, Blackwell, pp. 52–69.

Pempel, T.J. and K. Tsunekawa (1979), 'Corporatism without labor. The Japanese anomaly' in P.C. Schmitter and G. Lehmbruch (eds.), *Trends Toward Corporatist Intermediation*. Beverly Hills, Sage, pp. 231–70.

Skocpol, T. and M. Somers (1980), 'The uses of comparative history in macro-social inquiry', *Comparative Studies in Society and History*, 22(2), pp. 174–97.

Contrasts and comparisons in the analysis of conflict management

Sugimoto, Y. (1978), 'Quantitative characteristics of popular disturbances in post-occupation Japan (1952-1960)', *Journal of Asian Studies*, 37(2), pp. 273–91.
Turner, V. (1985), *On The Edge of the Bush*. Tucson, University of Arizona Press.

2 Patterns of Conflict and Conflict Resolution in Japan: Some Comparative Indications[1]

S. N. Eisenstadt

Conflict has recently surfaced as a major theme in studies of Japanese society, largely in reaction to the group (or harmony) model often attributed to Chie Nakane (1970), but which in fact goes further back and seems to have been prevalent in such studies for about two or three decades.

A survey of these studies and of the controversies they have engendered is beyond the scope of this chapter (see Mouer and Sugimoto, 1986). It is obvious that Japanese society was never without conflict. It is enough to peruse any book on Japanese history – ancient, medieval or modern – as well as the continuously expanding literature on conflict in Japanese society (Kraus, Rohlen and Steinhoff, 1984; Koschmann, 1978; Najita and Koschmann, 1982), to recognize the ubiquity of conflict in most periods of Japanese history and in different sectors of Japanese society. Yet, as the expanding literature on conflict in Japan attests, these conflicts had certain distinct characteristics in common, especially with respect to the definition of conflicts, the basic modes of conflict resolution, and the specific structural locations of conflicts found in different sectors of Japanese society.

The existence of specific definitions of conflicts, modes of their resolution, and their structural locations is not surprising. In Japan, as in any society, the problem with the analysis of conflict is not whether conflicts exist – basically a meaningless question – but how to explain their specific characteristics.

Is it due to some special cultural traits or traditions – an explanation often employed in the literature on Japan (a good analysis of these discussions can be found in Cole 1971, 1978) – or rather to some specific constellations of contingent historical and structural circumstances, as asserted by those scholars who do not accept the cultural explanations with respect to, for instance, the distinct characteristics of the Japanese patterns of industrial relations (see for discussion Cole, 1978; Cole and Karsh, 1968).

It seems to me, as in many other cases, that posing the question in such mutually exclusive and dichotomous terms is misplaced. The problem is not whether 'culture' or 'social structure' (or history) is the only explanation for specific institutional or behavioural patterns, but rather which are the processes through which cultural and structural dimensions of social action are interwoven in different social and historical settings, and how different modes of interweaving influence the specific patterns investigated.

A closer look at the abundant materials about conflict in Japan reveals a rather paradoxical picture of the place of ideals of harmony and group consensus in this context. The ideals are evident in the definitions of conflicts and of conflict resolution that have been prevalent in Japan: first, in the strong tendencies to minimize the legitimacy of direct, open confrontations; second, in the tendency to minimize the definition of differences of interests and opinions in terms of outright conflict or confrontation; and third, in the tendency to resolve many such differences in seemingly informal ways, based on presumptions of solidarity and harmony between the contestants (Smith, 1983, ch.2; Haley, 1982).

But the existence of such themes of harmony and consensus does not mean that they 'naturally' permeate all sectors of Japanese society, so as to minimize the development or expression of conflicts. Rather, as Upham (1986) in his recent analysis of law and social change in contemporary Japan has shown, and as has been illustrated in some studies of industrial conflict in Japan, such ideals of harmony, or of the benevolence of the rulers (Smith, 1984) (or of the 'bosses'), constitute models and symbols that are activated *in situations of sometimes very intensive conflict*, mainly by different groups of élites or of influentials, in order to bring about a certain mode of resolution, or even of suppression, of conflicts.

13

But this is not the whole story. These themes are also often used by the non-élite sectors, in situations of confrontations with the élites, and serve to justify demands made on the élites. This can perhaps best be seen if we look closely at the ideologies and symbols of protest and of rebellion, especially of peasant rebellion, which have been endemic in Japanese society.

A very common theme to be found in these ideologies and often seen also in other situations of protest and of confrontation is, to follow T. C. Smith's (1984) felicitious expression, the 'right to benevolence' of the leaders, élites and bosses. Such claims have often been connected with communitarian and millenarian orientations (Scheiner, 1978; Kelly, 1985; Walthall, 1986) but not, as in many European or Chinese rebellions, with strong utopian visions and strong class consciousness. Nor have such protests or rebellions usually been closely linked with intellectual élites and secondary (samurai) groups.

These themes have also been very important in the development of industrial conflict in Japan (see also Garon, 1987). However much the picture of the 'benevolent' patterns of industrial relations in Japan has been exaggerated, there can be no doubt that, despite many attempts by various radical and militant groups, especially in the twenties and during the late forties and fifties, the more 'harmonious' company–union type of industrial relations has been the predominant mode of resolving industrial conflict in Japan.

Many scholars, even those who have emphasized the importance of conflict in Japanese society, have inquired about the possible relationship of the frequency of these themes to some cultural orientations or premises prevalent in large sectors of Japanese society in most periods of Japanese history.

Victor Koschman addresses this problem in his introduction to *Authority and the Individual in Japan* (Koschmann, 1978). His views are presented by Ellis Krauss (1981, pp. 165–80) as follows:

> Koschmann presents the view that Japan's early socio-political development and escape from foreign invasion provided no alternative examples of political authority such as Europe experienced, and resulted in authority being perceived as a 'given', 'as an inalienable part of the natural order' (pp. 6–7).

Thus, no philosophy of transcendence and negation developed as in the West, and little differentiation between the sacred and the profane. The sacred and the profane were seen rather as immanent in group life and the heads of group acquired the role of intermediaries between their group and the gods. . . . The givenness of authority and its association with higher, sacred ideals therefore made individuality and opposition in the name of a transcendent principle exceedingly difficult.

A second characteristic of Japanese authority patterns is their basis in 'soft rule' (giving rise to expressive protest) (p. 12). In the West, force was frequently used to subjugate populations, whereas in Japan the tendency was to rule through ideology and persuasion, by faith rather than fear. Under the hard rule of élites in the West, conflict came to be taken for granted and contract became the device developed to achieve cooperation under Japan's soft rule, conflict came to be denied in the name of group unity and conciliation was the preferred means of conflict resolution.

Soft rule and given authority usually have been resisted either by separating oneself from the community, 'retreatism', or by private dissent but outward obedience, 'ritualistic conformity' (pp. 20–1). Active forms of protest that have occurred tend to be of the expressive rather than instrumental kind. Expressive protest brings outward behavior in conformity with internal belief, but more for the sake of proving one's sincerity of commitment than for accomplishing a particular goal through rational, organized action. Thus only the release of frustration is attained by meaningful social change. Although Koschmann believes such patterns of authority and protest remain influential through contemporary times, he sees more recent forms of dissent like citizens' movements as possibly breaking the mold of the Japanese political ethos.

These themes, as analysed by T. Smith, Koschmann – possibly in a somewhat exaggerated way, and often from a Western perspective – and many others (see Lebra and Lebra, 1986), are related to some of the basic cultural orientations that can be identified as predominant in most periods of Japanese history and in most sectors of Japanese society.

From a broader comparative civilizational perspective, the most important of these orientations have been: the relatively low level of tension between the transcendental and the mundane orders; a strong combination of this- and other-wordly orientations, together with a strong emphasis on delineation of realms of purity and of pollution and an emphasis on ritual activities as bridging between these realms; a strong commitment to the social and cosmic orders, extending from the family through various wider circles, in principle to the centre of the collectivity as a whole; a strong emphasis on group identity and on social contexts in general and on special combinations of vertical and horizontal loyalties, in particular as basic components of personal identity.

These orientations, and the concomitant themes of harmony, benevolence and the like, did not float in the air, generating the general ambience of Japanese society. They have been articulated by the major primary and secondary élites and counter-élites, and by different influentials prevalent in Japanese society and history, at least from the Kamakura period on. The orientations were closely related to some of the basic characteristics of these coalitions of élites and interwoven with the modes of control exercised by them.

The coalitions were composed of many different actors. The most important were the 'functional élites' – political, military, economic, and cultural–religious – as well as representatives of the family, village, feudal or regional – or, in modern times, different economic and bureaucratic sectors.

The common characteristic of these élites and of their major coalitions was their embedment in groups and settings (contexts) that were mainly defined in primordial, ascriptive, sacral and often hierarchical terms, and much less in terms of specialized functions or of universalistic criteria of social attributes.

The various specialized activities – economic, cultural or religious – were also often combined with strong achievement orientations (De Vos, 1985), but these were ultimately oriented in broader contextual settings imbued with strong solidary and expressive dimensions.

The structural characteristics of the major coalitions and counter-coalitions, and the cultural orientations and themes articulated by them, led to continuous recrystallization of the coalitions and to the crystallization of new alliances. Such alliances usually led to a reconstruction of primordial, sacral and interpersonal contextual orientations as criteria of membership

(Hamaguchi, 1985), but not to their transformation into more functionally specific or universalistic directions.

This tendency to define membership in coalitions in terms of some combination of primordial and sacral attributes and of achievement set within expressive solidary settings was closely interwoven with a strong predilection to the development of vertical, rather than horizontal, ties and loyalties, although it did not necessarily negate the existence and consciousness of horizontal divisions within Japanese society.

The characteristics of the major coalitions and counter-coalitions and the tendency to a continuous extension of membership in such coalitions beyond the nuclear family are indeed very close, though not entirely identical, to those of *ie* society or organization, as defined by Murakami, Sato and Kumon (Murakami, 1984) – the model of social organization they see as having been predominant in Japan since the early medieval period.

One of the important aspects of this model is that the members of different subgroups within any coalition were not granted autonomous access to the centres of power within them. Similarly, members of different sectors of Japanese society did not generally possess independent access to the collectivities in which they participated. The collectivities were themselves supervised by their hierarchical superiors – the Emperor or the Shogun.

In most sectors of Japanese society, social control was vested in the leaders of the respective communities, which were usually organized vertically. Although these vertical lines converged on the centre, access to the centre was based not on autonomous rights, but rather on the strong commitment to the groups and the broader societal settings, a commitment that the élites attempted to regulate and mobilize for their own aims, but which was also very often articulated in the demands made on the élites.

Linked to the characteristics of the coalitions and counter-coalitions prevalent in Japanese society was the relative weakness of autonomous cultural élites. True, many cultural actors – priests, monks, scholars, for example – participated in such coalitions; but, with very few exceptions, their participation was based on primordial and social attributes and on criteria of achievement and of social obligations according to which these coalitions were structured, and not on any distinct, autonomous criteria rooted in or related to the arenas of cultural specialization in which they were active. These arenas – cultural, religious, or literary – were themselves ultimately defined in primordial–sacral terms, notwithstanding the fact that many specialized activities developed within them.[2]

The combination of the basic cultural orientations, the characteristics of élites and coalitions (and their interaction with broader strata), connected as it was with the basic cultural orientations prevalent in Japanese societies and articulated by the major members of the coalitions and counter-coalitions that were predominant in most sectors of Japanese society, has also shaped some of the basic characteristics of institutional formations in most periods of Japanese history, as well as the strategies of action which were deemed appropriate within them, including the nature of conflicts and patterns of their resolution.

Some of the basic characteristics of the major institutional formations can perhaps best be analysed by their comparison with those in Western Europe, with which they have shared many common characteristics throughout their respective histories; although, in Japan, these formations were defined and regulated in different ways and according to different principles.

Thus, to give some illustrations, as Marc Bloch (1964) pointed out long ago, Japanese feudalism (Daus, 1976) never developed fully-fledged contractural relations between vassal and lord; Japanese vassals could have only one lord; fully autonomous Assemblies of Estates did not exist – the Emperor or Shogun never relied on consultation in the formal institutionalized way; and Japanese feudalism was much more centralized than the European version; there were at least two foci – Emperor and Shogun or Bakufu, even in many periods neither of them encompassed under his rule all the sectors of Japanese society.

Similarly, the Togukawa regime – while exhibiting, as T. Umesau (1964) and other scholars have shown, great similarities to European absolutist states – was not based on a definition of the 'state' and the public domain as being entirely different from the more 'private' or familial domain, and, instead of abolishing the feudal system, it superimposed strong centralist control on the feudal rule of the *daimyo* (Berry, 1986).

Again, while many of the Japanese rebellions had causes similar to those of peasant rebellions in the West (or in China), they never developed either strong utopian (as distinct from millenarist) orientations, or a strong class consciousness or linkage with intellectual élites and secondary (samurai) groups (Kelly, 1985; Walthall, 1986).

Similarly, the strong semi-autonomous and independent castle towns of pre-Togukawa and Togukawa-period cities never evolved – with the possible exception of Jansi – the conceptions and institutions of corporate urban autonomy and self-regulation (Eisenstadt and Shachar, 1987, ch.11).

Likewise, in contrast to Europe, Japanese social hierarchies placed less emphasis on horizontal and more on vertical lines as the basis for the organization of groups or strata, with autonomous access to the attributes of status and to the centre. Tendencies to horizontal organization were found in millenarian and populist organizations – and often erupted in the various rebellions – but not in more central institutional arenas.

The common denominator of all these arenas that were structurally similar to those of Western Europe was that they were not defined in terms that differentiated them sharply from those of other arenas. Instead they were defined in primordial, sacral or 'natural' terms and were seen as embedded in the overall societal contexts. They were regulated not by distinct autonomous, legal, bureaucratic or 'voluntary' associations – or by the market – but through various less formal arrangements and networks, usually embedded in various ascriptively defined social frameworks, even though the access to such frameworks was often attained by achievement and performance.

Concurrently, in Japan, there developed almost no distinction between the societal and cultural orders represented by the centre and those represented by the various types of collectivities on the periphery. A relatively close relationship evolved between the symbols of the centre and those of the peripheral groups, with the orientation of the centre constituting a basic component of the identity of most of these groups.

Accordingly, it is but natural that in structural–organizational terms the centres in pre-modern times in Japan showed some of the characteristics of various patrimonial systems, in which relatively little distinction existed between centre and periphery, and in which there was little permeation of the centre in the periphery or impingement by the periphery on the centre. In fact, however, the picture was much more complicated. In Japan – seemingly in common with some Axial civilizations, especially Europe – the centres continuously attempted to permeate the periphery, building to no small extent on the strong commitment to the centre. This permeation was, however, less oriented to the ideological restructuring of the periphery as in different imperial or feudal systems of Axial civilizations; rather, it focused on mobilizing the economic, political and military resources, as well as the loyalty and strong commitments of the different groups of the periphery to the centre, and it was based on the assumption of the basic symbolic identity between centre and periphery.

A basic institutional corollary of this specific mode of definition and structuring of major institutional arenas in Japanese society was that, in Japan, different institutional arenas were less separated than in other, structurally similar societies. The different sectors of society – be they feudal domains, companies or patterns of patron–client relations – were defined in some overarching contexts in interactional or primordial terms. The linkage between such arenas and markets has been very heavily dependent on various informal behaviour arrangements and networks, and much less on explicit, abstract, formal rules and perceived, functional frameworks.

One of the most important illustrations of this mode of definition of the major arenas of social interaction is the transformation or 'Japanization' of Confucianism and Buddhism, two of the major Axial civilizations (Eisenstadt, 1982, 1988). They expanded into Japan relatively early and were of crucial importance there. They were, however, transformed in ways that changed some of their most important Axial orientations and institutional implications.

On the institutional level, the transformation was manifest in the absence, in Japan, of the literati and the examination system (so important, even if in different ways, in China, Korea and Vietnam), as well as by the prevalence of a new type of Buddhist sectarianism characterized by strong group adherence with tendencies to hereditary transmission of leadership roles.

Some of the major premises or concepts of Confucianism and Buddhism were transformed in Japan. Here (following, for instance, Umehara, 1987 and Nakamura, 1964) we can note the transformation of transcendental orientations that stressed the chasm between the transcendental and mundane orders into a more 'immanentist' direction – as evident in the transformation of the conception of a chasm between culture and nature into a much stronger emphasis on the mutual embedment of the cultural and natural orders and on nature as a basic given. Such transformation had far-reaching impact on some of the basic premises and concepts of the social order – such as the Mandate of Heaven (Kemper, 1967), with its implication for the conception of authority and the accountability of rulers, as well as conceptions of community. Unlike in China, where in principle the Emperor, even if a sacral figure, was 'under' the Mandate of Heaven, the Emperor in Japan was sacred and seen as the embodiment of the sun and could not be held accountable to anybody. Only the Shoguns and other officials – in ways not clearly specified and only in periods of crises, as for instance at the end of the Tokugawa regime – could be held accountable.

Similarly, the transformation of Confucianism and Buddhism in Japan had far-reaching implications for the relations between the conception of the nation and the potentially broader religious or cultural (such as Buddhist or Confucian) communities. The strong universalistic orientations inherent in Buddhism, and more latent in Confucianism, were subdued and 'nativized' in Japan (Kitagawa, 1987, pp. ii, iii and iv). When Japan was defined as a divine nation, this meant a nation protected by the Gods, a chosen people in some sense, but not a nation carrying God's universal mission (Sonoda, 1987; Okada, 1987).

Yet, contrary to many non-Axial civilizations (for example, ancient Egypt, Assyria or Mesoamerica) – which, unlike Japan, were also pre-Axial civilizations – Japan evolved sophisticated intellectual, philosophical, ideological and religious discourses, as manifest, for instance, in the development of the intensive debates between different Neo-Confucian schools and schools expounding the so-called nativistic learning in the Tokugawa period.

The transformation of Confucianism and Buddhism in Japan represents the de-Axialization of Axial religions, not in the local or peripheral arenas or 'small traditions' of Axial societies, but in the Great Tradition of a 'total' society.

The transformation illustrates one of the major characteristics of Japanese history – the openness to outside influences and their 'domestication' or 'Japanization'. Throughout its history Japanese society has been characterized by its openness to outside influences, continuous internal change and innovation. This openness has often, and mistakenly, been designated as borrowing or imitation. Yet, as the transformation of Buddhism and Confucianism in Japan attests, this openness and incorporation of foreign influences were usually accompanied not just by the addition of local colour, but above all by their transformation according to the basic premises of Japanese civilization.

These modes of structuration of the major arenas of social interaction, connected as they were by the combination of the basic cultural orientations, the characteristics of élite and coalitions and their interaction with broader strata, greatly influenced also the definition of conflict and the modes of conflict resolution in most sectors of Japanese society.

The élites and their coalitions, as they emerged in different periods of Japanese history and in different sectors of Japanese society, attempted to mobilize the resources of the periphery and resolve social conflicts in the direction of the ideas of group harmony – as interpreted by them. Yet, obviously enough, they were not always successful in this. These specific definitions of institutional arenas as well as the modes of control exercised by the elites often generated distinct foci and loci of conflict.

Conflict tended to emerge in Japan between the hierarchical principles of any group represented by its designated (ascriptive or elected) leaders and the more egalitarian, horizontal tendencies within it. There was conflict between the concrete application of such principles and the interests of various subgroups within any broader setting – family, village group, or company. There was conflict between the internal solidarity and interests of any such group or company – defined mostly in terms of some hierarchical vertical order – and broader settings that necessarily extracted resources from the family or the village, or the workers in a factory, and there was conflict focused on specifying the exact locus of vertical networks and the mutual obligations of lower and higher echelons within them.

The very fact that so much in the structure and working of Japanese society depended on such multiple, often informal, contexts and vertical coalitions meant that when these broke down – or were not yet crystallized – intensive confrontations might emerge which could not be dealt with within the existing frameworks.

Just because the overt ideology of such obligations tended to stress mutual harmony and benevolence, and because the emphasis on harmony prevented readiness to admit that conflicts existed in situations of sharp confrontation, there were few institutional mechanisms to cope with such situations.

Indeed, whenever different vertical links were weakened, as, for instance, after the occupation, when the pinnacle of these links was removed from his former symbolic role (Ishida, 1984), when combined with the ideological emphasis on harmony and avoidance of conflicts could exacerbate the situations of confrontations and breakdown that develop in many situations of social change or upheavals.

These situations often spawned attempts to change some of the basic premises of the Japanese system, so that a combination of the communal–egalitarian themes – together with potentially more universalistic orientations – challenged the basis of vertical hierarchies.

Such developments took place in many of the peasant rebellions and popular uprisings both under the Tokugawa (Scheiner, 1978; Kelly, 1985) as well as in the early Meiji period. They developed in the first decade of the Meiji era before the crystallization of the Emperor system (Wray and Conroy, 1983, pp. iii and iv; Gluck, 1985), and later during the Taisho period (Wray and Conroy, 1983, p. vii), when attempts were made to undermine the 'Emperor system' and establish some type of liberal democracy.

The most important such development occurred immediately after World War II, when, under the impact of the loss of the war and the American occupation, many old institutions and institutional premises lost some of their legitimacy, and new directions of organizing social and political life opened out. During this period, a major upsurge of new forms of political and industrial organization took place, and the Socialist Party emerged as a potentially strong and innovative force (see, for instance, Garon, 1987).

In these situations, many different ideological and institutional options seemed available. Such options were often articulated by various groups of intellectuals, which could be defined as autonomous – and oppositionary. The same could be said of some Buddhist monks and Confucian scholars in different periods of Japanese history.

Yet, such confrontational situations and breakdowns did not lead – at least for any length of time – to the institutionalization of entirely new modes of conflict resolution – in more formalistic legal or universalistic directions – even if some institutions structured according to such criteria were adopted. Such openings and the more formal modes of conflict resolution expanded with the development of bureaucracy were usually 'closed up' relatively quickly by some old or new coalition or counter-coalition. Most of these coalitions were restructured according to recombinations of the primordial–sacral and ascriptive symbols and criteria and of achievement orientations embedded in solidary frameworks. The resolution of the conflicts that emerged in such situations tended to re-establish some of the vertical hierarchical principles, even if in new – often more formal – organizational or institutional configurations and with different ideological underpinnings and definitions. Horizontal or egalitarian solidary–communitarian orientations – often imbued with millenarian but only very rarely with utopian themes – were indeed evident in peasant rebellions, or, in modern times, in different protest movements, such as, for instance, the movements of citizens' rights (Huffman, 1983; Bowen, 1980). They constituted a reservoir of cultural themes and served as important components of collective actions, but they were not on the whole effective in changing the basic premises of Japanese society and the patterns of regulation of conflicts prevalent in it, although they constantly necessitated the reformulation of such premises.

In order to understand how most confrontational conflicts in situations of change – as well, of course, as the more 'routine' conflicts in more 'stable' situations – came to be resolved in the ways discussed above, it is necessary to consider in greater detail the modes of control exercised by different élites and counter-élites in most sectors of Japanese society and, above all, the place of coercion within them.

Coercion was employed by the élites in Japan, as in all other societies, in order to resolve conflicts in the direction most amenable to them. But different societies differ in the mode in which coercion is employed and interwoven with other means of social control. In most periods of Japanese history, even in those characterized by intensive internal strife and violent conflicts, the coercive measures employed by different élites were usually closely interwoven with other modes of social control. These modes taken together seem to have been much more prevalent in Japan than in other societies.

The processes of control employed by the élites at different levels of Japanese society continuously mobilized group commitments and the themes of harmony and common group or network obligations. These themes were related to the relatively strong degree of cohesion among the major social groups and relied heavily on strong vertical relations between different groups. Such cohesion and vertical relations, when reinforced by governmental policies – above all in the Togukawa period – led towards relatively far-reaching self-regulation and responsibility within many sectors of Japanese society. The control of such self-regulation was vested in (associated with 'honour', 'fierce family pride' and so on) the leaders, whether hereditary or elected, or collectivities – families, extended families, villages and towns, later of various 'modern' occupational groups and sectors, which were usually organized vertically. Although the vertical lines converged on the centre, access to the centre was based not on an autonomous approach of members of the group to it, but rather on a strong commitment to the authorities of the groups or networks.

This strong degree of commitment to the group or networks and to their solidarity enabled the leaders of these groups to enforce their self-made laws and impose sanctions on transgressive members. Yet at the same time such headmen or other middle-echelon intermediaries, or their modern equivalents, often became the focus of conflict and ambivalence, and were caught in the middle of confrontational situations.

Yet, the fact that very often such approaches by various leaders stressing the harmony–consensus theme found enough response from wider sectors of the population seems to indicate that they fell on receptive ears, i.e. that they evoked some resonance from some deep-seated orientations or predispositions among the members of many groups or sectors in Japanese society – orientations which were presumably inculcated through processes of socialization and education, and which were rooted in the basic conceptions of personality, self, social obligation, interaction and of nature, so abundantly analysed by many studies of Japanese behaviour (Lebra and Lebra, 1986; Hsu, 1975; R. Smith, 1983; Berque, 1986; Rohlen, 1987).

Such resonance, however, was not assured automatically. It depended on a certain responsiveness of the élites to the very themes they evoked and to the concomitant demands voiced by members of different groups in situations of conflict. This responsiveness of élites was manifest in the acceptance of many of the demands voiced by such groups in situations of conflict, and by the selective co-optation of members of such groups by the élites. Such acceptance and co-optation were usually effected in very specific ways. Demands were usually acceded to as long as the authorities or élites were left in charge, above all, of the right to define such demands and their legitimacy – and often after some of those who voiced these demands were punished.

The co-optation of various members of broader groups by existing élites was usually effected by activating vertical-hierarchical ties and appropriate 'contextual' orientations; at the same time, the structure of such ties tended under the impact of such co-optation to become more dispersed and diversified.

This mode of acceding to the demands of different groups and their co-optation into continuously expanding networks was usually connected with the expansion of the range of legitimate discourse, activities and life-styles of the major sectors of Japanese society.

Such patterns of co-optation were also reinforced by the tendency of the victors in any confrontation (as Ben-Ami Shillony shows in Chapter 6) to leave some living space to the losers, emphasizing their belonging to the same framework.

Thus it was in so far the employment of these types of social control that assured the relative – of course only relative – success of the élites in the effective mobilization of motivation, commitment and group loyalties of wider sectors of the population.

The mutual responsiveness of leaders, influentials and broader sectors, however unstable and fragile it might have been, was in its turn dependent on the extent to which the interaction between the élites or influentials and the broader sectors were interwoven, and was characterized by a certain type of process of social interchange.

The special characteristics of these processes in large sectors of Japanese society, analysed in this volume above all by Harumi Befu (Chapters 8 and 10) (see also Hamabata, 1986), does not lie, of course, in the nature of the resources – power, trust, prestige, information or instrumental resources – that are exchanged through them, but in the modes in which these resources are combined in them.

The special characteristic of this combination is the prevalence, in most patterns of exchange or social interaction, in the many sectors of Japanese society of a certain type of package deal in which solidarity, power and instrumental resources are continuously interwoven and organized in relatively enduring frameworks, oriented to longterm interaction. Unlike in many other, especially modern, societies, these different types of resources are not organized in separate ad-hoc discrete activities and distinct organizational frameworks which are then connected through such formal frameworks as legal agencies, bureaucracies or the impersonal market (see also Dore, 1983 and 1986; and, for these characteristics in the structure of the Tokugawa State, Berry, 1986).

The most crucial aspect of this combination is the continuous reconstruction and broadening of the range of trust in terms of the extension of primordial, sacral and ascriptive – and not transcendental – criteria, closely connected with an emphasis on achievement set within expressive and solidary settings defined in these terms. This reconstitution makes the extension of trust seem to flow naturally from one setting to another, from one context to another – and, seemingly, not questioned.

The prevalence of such a mode of interaction or exchange does not mean that no competition or conflicts develop between different groups in Japanese society. What it means is that competition is regulated in a distinct way and that even if confrontational situations develop out of such conflicts, it is the re-establishment of trust that often constitutes a major objective of the contestants.

This mode of exchange is closely linked to that of the structure of relations between the major dimensions of status – wealth, power and prestige – as they have developed in Japanese society. Of special importance here is the rather far-reaching limitation on the tendencies to congruence between these different dimensions of status, and the concomitant limitations on the degrees to which the respective resources – wealth, power and status – can be converted into one another.

This pattern of structuration of social status was already prominent in Japan in the early feudal system (Hall and Maas, 1974); it seems to have continued, despite continuous changes in the specific contents and organization of these arenas and markets, through most periods of Japanese history, up to the present-day industrial society.

A good illustration of these patterns of interaction is the special pattern of patron–client relations that has developed in Japan (Eisenstadt and Roniger, 1984, pp. 144–5).

> Clientelistic relations emphasize to an even greater degree than those found in other settings the combination of voluntary undertaking of such links with strong elements of inequality in hierarchical standing of the partners, and the recognition by the clients of the patrons' rights to control the avenues and terms of exchange and flow of resources. In the case of Japanese *oyabun-kobun* links, this even occurs in spite of actual changes in the market positions of the partners. In addition, through such relations, and as in other clientelistic ties, clients gain some measure of protection against the uncertainties of markets and of nature, and against the arbitrariness and demands of centre, groups, organizations or individuals.
>
> In spite of these similarities, however, and as against clientelistic relations found in Latin America, Southeast Asia or in the Mediterranean, by being involved in *oyabun-kobun* relations, Japanese 'clients' are not only granted a certain degree of security, of control over sources of uncertainty, of protection or of delegation of power, but also have certain obligations that are not typical of other patron–client relations.
>
> While in other clientelistic societies the reflection of the patron's 'social visibility' and power is sometimes used to enlarge the degree of low standing, Japanese clients are required to adhere to certain standards in performance of duties in wider frames. Not only are *kokata* requested, like their Latin American or Southeast Asian peers, to deliver resources and services, according to their patrons' wishes and priorities, but they are also accountable to the *oyabun* for responsible social behaviour in broader institutional spheres. The *oyabun* is expected to guide them as to the proper forms of behaviour in these areas, as institutions and people will address complaints to him on inadequate performance by his *kokata*. In other words, people attached to an *oyabun* feel less

free to indulge in individualistic behaviour and are expected to be more committed to the proper performance of duties, in which they will have a greater emotional involvement. In E. Goffman's formulations, they will be expected to be more tightly related to social situations and interactions. In addition, the *oyabun* is, in some sense, seen as responsible before people higher in the social hierarchy for the behaviour of his dependents, since he is supposed to guide and control them on responsible conduct, and their irresponsible acts may therefore endanger his own market position.

In addition, the *oyabun-kobun* links do not constitute a central organizing principle in articulating different levels of interaction and exchange in Japanese society, despite their strong binding hold on the individuals involved in these links. Accordingly, these Japanese relations have lacked the pyramidal tendency of Latin American or southern European clientelism, and the networks have remained dispersed and, as a rule, not integrated into wider chains. In relation thereto, the gaining of access to the centre and to the resources it commands does not appear to be a main motive for undertaking such relations in Japan, nor do these relations ensure such access.

The emergence of Japanese hierarchical links has been fostered and reinforced, to a great extent, by the widespread acceptance of certain cultural orientations, among which stand out the recognition of authority, commitment to it, and to the norms upheld by its strong emphasis on seniority, on harmony and on *giri* obligations, and the high value placed on filial piety and paternalism. It is therefore the *oyakata* who seem to invest time and resources in maintaining the *kokata*'s long-term commitment. This is done by renouncing in the short term the use of the differential ranking advantages they have, and by stressing the highly expressive content of the relationship, shaped around values of long-term recognition of paternalistic authority. This phrasing of the relations confers expressive gratification upon clients and an egalitarian aura, despite their hierarchical inequality.

It is in so far as the various élites and influentials in different sectors of Japanese society employ these various modes of social control, of responsiveness to the demands of various sectors and engage in the modes of exchange specified above, that they may be able to activate, among the members of such sectors, the responsiveness to the themes of harmony and consensus.

The continuous eruption of many severe confrontational situations in different sectors of Japanese society attest to the fact that very often the élites did not behave in these ways. At the same time, however, it is one of the most important aspects of Japanese history that, as we have seen, the outcome of most of such confrontational situations has been the reconstruction – often by some new élite groups or persons – of the primordial–sacral hierarchical criteria and some vertical–hierarchical arrangements – albeit usually in highly reformulated ways, broadening the scope of social activity; incorporating new ideological themes and sectors of society.

But even when successful, these modes of control, just like any other such modes, generate continuous tensions. Such tensions can be identified in various liminal, ritual and therapeutic situations – in all those interactions in which 'society reflects on itself'.

Some of these situations are analysed in this volume in chapters 5 and 9 by E. Ben-Ari and M. Ashkenazi. Their analysis, as that found in many other descriptions of such situations in Japanese society (see, for instance, Lebra and Lebra, 1986, p. iv) indicates that in all these situations, side-by-side with the articulation of the tensions generated, there is a continuous emphasis on symbolism of trust and its extension, on the conceptions of self as embedded in social nexus and on the obligations pursuant on these conceptions.

It is in such situations that, as E. Ben-Ari (1986) has put it, a meta-language of group – or, to use E. Hamaguchi's (1985) expression, of contextual – orientations is continuously promulgated and reinforced, thus both allowing the expression of the tensions as well as seemingly resolving them according to such principles.

The picture of conflict in Japanese society is thus very complex, but in principle it does not differ from conflict in other societies. Conflict is innate in Japanese society – as to any society; the major difference is in the location, definition and modes of resolution of conflict. These differences are related to the basic cultural orientations and institutional premises of Japanese society and the ways in which they are worked out in different concrete situations.

Within the framework of these orientations, the ideals of group harmony, rights to benevolence and so on constitute an important component that greatly influences the definition of conflicts and the modes of their resolution.

But these themes do not constitute a mechanism that inhibits automatically the development of conflicts. Rather, they constitute a reservoir of powerful themes that can be mobilized in situations of conflict, many of which have been frequently generated by institutional derivations of the specific premises of Japanese society – and in which confrontational attitudes and behaviour may become intense.

The success of the élites and influentials in activating these themes of harmony as components of modes of conflict resolution builds on very strong predispositions, rooted in the basic conceptions of self, society and nature inculcated through socialization, education and communication. But these conceptions do not assure, as it were, the automatic compliance of the different sectors of the society and the wishes of the élites.

Rather, these conceptions define the criteria of legitimation of élites; hence, on the one hand, they limit and direct the ways in which they exercise power, while, on the other hand, they influence the demands made on them. It is only in so far as the élites and influentials exercise their power accordingly and accede to the demands made on them – and sectors of Japanese society do engage in specific modes of interaction and exchange of ritual and liminal situations analysed above – that themes of harmony and consensus may become effective in a process of resolution of conflicts.

It is through such processes of interaction that the various components of the picture presented above – namely, the basic cultural orientations, the institutional premises, the symbols of harmony, and the structure of élites – are brought together. These processes tend to generate both special types of conflicts and the modes of their definition and resolution, as well as possible breakdowns of such resolutions.

It is also the combination of these various components that has generated strong dispositions to change in many sectors of Japanese society throughout Japanese history; at the same time, it assured that the outcomes of such changes were reconstructed according to the continuously reformulated basic premises of Japanese society.

It is such extension of trust defined in flexible primordial, sacral or traditional settings of interaction, closely connected with an emphasis on achievement set within expressive and solidary settings, that constitutes the very crux of these patterns of interaction.

Such coalescence between these different components is not automatic or generated by some metaphysical necessity. It is rather based on a series of elective affinities between these different components – the élites, groups and societies – that have been brought together in specific historical circumstances.

Once brought together, they generated processes that produce feedback among these components – a feedback that is not automatic, but rather is continuously reflexive and which may break down precisely because of this very reflexivity.

Notes

1 I am indebted to Harumi Befu, Peter Duus and Ben-Ami Shillony for their insightful comments on a draft version of this chapter.
2 The best illustration of the weakness of such actors is the Meiji Restoration, where no groups of this sort played an independent, firmative role.

References

Ben-Ari, E. (1986), 'A sports day in suburban Japan: leisure, artificial communities and the creation of local sentiments' in J. Hendry and J. Webber (eds.), *Interpreting Japanese Society: Anthropological Approaches*, JASO Occasional Papers, Number 5, pp. 211–26.

Berque, A. (1986), *Le Sauvage et l'Artifice – Les Japonais devant la Nature*. Paris, Gallimar.

Berry, M.E. (1986), 'Public peace and private attachment: the goals and conduct of power in early modern Japan', *Journal of Japanese Studies*, 12(1).

Bloch, M. (1964), *Feudal Society*. Chicago, University of Chicago Press, Vol. II, pp. 446–97.

Bowen, R. (1980), *Rebellion and Democracy in Meiji Japan*. Berkeley, University of California Press.

Cole, R.E. (1971), 'The theory of institutionalization: permanent employment and tradition in Japan', *Economic Development and Cultural Change*, 20(1), pp. 47–70.

Cole, R.E. (1978), 'The late-developed hypothesis: an evaluation of its relevance for Japanese employment patterns', *Journal of Japanese Studies*, 4(2), pp. 247–65.

Cole, R. and E. Karsh (1968), 'Industrialization and the convergence hypothesis', *Journal of Social Issues*, 24, pp. 45–64.

De Vos, G. (1985), 'Dimensions of self in Japanese culture' in J. Marsella, G. De Vos and F.L. Hsu (eds.), *Culture and Self – Asian and Western Perspectives*. New York and London, Tavistock Publications, pp. 141–85.

Dore, R.P. (1983), 'Goodwill and the spirit of market capitalism', *British Journal of Sociology*, 34(4),pp. 459–82.

Dore, R.P. (1986), *Flexible Rigidities*. Stanford, Stanford University Press.

Duus, C. (1976), *Feudalism in Japan*. New York, A. Knopf.

Eisenstadt, S.N. (1982), 'The axial age: the emergence of transcendental visions and the rise of clerics', *European Journal of Sociology*, 23(2), pp. 294–314.

Eisenstadt, S.N. (ed.) (1986), *The Origins and Diversity of Axial-Age Civilizations*. Albany, SUNY Press.

Eisenstadt, S.N. and L. Roniger (1984), *Patrons, Clients and Friends*. Cambridge, Cambridge University Press.

Eisenstadt, S.N. and A. Shachar (1987), *Society, Culture and Urbanization*. Beverley Hills and London, Sage Publications.

Garon, G. (1987), *The State and Labor in Modern Japan*. Berkeley, University of California Press.

Gluck, C. (1985), *Japan's Modern Myths: Ideology in the Late Meiji Period*. Princeton, Princeton University Press.

Haley, J.O. (1982), 'Sheathing the sword of justice in Japan – an essay on law without sanctions', *Journal of Japanese Studies*, 8(2), pp. 265–81.

Hall, J.W. and P.J. Mass (eds.) (1974), *Medieval Japan: Essays in Institutional History*. New Haven, Yale University Press.

Hamabata, M.H. (1986), 'Ethnographic boundaries, culture, class and sexuality in Tokyo', *Qualitative Sociology*, 8(4), pp. 354–71.

Hamaguchi, E. (1985), 'A contextual model of the Japanese: toward methodological innovation in Japan studies', *The Journal of Japanese Studies*, 2(2).

Hsu, L.K. (1975), *Iemoto – The Heart of Japan*. New York, Halsted Press.

Huffman, J.L. (1983), 'The popular rights debate – political or ideological' in H. Wray and H. Conroy (eds.), *Japan Examined – Perspectives on Modern Japanese History*. Honolulu, University of Hawaii Press, pp. 98–107.

Ishida, T. (1984), 'Non-confrontational strategies for management of interpersonal conflicts: Omote-Ura and Uchi-Soto relations' in E.S. Krauss, T.P. Rohlen and P. Steinhoff (eds.), *Conflict in Japan*. Honolulu, University of Hawaii Press, pp. 16–39.

Kelly, W.W. (1985), *Deference and Defiance in Nineteenth-Century Japan*. Princeton, Princeton University Press.

Kemper, U. (1967), *Arai Hakusaki und Seine Geschichts Auffassung*. Wiesbaden, Harvasovitz.

Kitagawa, J.M. (1987), *On Understanding Japanese Religion*. Princeton, Princeton University Press.

Koschmann, J.V. (ed.) (1978), *Authority and the Individual in Japan: Citizen Protest in Historical Perspective*. Tokyo, University of Tokyo Press.

Krauss, E.S. (1981) "Koschmann, ed.: Authority and the Individual in Japan", *Journal of Japanese Studies*, 2(2).

Krauss, E.S., T.P. Rohlen and P.G. Steinhoff (eds.) (1984), *Conflict in Japan*. Honolulu, University of Hawaii Press.

Lebra, T.S. and W.P. Lebra (1986), *Japanese Culture and Behaviour*. Honolulu, University of Hawaii Press.

Mouer, R. and Y. Sugimoto (1986), *Images of Japanese Society*. London and New York, Kegan Paul International.

Murakami, Y. (1984), 'The *Ie* society, as a pattern of civilization', *Journal of Japanese Studies*, 10(2), pp. 279–364.

Najita, T. and J.V. Koschman (eds.) (1982), *Conflict in Modern Japanese History*. Princeton, Princeton University Press.

Nakamura, H. (1964), *The Ways of Thinking of Eastern People: India – China – Tibet – Japan*. Honolulu, University of Hawaii Press.

Nakane, C. (1970), *Japanese Society*. London, Weidenfeld and Nicolson.

Okada, S. (1987), 'The development of state ritual in ancient Japan', *Acta Asiatica*, 51, pp. 22–41.

Rohlen, T.P. (1987), 'Social Order in Japanese Society – Questions and Observations Aimed at Developing an Approach to Adult Society that Benefits from Studies in Early Education'. Ms.

Scheiner, I. (1978), 'Benevolent lords and honorable peasants: rebellion and peasant consciousness in Tokugawa Japan' in T. Najita and I. Scheiner (eds.), *Japanese Thought in the Tokugawa Period*. Chicago, University of Chicago Press.

Smith, R. (1983), *Japanese Society – Tradition, Self and the Social Order*. Cambridge, Cambridge University Press.

Smith, T.C. (1984), 'The right to benevolence: Dignity and Japanese workers, 1890-1920', *Comparative Studies in Society and History,* 26, pp. 587–613.

Sonoda, M. (1987), 'The religious situation in Japan in relation to Shinto', *Acta Asiatica,* 51, pp. 1–21.

Umehara, T. (1987), 'Shinto and Buddhism in Japanese culture', *The Japan Foundation Newsletter,* 15(1), pp. 1–7.

Umesao, T. (1984), *La Formation de la Civilisation Modern au Japon et son Evolution.* Leçons Données au College de France.

Upham, F.K. (1986), *Law and Social Change in Postwar Japan.* Cambridge, Mass., Harvard University Press.

Walthall, A. (1986), *Social Protest and Popular Culture in Eighteenth-Century Japan.* Tucson, University of Arizona Press.

Wray, H. and H. Conroy (eds.) (1983), *Japan Examined – Perspectives on Modern Japanese History.* Honolulu, University of Hawaii Press.

Part Two
INSTITUTIONAL FORMATION AND
CONFLICT RESOLUTION IN THE
ECONOMIC SPHERE

3 The Japanese Economy: A Different Kind of Capitalism

Ch. Johnson

To talk about the economic challenge of Japan has become almost trite. We have all become familiar with the growing body of literature devoted to detailing various aspects of Japan's economic achievements: Japan has the world's highest rates of personal savings; it has tranquil and almost strike-free labour relations; its rates of unemployment are at least five points under those of other advanced industrial democracies; it is, today, the world's leading creditor nation, with net capital exports during 1986 of $131 billion; it has an enviable reputation for high quality and price competitive manufactured goods; it is the world's preferred supplier of automobiles and consumer electronics; and the list goes on and on.[1] What is perhaps less well known is how utterly controversial and even ideological the *explanation* of Japan's economic performance has become, particularly among Japan's competitors, and above all in the United States.

Mainstream neo-classical economists in the United States are, with a very few exceptions, unanimous in arguing that the Japanese 'challenge' is really not a challenge. They maintain that the Japanese achievements are merely the result of 'getting the prices rights', while other nations are getting them wrong. And to raise the idea that Japan may have invented a different *kind* of capitalism is to risk being accused both of committing an economic heresy and of taking the first step down the political road to serfdom. As Robert Kuttner puts it (1985, p. 82), 'Economics knows only that Japanese economic planning didn't help, because it couldn't have, *a priori*.'

Perhaps I can illustrate this growing controversy with a few personal anecdotes. My experiences as a writer on Japan's economic performance are neither exceptional nor unusually unpleasant; I discuss my own case simply because it is the one I know best. More than fifteen years ago, in 1972, I began doing research in Tokyo on the Japanese Ministry of International Trade and Industry, or MITI as it is commonly known, investigating above all MITI's role as the 'pilot agency' that had guided Japan's post-war economic reconstruction and growth. MITI is the most important policy-making agency within the Japanese economic bureaucracy, and it is the main governmental centre for the formulation and execution of industrial policy. In 1982, I published a book entitled *MITI and the Japanese Miracle* on the history of MITI and Japan's long experience with industrial policy and the conscious change of industrial structure. The book was quite well received in East Asia. A group of young MITI bureaucrats even undertook to translate it into Japanese, and today the ministry itself assigns my book to newly hired officials so they can learn about their ministry's glorious past. (Incidentally, I made a point of never visiting the ministry until after writing my book, in order to avoid charges that I was biased.) My book was also translated into Korean and Chinese. But in the United States, the reviews were, as they say, 'mixed'.

An editor of *Fortune* magazine (Sept.6, 1982) initially took the view that the book contained an important message. 'In Johnson's view the critical element in the process [that is, "Japan's emergence as a great economic power"] has been the collaboration between the government and business, which are bonded together in what he calls a "state-guided market system" dedicated to rapid growth.' That is indeed what my research revealed, and I suggested that Japanese capitalism displayed a configuration quite different from that in the United States. I called it the 'capitalist developmental state'.

However, a year later, one David R. Henderson, an economist attached to the president's Council of Economic Advisers, wrote (also in *Fortune*, Aug.8, 1983):

> In his favourable review of Chalmers Johnson's *MITI and the Japanese Miracle*, Robert Lubar, a member of *Fortune*'s board of editors, accepted Johnson's view that Japan's post-war success is largely due to MITI's central planning. Many American business executives and politicians go further, urging the US government to follow the example of 'Japan Inc.' and subsidize industries it thinks will succeed. They are wrong. The

idea that central planning is responsible for Japan's success is a
myth. MITI has made no contribution to many of Japan's
biggest industrial successes. What's more, it isn't that powerful.
The real explanation for the Japanese economic miracle is the
country's *laissez-faire* policies on taxes, anti-trust, banking, and
labour. Japan teaches a lesson not about the value of economic
planning, but about the vitality of the free market.

Mr Henderson is exceptionally careless – neither the term nor
the idea of central planning ever appears in my book – and he
gives us not the slightest evidence of why he should think that
MITI is 'not that powerful'. But leaving these points aside, I
would suggest that if Mr Henderson really believes that Japanese
banking (which the US government has been prodding Japan for
years to deregulate), together with their tax policies, labour
markets, and industrial competition, are examples of '*laissez-
faire*', then perhaps he does not know French.

But *Fortune*'s obvious fear that it had blotted its ideological
copybook was only the beginning. In early 1984, the Institute for
Contemporary Studies in San Francisco got the idea that it should
sponsor an election-year volume on industrial policy and asked
me to edit it. The ICS is the think-tank created by Edwin Meese
and Caspar Weinberger for Ronald Reagan when he was
governor of California, and it reflects the views of the Reagan-
wing of the Republican Party. It seemed to me then (as it still
does) that the Republicans were utterly justified in denouncing
the industrial policy proposals of Walter Mondale as reflecting
vested interests and being little more than new names for
protectionism. However, the Republicans were going too far and
were in fact painting themselves into a corner by asserting that
there was no such thing as industrial policy and that the United
States did not need one. It seemed clear to me that the United
States already had an industrial policy – an inevitability, given the
fact that the US government controls well over a quarter of the
gross national product. What the United States needed was a
new, lean, effective industrial policy – one that addressed global
competition, the chaotic shift of industry from the rust-belt to the
sun-belt, and other well-known American economic problems.

The book that I edited for the ICS, entitled *The Industrial
Policy Debate*, in fact contained several essays suggesting that the
United States should not create or implement a Japanese-style

industrial policy. These were included to balance my and others' arguments that a new industrial policy – smooth government–business relationships, a long-term economic strategy for the country, and attentiveness to the problems of industrial location and relocation – was precisely what was needed. None the less, the book immediately caused concern in Republican circles in Washington. Those of us who had the temerity to suggest that there was an alternative to either the neo-classical status quo or protectionism were dismissed as crypto-socialists.[2]

Needless to recall, the issue of industrial policy never really got on the agenda of the 1984 presidential election campaign. Americans decided to forget about the performance of the economy until after the re-election of President Reagan, when all the old issues and a few new ones again came to the fore. These included a catastrophic 1984 American trade deficit (which the politicians tried to blame on the seller, Japan, rather than the buyer, the United States); huge governmental budget deficits that mortgage the future; the discovery that the American tax code contains inequities and irrationalities that affect American economic performance; and the fact that during 1985 the United States became, for the first time since 1919, a debtor nation. Still, the economists refuse to study or learn from Japanese achievements, since these cannot be squared with neo-classical economic theory. Instead they argue that the Japanese must be 'cheating', a conclusion that also conveniently lets American politicians off the hook.

Even the Japanese have got into the act. They could never really decide whether it was a good thing or very dangerous for Americans to start thinking about industrial policy. During 1983, Lionel H. Olmer (1983, p. 419), the Under-Secretary of Commerce for International Trade, declared that 'Government-directed industrial policy and how it affects Japanese performance in the United States is more important than the openness of the Japanese markets. The Japanese government doesn't understand the extent to which industrial targeting is an issue in the United States.' This statement divided the Japanese government in terms of its response. The Japanese Ministry of Foreign Affairs launched a campaign to deny the very concept of industrial policy, whereas MITI instead chose to defend it, arguing that Japan simply had a better one than the United States and that it was a legitimate arena of competition among capitalist nations. My book *MITI and the Japanese Miracle* became a weapon for both sides. The Ministry of Foreign Affairs, through its registered agent in Washington, DC, the Japan Economic Institute of America, published an English-language pamphlet entitled *Japan's Industrial Policies*, which rather confusingly denies that Japan ever had any, or that they made any difference, or that they were any different from those of the United States. The Foreign Ministry was clearly worried that readers of my book on MITI might use it as source material for new protectionist measures against Japan.

A few months later, however, the Japan External Trade Organization (JETRO), an organ of MITI, published, also in English but under its own name, another pamphlet entitled *Japan's Postwar Industrial Policy*, which, it says, was 'produced in response to [the] strong interest of developing countries in the policies of the Japanese government.' This is a sort of 'how to' handbook, and the only English language work it cites that is not an official Japanese government publication is my *MITI and the Japanese Miracle*.

What is the larger meaning of this controversy? Does it have any significance beyond the usual disagreements among scholars? Yes, it does. Economists are not alone in their myopia, and it is not my intention here to single out economists for criticism. Virtually the entire social science establishment can be faulted for its hostility to the study of institutions. All the social sciences have tended to be blind to the implications of different institutions performing the same or similar functions for different but similar societies. The social sciences have been preoccupied with elaborate theoretical structures but have been indifferent to the institutions through which these theoretical propositions are actually manifested in living societies. As a result, all the social sciences have taken too long to recognize that although Japan is an advanced capitalist democracy, the institutions of capitalism that it has built through its industrial policies differ fundamentally from those encountered in American capitalism.

Institutions in Japan such as 'labour unions', 'joint stock companies', and the 'banking system' may have the same names in Japanese that we use in English, but they none the less function in quite different ways. Japanese unions are company unions, and organized labour in Japan has *no* role or voice in politics. Joint stock companies may be 'owned' by shareholders, but at least 70 per cent of the shares of Japan's most important companies are owned by competing companies and are never traded, regardless of price. Japan's banking system is the primary means whereby the Japanese transfer savings to industry, instead of using capital markets. These are *fundamental* differences.

We are only beginning to recognize that Japan has invented and put together the institutions of capitalism in new ways, ways that neither Adam Smith nor Marx would recognize or understand. This is not due to some mystical difference known as Japanese culture or Japanese social character. Nor does Japanese capitalism work according to different economic or political theories from those that pertain in the West. It is rather that the common capitalist and democratic theory is realized in Japan through different institutions from those in the West – and with markedly different trade-offs, above all, greater and more rational economic performance, but with considerably less popular participation in economic policy-making. Institutions are the key variables. This understanding leads to two related axioms. First, capitalist economic theory is an utterly abstract and even utopian body of thought until it is translated into action through concrete institutions. Second, any set of institutions that ignores economic theory will eventually bankrupt a nation in which it is established, other things being equal. Both of these propositions recommend the comparative study of economic and political institutions.

Let me try to illustrate some of these ideas about Japan by briefly describing some ten institutions that are intrinsic to the Japanese economy but virtually unknown in the United States. It should be stressed that each of these institutions is the product of quite recent Japanese history and of conscious innovation. None of them has existed unchanged for more than a few decades, and none of them can be traced to traditional organizations (with the possible exception of the official state bureaucracy, which clearly has its roots in the old samurai class). These institutions are not the product of Japan's unique culture, although they obviously do not clash with that culture. Japan is currently being emulated by South Korea and Taiwan, both of which have very different cultural roots from Japan and both of which are attempting to improve on many features of the Japanese model.

The theory that Japan's institutions are to be explained by its culture is essentially an ideological way of avoiding the competitive implications of Japan's institutional innovations. It is these institutions that are the real Japanese challenge to the rest of the world. Each of them identifies a dimension on which Japan's competitors must match or meet (although not necessarily copy) Japanese performance. That is precisely what international economic competition is all about.

The first set of institutions I want to mention is crucial and thus requires a somewhat longer discussion than the others. This is the Japanese financial system. Instead of relying on a highly developed capital market, such as the New York Stock Exchange, Japan transfers its savings to industry through its banking system. Japan has a stock market, the Tokyo Stock Exchange, but it has never even come close to equalling bank loans or corporate bonds as a source of external funds for Japanese companies. Even though Japan's banking system is starting to undergo deregulation and internationalization, there is not the slightest chance that it will come to look like that of the United States until well into the next century (if ever). Moreover, some of the core elements of the Japanese system, such as the government-owned Japanese Development Bank, are exempt from deregulation.

Japan's choice of different institutions from those in the United States to finance its industries has many implications. I shall discuss four of them. First, through its system, Japan avoids the short-term bias inherent in the American stock market. No manager or chief executive officer of a Japanese corporation begins the morning by looking at his company's stock quotations. Such information is irrelevant to him because it is irrelevant to the bankers who have lent his firm its capital. What the bankers are concerned about is the company's market share and its ability to repay its loans over the long term, and these depend upon how well the company is doing in developing new products, controlling costs and quality, and preparing its work-force for the future. These are the criteria of good management in Japan. They are utterly different from those in the United States because the American institutions of industrial financing impose short-term incentives on managers.

Second, Japan avoids the waste of capital and talent inherent in the 'paper entrepreneurialism' (in Robert Reich's apt phrase) that the American system generates. There is no shortage of capital in the United States, but in recent years a good part of it has been mobilized for hostile takeover bids, buyouts of corporate raiders, 'greenmail', the wooing of white knights, paying for 'golden parachutes', and all the other devices of price manipulation inherent in a capital market. These things do not happen in Tokyo, even in firms that are highly capitalized, for the simple reason (as Rodney Clark, 1979, p. 86, puts it) that 'unlike Western institutional shareholders, which invest largely for dividends and capital appreciation, Japanese institutional share-holders tend to be the company's business partners and associates: shareholding is a mere expression of their relation-ship, not the relationship itself.' In other words, the concept of 'ownership' has become irrelevant to Japanese capitalism, where the managerial revolution has been carried to greater lengths than it has in competing systems.

Third, neo-classical economists argue that even though Japan may not have to contend with some of the unintended consequences of a capital market, it none the less loses the benefits of such a market, above all the *information* that capital markets generate about which new technologies have real commercial potential and which ones do not. This proposition is true, but the Japanese have invented quite effective substitutes for the information-supplying function of a capital market. These substitutes include: Japan's elaborate apparatus of industrial policy within MITI; several dozen forums for public–private consultation; the most effective organization of the private sector of any capitalist country, namely, Keidanren, or the Federation of Economic Organizations; thousands of semi-official trade organizations; and the information collecting, processing, and disseminating capabilities of the general trading companies and JETRO. Taken together, these institutions are more than adequate to signal investors about promising new prospects. In the United States, venture capital to finance new products is supplied through the market, and theorists tell us that it could not possibly be supplied as efficiently in any other way. In Japan, a good part of venture capital is supplied by the Japan Development Bank (*Japan Economic Journal*, July 19, 1983; Nihon Kaihatsu Ginko, 1984).

Fourth, despite the growing internationalism of Japan's financial system, the cost of capital is still significantly lower for Japanese industry than it is for Japan's competitors. This is because many interest rates are still officially administered in

Japan, because different industries and enterprises have different degrees of access to the Japanese financial system, because of the ease with which Japanese industrial policy authorities can 'guide' capital, and because of the continuing undervaluation of the yen despite the existence of 'floating' exchange rates for more than a decade. Any industrialist understands what a competitive advantage his Japanese counterpart enjoys in significantly cheaper prices of capital (Rappa, 1985; Tsongas and Hatsopoulos, 1984).

In bringing this discussion of Japan's financial system to a close, let me make clear that Japan's institutions are not necessarily *preferable* to those of the United States. My point is rather to stress that US institutions must be modified or replaced by others in order to give managers real long-term incentives, to end paper entrepreneurialism, and to bring the cost of capital into line with the competition.

A second set of unusual institutions in Japan is the 'industrial groups', known in pre-war Japan as *zaibatsu* (financial cliques) and in post-war Japan as *keiretsu* (lineages) or *kigyo shudan* (enterprise groups). The most famous of them are the Mitsubishi, Mitsui, Sumitomo, Hitachi, Yasuda, and similar groups. They are perhaps most accurately called 'developmental conglomerates', because they concentrate huge amounts of capital and then use it along with their well-established industries to finance risky, new ventures. The industrial groups are a specific Japanese invention dating from the nineteenth century, when Japan launched its drive to catch up with the advanced industrial nations that were threatening it. Their contemporary successors have been modernized: they have eliminated the old family holding companies in favour of guidance through banks and trading companies. Perhaps the most important feature of the *keiretsu* system in Japan is that there is more than one group: only one conglomerate would lead to monopoly, but five or more involved in every industry in fact generates cut-throat competition. Incidentally, these institutions are today being duplicated in South Korea, but the Koreans have made some subtle improvements on the Japanese prototypes.

Many significant implications flow from this form of industrial organization. Let us consider just one. The industrial groups are relatively impervious to the effects of the international business cycle because of their large concentrations of capital and conglomerate structure. This means that they can leverage their positions during the business cycle to gain advantages over their international competitors. Japanese firms in the *Keiretsu* can continue to invest in R & D and productive capacity right through a cyclical downturn, whereas their American competitors, without comparable backing, will be forced to lay off workers, reduce investment, and cut back on research. When the recession is over, the Japanese will be ready to meet renewed demand, often with better prices and higher quality products. In the semiconductor industry, for example, the Japanese have pulled this stunt at least twice (with 64K and 256K memory chips). They are able to do so because the industrial groups can free leading enterprises from short-term profitability considerations.

A third key institution in Japan is the postal savings system, through which the government invests the people's savings in projects that the industrial policy organs have designated as strategic. At the end of 1984, the deposits in the postal savings system amounted to some ¥86.3 trillion (*c.* $350 billion), or two-and-a-half times the assets of Citicorp. These deposits form the basis of the Fiscal Investment and Loan Program, a financial institution that is wholly in the hands of Japan's industrial policy bureaucrats. It is, in fact, the largest single financial organ in the world today.

Japanese citizens save at their post offices, because the system offers higher interest rates and better terms than the government allows the commercial banks to offer, and because the Japanese cannot freely invest their money abroad, in, say, US banks, where they might get still higher rates of interest. The Japanese government also induces its people to save by not providing the full range of welfare and retirement services found in most other democracies. During the 1950s, at the start of high-speed growth, postal savings contributed some 40 per cent of all investment in Japan's priority industries. That figure is much lower today, not because postal savings are smaller but because bank lending has grown phenomenally. The postal savings system, given its size and the bureaucrats' track record in managing it, still possesses almost irresistible powers of guidance for the economy as a whole.

The fourth set of institutions I would like to mention are the official forums through which bureaucrats, businessmen, experts, journalists, and representatives of the people consider and decide on virtually all public policies. These are the *shingikai*, or 'deliberation councils', of which, during 1984, there were some 214. At present the Ministry of Finance operates fourteen of them, MITI twenty, the Ministry of Agriculture fourteen, the Ministry of Transportation eleven, the Economic Planning Agency three, and so forth (Japanese Government, Prime Minister's Office, 1984). The *shingikai* contribute to the smooth government–business relationships of Japan, which is a distinct comparative advantage when Japan is competing with systems that cannot produce widely supported or effectively implemented public policies. In the US, similar deliberations on laws go on in Congress and are subjected to the full range of lobbying pressures, including pressure from foreign lobbyists. In Japan, they are conducted in private, shielded from interest groups or the press and under the control of Japan's élitist state bureaucracy. By the time a proposed Japanese law gets to the Diet, it has already been thoroughly debated and a decision has been reached. All Japan's elected legislators do is to rubber-stamp it.

The fifth institution on my list is actually one of the 214 deliberation councils. This is the Tax System Investigation Council (*Zeisei Chosakai*), which is the key Japanese organization for trying to depoliticize the national and local tax systems and to make them as economically rational as is possible in a democracy. No tax system is politically or economically neutral, certainly not Japan's. But Japan's system is more closely coordinated with industrial policy than in other countries, and its overall tax burden is the lowest of any OECD nation. One of the ways Japan achieves these things is through its very prestigious Tax System Investigation Council.

In its current form the Council came into being in April 1962. It is composed of some thirty tax experts, representatives of enterprises, bankers, and opinion leaders who are appointed for three-year terms by the Prime Minister on the recommendation of the tax bureaux of the Ministries of Finance and Home Affairs (the latter representing local governments). The Council deliberates in secret and each year produces a long report of recommended revisions to the tax codes. Many of these changes are timely, narrowly focused tax breaks for industry, such as the temporary removal of excises to help enlarge the market for a new product or the authorization of a new and often quite unorthodox tax-exempt reserve fund to finance some new activity. The Council's recommendations are communicated directly to the Diet, where, with very rare exceptions, they are automatically enacted into law.

The Council is influential because of the reputations of its members and because of the relative invulnerability of its sponsoring ministries to lobbying. There has been some increase over the years in the representation of politicians on the Council, but during the 1980s its head was the country's most distinguished former Vice-Minister of Agriculture, Ogura Takekazu. Members included editors from the Sankei, Mainichi, Yomiuri, Nihon Keizai, and Asahi newspapers; professors from Tokyo, Keio, Nagoya, and Osaka universities; the governor of Kagoshima prefecture; and the chief executive officers of Toshiba Electric, Komatsu Tractors, Mitsui Bank, and Suntory Whisky (Japanese Government, Prime Minister's Office, 1984, pp. 28–9). The Council has more authority in the eyes of the public than any group of elected politicians, and this is the key to its success. The Diet has the legal power to overrule the Council, but it rarely does so because of the rationality and seriousness of the Council's recommendations.

A sixth set of very important institutions in Japan are those concerned with labour relations. Nowhere does Japan achieve a greater comparative advantage over its competitors than in its utterly flexible, strike-free ways of avoiding labour conflict. Many people in the West who have not known Japan over the whole post-war era conclude that Japan's tranquil labour relations must be a reflection of cultural propensities. None the less, the evidence is building daily that Japanese-run factories in the United States and elsewhere also achieve greater loyalty and commitment from their workers than do factories under ordinary American management. Culture thus has little or nothing to do with Japan's achievements in this area.

During the late 1940s and all of the 1950s Japan was torn apart by very violent labour strife. The result of this era, however, was a decision by management not to buy the unions off (as in the American steel and automotive industries) but to fight them to the bitter end. The end came with a bloody strike at the Mitsui Miike coal-mine that lasted throughout much of 1960. At Miike, management broke the hold of the most leftist, horizontally-structured federation of industrial unions, Sohyo. Since then trade unions in Japan have been replaced with enterprise unions, which are supported by the workers because of a simultaneously enlarged career employment system for male heads of households. The result is a labour force that is sensitive to international competition in order to keep their enterprises healthy, that has no incentive to oppose technological innovation of even a labour-saving type (such as robotics) because of career job security, and that does not have or seek a major role in politics. This last achievement is critical to Japan's success with industrial policy. Japan does not exploit its labour, but it also does not give labour a veto power over its industrial policy initiatives – and that is a real competitive advantage.

The seventh set of institutions to consider are conspicuous by their absence. That is to say, Japan garners some advantages by *not* allowing certain American-type institutions to flourish. These are the institutions of anti-trust and anti-monopoly policy, which Americans claim are needed to promote competition. Japan actually achieves much more vigorous domestic competition for an advanced, oligopolized industrial economy than the United States does, but it manages to do so without the benefit of thousands of anti-trust lawyers. Japan has an Anti-Monopoly Law and a Fair Trade Commission to administer it, both of them supplied for the first time in Japan by American reformers during the Allied occupation. But nobody in Japan regards either of them as very important – Keidanren is openly contemptuous of the Anti-Monopoly Law – and Japan relies on lawyers and the courts to maintain competition only in extreme cases.

Japan in fact generated its vigorous domestic competition through industrial policy and its structure of industrial groups. When one of MITI's deliberation councils designates a particular industry as important for Japan's future growth, industrial groups vie with each other to enter it. This is because of the reduced risks that follow from investment in a designated industry and because of the longer time perspectives of Japanese managers. At the same time, given a less legalistic orientation than the United States, Japan is able to employ all manner of cartels – recession, export, import, rationalization, research, and so forth – to implement its policies. Each of these is authorized as an exception to the Anti-Monopoly Law, usually for fixed, relatively short periods of time. Japanese economic ministries also tailormake policies for particular industries or enterprises through discretionary and non-justiciable 'administrative guidance'. Above all, Japan is not burdened with the huge and wasteful diversion of human resources into the legal profession that is so conspicuous a part of the American economic system. Incidentally, even though the Japanese do their best to avoid litigation in their own economy, when they go abroad they adapt readily to foreign practices. Japanese companies and trade associations operating in the United States hire the best (and most expensive) lawyers they can find to represent them.

An eighth set of Japanese institutions illustrates the country's creative use of cartels. These are the 'research cartels' (*kenkyu kumiai*) that the Agency for Industrial Science and Technology, an integral part of MITI, authorizes and funds in order to promote Japan's research and development. Such cartels allow competing firms to collaborate on specific research projects – projects that may advance Japan's overall technological level but that, in any case, save Japanese firms the costs of duplicating R&D. Research cartels are currently authorized for a range of microelectronics, biotechnology, telecommunications, new materials, and energy conservation projects. The government also sponsors a group of closely related R&D efforts, including the well-known attempt to build a 'fifth generation' computer and one to give Japan its own capacity to produce and launch telecommunications satellites.

Japan's public financial support for R&D is less than that in the United States, just as the Japanese spend less on subsidies for various industries. But this does not mean that Japanese R&D is less effective. In Japan, R&D is much more evenly addressed to *all* aspects of the industrial process – basic research, applied research, product development, and manufacturing and marketing. Japanese R&D is also oriented more towards product engineering than towards 'pure science' of the Nobel prize variety. Finally, Japan's R&D avoids the distortions that much American R&D suffers as a result of being paid for and administered by the Department of Defense.

A ninth set of Japanese institutions are those that supply domestic information, intelligence, publicity, and propaganda concerning commercial trends and new economic challenges. Japan actually operates something similar to the National Security Council, the Central Intelligence Agency, and the Rand Corporation in the industrial and commercial spheres. In Japan, however, these kinds of operations are not secret; instead they are aimed at achieving the greatest possible publicity.

Among Japan's information organs there are: the Trade Council (known as the 'Supreme Export Council' before 1980), which is led by the Prime Minister and the cabinet and is intended to give maximum authority and publicity to national economic initiatives; the Economic Planning Agency, which is an organization for economic monitoring and analysis, one that is infinitely more effective than the American Council of Economic Advisers precisely because it is not authorized to give advice; JETRO, which is a worldwide commercial intelligence and support organization for Japanese importers and exporters; and MITI, the Ministry of Finance, the Bank of Japan, and the semi-official Bank of Tokyo, each of which produces innumerable 'visions' of the future, indicative plans, and analyses of various industries and markets. All of this material is readily available in any Japanese bookstore. The Japanese businessman who does not know what his foreign competitors are doing, or who does not know where to turn if he wants more information, is probably illiterate. (Unfortunately, such illiteracy is the common lot of foreign businessmen in Tokyo who read and speak no Japanese.)

The tenth and final set of institutions to be discussed in this survey are those charged with making and implementing industrial location policy. These institutions are particularly relevant to the United States because of the very high social and political costs associated with the shift of American industries from the rust-belt to the sun-belt. In Japan, industrial location policy is as politically salient an issue as it is in the United States. This is because of the depression during the 1960s of Japan's old coal-mining areas, because of the controversy over the industrial pollution that accompanied high-speed growth, because of the overconcentration of industries in the Tokyo–Kobe corridor, and because of the lack of job opportunities in some of Japan's rural and coastal prefectures. The Japanese answer to these problems has been a combination of local initiatives, massive government investments in infrastructure to assist relatively backward areas (for example, the bullet trains to the north-east, the bridges to Shikoku island, and the world's longest tunnel connecting Honshu and Hokkaido), and the establishment of a number of public corporations to provide incentives for labour mobility, relocation of industry, and foreign investment.

Perhaps the best example of a local prefecture taking the lead in attracting new industry is Oita in north-eastern Kyushu. The area was long a region of labour exodus and stagnation. This began to change in 1979, when Hiramatsu Morihiko, a former high-ranking MITI official, was elected governor. While at MITI, Hiramatsu was notorious for his hostility to foreign firms, particularly IBM, but as governor he set out to get them to locate in his province. By offering free space in fully developed industrial parks, he attracted Texas Instruments, Material Research Corporation, and many others to his area. Oita is today one of Japan's more flourishing new industrial areas.

In implementing its industrial location policies, Japan relies primarily on public corporations. This means that although politicians establish industrial location policy – something particularly true under the leadership of former Prime Minister Tanaka Kakuei – the actual implementation is fairly depoliticized and technocratic. The most important public corporations in the industrial location field include the Japan Regional Development Corporation, which traces its history back to 1962, when the country started to try to invigorate the depressed coal-mining areas; the Japan Highway Public Corporation, established in 1956; the Hokkaido and North-East Development Fund, also established in 1956; the Employment Promotion Projects Corporation, an organ supervised by the Ministry of Labour and intended to help finance the retraining and relocation of workers; the Japan Railway Construction Corporation, which builds the bullet train rights-of-way; and the Honshu-Shikoku Bridge Authority, which is in charge of the massive series of bridges being built between Japan's least and most developed islands.

In addition to the activities of these organizations, in 1983 the Diet passed a MITI-sponsored law to create and give tax benefits to some fifteen high-tech cities throughout the country, known as 'technopolises'. The technopolises are modelled on California's Silicon Valley and are based on the hopeful idea that high-technology industries located adjacent to each other will generate synergisms of innovation and new jobs. One of the Japanese technopolises, Miyazaki city in Kyushu, even claims that it lies in the same 'isothermal zone' (in other words, has the same weather) as Silicon Valley, which is thought to be of possible advantage to it, or perhaps just a good omen. To celebrate this latest aspect of industrial location policy, MITI, during 1985, sponsored a high-tech world fair at Japan's first 'science city', Tsukuba, where from the early 1970s MITI has located many of its most important laboratories and research cartels.

At least two lessons seem to emerge from the Japanese experience with industrial location and relocation activities. First, political initiative is necessary to get anything done. The leader in Japan was Tanaka Kakuei, who, as Prime Minister from 1972 to 1974, made industrial dispersal one of his main priorities. Second, local initiative is equally important; the central government is responsive not just to depressed areas but also to those areas that are most active in terms of self-help. Japan's programmes have not been perfect, but the most pervasive impression one gets of the country as a whole is of the relatively equitable distribution of income and amenities.

The ten sets of institutions outlined here of course do not add up to the totality of the Japanese industrial system. Aspects that have not been mentioned include measures for the relief of structurally recessed industries, Japan's trade policies, and its measures for administering economic diplomacy (unlike the United States, Japan never entrusts its foreign economic diplomacy to its Ministry of Foreign Affairs). Equally to the point, not everything the Japanese do in the name of industrial policy succeeds. Some examples include Japan's refusal during the 1960s to revalue its undervalued currency (this failure led to the collapse of the international system of fixed exchange rates), the poor engineering of the atomic ship *Mutsu*, the oil importers' manipulation of MITI during the early 1970s to fix prices, the inability of the government to build an airport for its capital city that is as convenient as and has the capacity of other international airports, and the continuing subsidization of what is one of the world's most inefficient agricultural sectors.

In my opinion, what does emerge from the Japanese case is that the Japanese government takes its responsibilities in the economic sphere more seriously than do most other democratic governments: it staffs its government with the best minds in the country; it tries to depoliticize important economic decisions; it publicizes the government's own economic intentions and then sticks to them long enough for households and enterprises to adjust; and its interventions in the privately managed economy are market-conforming rather than market-displacing. Firms or nations wanting to compete with the Japanese must become at least as serious.

The key to what makes Japan so different from the other advanced industrial democracies is its institutional innovations. Japan has outperformed the rest of the world in inventing new institutions through which the relationships of modern capitalism are realized. Japan has altered, experimented with, and reinvented both democracy and capitalism to such an extent that it has evolved a qualitatively different structure as a nation state from the norm in the West. This different structure has many important implications for social conflict and its study in Japan.

The most obvious one is that many of the conflicts found in the West do not occur in Japan because Japan's institutions were designed in part to avoid creating the same tensions that occur in the West. Thus, as we have seen, labour disputes in Japan are very different from those in the West. Through its innovations in this area, Japan has sought to avoid long strikes or the attempts by industrial and craft unions to obstruct technological innovation in order to save jobs. At the same time, Japan's institutional answer, enterprise unions and job tenure, create new sources of conflict. Japan finds it much harder than the West to merge firms, and hostile takeovers or buyouts are virtually unknown – partly because of the inability of Japanese managers to discharge unneeded workers. The enormously inefficient Japanese National Railways, for example, were propped up much longer by the government than made any economic sense (until 1987, when they were broken up into smaller regional companies), because Japan did not have the means to handle the conflict inherent in large scale lay-offs of workers.

Another implication arises from the fact that Japan's conflicts are usually rooted less in disagreements over principle than in complaints that some person or agent is disrupting settled practices or disturbing social harmony (*wa*). Because Japan's history of institutional inventiveness has largely been undoctrinaire and based on borrowings from many different cultures, matters of principle rarely enter into these institutions or the disputes they generate. Conflicts based on religious differences, for example, are all but unknown in Japan. Instead, conflicts based on different interests predominate; and, not being based on principles, they are often harder to resolve than in the West, where legal norms and institutions are likely to prevail.

Thus, for example, one of the most common forms of conflict in Japan is between and among the various ministries of the national government, where principles of rationality and national purpose commonly give way to the bureaucrats' incessant struggle to preserve their particular jurisdictions (what the Japanese call *nawabari*, or 'roped-off areas').

A third implication of Japan's different institutional structure is that foreigners often make errors in attempting to understand Japanese society because they tend to project onto it expectations derived from their own, superficially similar but actually very different, societies. Thus, for example, Japanese households spend about a third of their income on food, but there is no serious consumer protest movement, as would be expected in the West, because Japanese consumers' perceptions of their advantages have been structured differently by their institutions. Similarly, discrimination against women in the workplace is widespread and routine in Japan, but it has not generated a movement for women's rights because the Japanese link this practice to the maintenance of their racially homogeneous society and their prohibition against virtually all legal forms of immigration into Japan. The employment of women in low-end jobs is thus seen by large sectors of the population as a legitimate trade-off to be paid in order to prevent the conflicts associated with multi-ethnicity. Foreigners should not expect to see the same kinds of conflicts in Japan as in other advanced industrial democracies, because Japan relies on different institutions. Conversely, these institutions in turn generate conflicts in Japanese society that are different from or not so intense as those in the West – for example, the conflicts associated with Japan's rigidly tracked and tested elementary school system. The demand for conformity in Japan's schools is so intense that it has generated a peculiarly Japanese form of social conflict, best described by its Japanese name *ijime* (roughly, 'bullying').

There are many other aspects of the relationship between Japan's institutional structure and social conflict. These include Japan's relatively slight reliance on the rule of law in social regulation, the marked distinction in all aspects of Japanese life between *tatemae* (formal aspiration or pretense) and *honne* (actual practice), and the widespread reliance on intimidation of weaker parties by stronger ones to structure social relationships. These features often lead to seemingly paradoxical situations that have to be socially unmasked before they can be studied. For example, Japan is widely regarded and regards itself as one of the safest societies on earth, above all in the sense of the comparative rarity of street assaults. At the same time and counter-intuitively, Japan tolerates one of the largest and most active organized criminal underworlds of any advanced social system. Are these two facts related? Does one help to explain the other? Or are Japan's safe streets better explained by its police institutions and alleged mono-ethnicity? My intention here is not to try to answer such questions. It is only to establish that the recognition of Japan's institutional differences is preliminary to any study, even to any identification, of Japanese social conflict.

Notes

1 See, *inter alia*, Frank Gibney, *Miracle by Design: The Real Reasons behind Japan's Economic Success*. New York, Times Books, 1982; Julian Gresser, *Partners in Prosperity: Strategic Industries for the US and Japan*. New York, McGraw-Hill, 1984; William Ouchi, *The M-Form Society: How American Teamwork can recapture the Competitive Edge*. Reading, MA, Addison-Wesley, 1984; Bruce R. Scott and George C. Lodge, (eds.) *US Competitiveness in the World Economy*. Boston, Harvard Business School Press, 1984; Ezra Vogel, *Comeback: Building the Resurgence of American Business*. New York, Simon & Schuster, 1985; Kozo Yamamura, (ed.), *Policy and Trade Issues of the Japanese Economy*. Seattle, University of Washington Press, 1982; and John Zysman and Laura Tyson, (eds.), *American Industry in International Competition*. Ithaca, NY, Cornell University Press, 1983.

2 See, for example, 'Influential Conservative Group Rethinking Economic Policy', *United Press International*, May 13, 1985; 'A *Republican* Industrial Policy?' *Washington Times*, May 22, 1984; 'Illiterate Journalists Compound National Stupidity', *Washington Times*, June 20, 1984; and *Business Week*, Sept.24, 1984.

References

Clark, R. (1979), *The Japanese Company*. New Haven, Yale University Press.

Japan Economic Institute of America (1984), *Japan's Industrial Policies: What Are They? Do They Matter? Are They Different from Those in the United States?*. Washington, DC, Japan Economic Institute of America.

Japan External Trade Organization (1985), *Japan's Postwar Industrial Policy: Economic Programs in the Reconstruction and Expansion Periods*. Tokyo, JETRO.

Japanese Government, Prime Minister's Office, General Affairs Agency (1984), *Shingikai Soran* (Survey of Deliberation Councils). Tokyo, Okura-sho Insatsu-kyoku.

Johnson, C. (1982), *MITI and the Japanese Miracle*. Stanford, Stanford University Press.

Johnson, C. (ed.) (1984), *The Industrial Policy Debate*. San Francisco, Institute for Contemporary Studies.

Kuttner, R. (1985), 'The poverty of economics', *Atlantic Monthly*, February 26.

Nihon Kaihatsu Ginko (1984), *Nihon Kaihatsu Ginko no Genjo* (Current State of the JDB). Tokyo, JDB.

Olmer, L.H. (1983), 'Japanese industrial policy', *National Journal*, February.

Rappa, M.A. (1985), 'The cost of capital in the Japanese semiconductor industry', *California Management Review*, 27, 85–99.

Tsongas, P.E. and G.N. Hatsopoulos (1984), 'Capital: the price is too high', *Washington Post, National Weekly Edition*, October 29.

4 Class Conflict, Corporatism and Comparison: A Japanese Enigma[1]

M. Shalev

The 'Japanese enigma' which concerns this chapter is this: in a society in which the labour movement has been almost continuously excluded from political power and where labour unions are weak, politicized and competitively divided, the political economy nevertheless generates outcomes characteristic of Sweden, Norway and Austria, countries in which class conflict is managed by 'corporatist' arrangements which emerged against a backdrop of political dominance by strong labour movements. The mix of outcomes quintessentially associated with modern social democracy includes longterm full employment and relatively equal distribution of income; and also, in the period following the economic shocks of the early 1970s, successful attempts at stabilization on the basis of organized labour's consent to the sacrifice of immediate wage gains and its use of the strike weapon, for the sake of preserving jobs and reviving investment and growth. Japan shares precisely these features, although, curiously, it lacks one other hallmark of the social democratic model: a big welfare state which plays a major role in the (re)distribution of income and the patterning of ordinary people's life chances and living standards.

The dissonance, from this comparative perspective, between the characteristics of the state and state/society relations in Japan, and Japan's favourable employment and growth record and relatively high level of economic consensus, has yet to be resolved in comparative studies of the political economy of the advanced capitalist democracies. This essay will review the puzzle, and argue that several earlier attempts to resolve it – including notions of some kind of a 'Japanese-style' equivalent to Western European corporatism – have been ill-conceived.

Instead, I propose a perspective which integrates analysis of labour markets and the state arena, and thereby renders the Japanese case comprehensible in terms which are also applicable to other nations, yet need not devalue the power of the analytical tools developed by modern comparativists. The lessons suggested by this exercise may be enlightening both to students of Japan and to scholars for whom Japan is merely a perplexing case which it is necessary to accommodate in models of a far broader research universe.

Comparative Political Economy

An important contemporary stream of the comparative study of political economy emerged in response to the puzzle of why the democratic capitalist societies of the West diverged so markedly in their adjustment to the global economic 'shocks' of the 1970s. The concerns of this literature have not only been confined to issues of economic adjustment and stabilization, but also include a quest for the origins of political stability and social peace. Indeed, insistence on linking distributional conflict and consensus with economic performance in a single causal argument is the very foundation of the political-economic approach. One particularly influential model of the political underpinnings of socio-economic stability has been the resurrection and adaptation (to modern democratic conditions) of the concept of *corporatism*. However, this contemporary revival has been motivated by at least two different intellectual agenda. For analysts of interest group politics, it originates in a longstanding unease with the pluralist model, which tended to portray the state as a neutral arbiter among competitive pressure groups (Schmitter, 1974). Yet as experience in Continental Europe and Scandinavia seemed to suggest, such a view may obscure powerful interlocks and interdependencies between the state and interest organizations, and it fails to account for the continuing importance of corporate (encompassing, monopolistic and internally hierarchical) forms of 'associability' in many modern liberal democracies.

Alongside this concern to revise the political analysis of state/society linkages in the Western nations, there also emerged a fascination with the corporatist model as a form of conflict resolution and, in particular, as a metaphor for a distinctive form of political management of class conflict (Crouch, 1977; Panitch, 1981). Since about the mid-1970s, many analysts, with their eyes quite clearly fixed on the small 'successful' states of Western Europe and Scandinavia, have posited a close relationship between the class representation of labour, political bargaining between state and associational élites, peaceful industrial relations, and effective management of the macro-economy. In some versions, it was pointed out that the strong labour movements of Norway, Sweden and Austria had constructed a 'virtuous circle' (Castles, 1978) based on longterm cooperation between unified and powerful peak union organizations and Social Democratic governments, in the context of which workers were willing to exercise self-restraint in the labour market and throw their electoral weight behind the left in return for public policies sustaining the full-employment welfare state (Korpi and Shalev, 1980). In other versions, it was suggested that corporate forms of labour representation and quiescent industrial relations prevail not only under Social Democratic regimes but also in the consociational polities of Switzerland and the Netherlands. Despite labour's relative political and organizational weakness in these societies, its representatives are integrated into policy-making networks, and a high degree of political consensus is evident on economic issues (Katzenstein, 1985).

In cross-national mappings of the outcomes which have been of central interest to the new political economists, the case for the corporatist paradigm has been empirically quite striking (for example, Goldthorpe (ed.), 1984; Lehmbruch and Schmitter, 1982). The five European countries named above as 'corporatist' stand out in their comparatively low levels of labour disputes, successful maintenance of full employment, big welfare states, and relative success in avoiding economic 'misery' in the form of stagflation. The fit between outcomes and expectations is, however, rather less impressive for the consociational cases than for the Social Democratic ones. Switzerland's welfare state is generally evaluated as the smallest in the West, while by the 1980s the Dutch commitment to full employment had proved to be painfully fragile. While this slippage might be regarded as merely a vindication of the distinction between the two subtypes of corporatism, the empirical credentials of the theory are much more seriously called into question by a potentially crucial case, which in many ways exemplifies the favourable outcomes attributed to corporatism, while diverging quite markedly from its political and institutional traits. This case is, of course, Japan, in which a weakly mobilized and internally divided working class has been largely excluded from both political power-holding and participation in policy networks – and yet unemployment is low, economic growth is the highest in the OECD bloc (albeit far below the spectacular levels of the 1960s) and, since the late 1970s, both inflation and overt industrial conflict have been well nigh eradicated.

The Treatment of Japan in Empirical Studies

The notion of corporatism, as it is by now widely known, has been conceptualized in diverse ways, with correspondingly eclectic implications for empirical measurement – even when the focus is confined, as it is here, to the implications of corporatism for labour market phenomena. In some versions, corporatism is seen as virtually a corollary of the 'social democratic model' (Shalev, 1983a). A recent exemplar is Czada's (1987) study, in which corporatism is treated as the pinnacle of a hierarchy of attributes encompassing almost all of the distinctively Social Democratic features of working class mobilization (broadly-based and highly centralized trade unions as well as a dominant party of the left). In an earlier contribution by Cameron (1984), on the other hand, it was argued that Social Democracy ought to be viewed as no more than a special case of labour movements enjoying a high degree of 'organizational power' (in effect, corporatism by another name). But the contrast between these two studies at the theoretical level is invisible in their empirical work. Both Czada and Cameron generated almost identical scaling of the 16–18 OECD countries of Europe, North America and the Pacific, which are the common research universe of the studies under review.[2] Not surprisingly, they both classified Japan as minimally corporatist.

In a seminal although unpublished attempt at quantifying corporatism, Crouch (1980) anticipated Cameron's approach of evaluating corporatism in terms of the institutions of trade unionism and collective bargaining, rather than the political power of the left. Again, Japan appears at the negative pole of the continuum. Crouch, however, also pointed out that labour representation and cooperative bargaining – among the hallmarks of corporatist industrial relations – are in some settings to be found at the enterprise level as well as, or instead of, in the national political arena. In an application of the Crouch scale by Bruno and Sachs (1985) which incorporated this additional factor, Japan was shifted somewhat away from the non-corporatist extreme on account of the regime of enterprise-level relations prevailing in its big private firms.

A final cluster of comparative studies sets out from rather different premises about the nature of corporatism, proposing criteria based on processes and outcomes of relations between labour capital and the state, rather than either the structure of working-class representation or the balance of class political power. For Manfred Schmidt (1982), the management of class conflict may be described as corporatist in those contexts where organized labour exercises restraint as a consequence not of coercion but rather out of commitment to a 'social partnership' ideology. And while this kind of outlook is common in countries with highly developed tripartite bargaining among union, employer and state élites, Schmidt argued that it could also be observed in the 'paternalist' societies of Switzerland and Japan. The economist Ezio Tarantelli (1986) also came to the conclusion that Japan should be evaluated as a paradigm case of neo-corporatism. He proposed that the Japanese system of industrial relations not only exhibited a high degree of harmony between labour and management, but in several respects was closer to the Scandinavian and Austrian corporatist model than was generally believed. Tarantelli argued (citing Shimada, 1983) that the annual 'spring wage offensive' functions in effect as a system of centralized wage bargaining, complemented in the 1970s by the co-optation of organized labour into a tripartite, if informal, system of national policy-making. He thereby stood on its head Pempel and Tsunekawa's (1979) widely cited characterization of Japan as a case of corporatism *without* labour.

It is clear from this brief survey that the Japanese case exposes more than any other the contingent character of the notion of corporatism. We may go even further than this and suggest that

Japan is the veritable achilles heel of empirical operationalizations of corporatism. For, in spite of the substantial conceptual and methodological differences among the studies reviewed here, they approach a quite pronounced consensus on the ranking of every one of the core OECD countries *except Japan*. The point may be demonstrated statistically by a factor analysis of seven different measures (those of the six authors cited here, plus a study by Lehner (1987). Most of the variance between scores is accounted for by a single factor on which every one of the corporatism scales 'loads' strongly. However, if Japan is included in the analysis (and *only* if it is included), then a second significant factor is also present – one on which the loading of each author's scale can be perfectly predicted by its treatment of the Japanese case!

Japanese Puzzles

What substantive difference does it make whether Japan is ranked as strongly or weakly corporatist in comparative studies of political-economic outcomes? That of course depends on the outcome which is of interest and how it, in turn, is defined and measured. For instance, strike activity in Japan has experienced quite dramatic shrinkage since 1975. But before then, the Japanese pattern of industrial conflict resembled the French and Italian profile of a high level of worker participation in broad but brief disputes (Korpi and Shalev, 1980). From this perspective, Japan would not have made sense as anything but the antithesis of corporatism. Similarly, an argument commonly voiced in the seventies was that inflationary bubbles had been prevented by 'social contract bargaining' in the corporatist democracies, and were most likely to develop where labour was alienated from parliamentary politics and accustomed to pursuing wage demands by work stoppages. The Japanese case, *circa* 1974, provided it was again viewed as non-corporatist, offered tangible supportng evidence for this hypothesis (as in Crouch, 1980).

Not only did Japan experience a surge of rising prices in the short-term aftermath of the first oil shock; it also suffered a very sharp decline in its previous growth rate. In these terms, Japan in the mid-1970s appeared to belong to that unenviable group of nations suffering the double-headed misfortune of stagflation; and here too, a non-corporatist Japan provided the best fit with observed outcomes. This was empirically demonstrated in a widely read volume by Bruno and Sachs (1985; see especially p. 228). Here Japan appeared to vindicate the view that only real wage moderation could ward off the disastrous economic effects of an external shock; but that in most instances, such moderation would only be forthcoming under conditions of highly centralized pay determination and a high degree of social consensus (that is, under corporatism). If on the other hand, a desirable stabilization policy was defined as one which permitted the economy to continue to grow and prevented rising unemployment – then Japanese developments, even in the early years of the crisis, had to be described as a success story. In this instance, a convincing cross-national argument required that Japan appear in the guise of a strongly corporatist nation – which indeed it did in several relevant studies (such as those of Tarantelli and Schmidt).

Thus, whether by luck or design, most researchers succeeded in verifying the associations which they hypothesized, despite their confusion as to whether Japan was or was not corporatist, was or was not a case of successful economic stabilization. It is true that scholars had to contend with a very fluid reality, in which Japan's economic position improved in the 1980s. Nevertheless, this is not the whole of the story. If Japan is (as we argued at the beginning of this chapter) an anomaly, then little is to be gained by disguising the problem, whether by more 'appropriate' coding or by hiding Japan behind measures of average effects for many countries. On the contrary, it is necessary – and, moreover, can be extremely fruitful for those in search of wider generalizations – to confront what are apparently deviant cases head on. The result, in at least some recent comparative research, has been to recognize what was always an obvious logical possibility – namely, that identical outcomes in different countries may well have divergent causal antecedents. A good example is Goran Therborn's study of the determinants of the contemporary divergence across OECD nations in the severity of unemployment. In Therborn's (1986, pp. 23–4) summary, during the post-war period:

Full employment was institutionalized for two major, quite

different reasons. One was an assertion of working-class interests. It owes its success to a politically dominant labour movement [as in Sweden and Norway]. . . . The second reason . . . was a conservative concern with order and stability as being of equal importance to capital accumulation. Full employment in Japan and Switzerland has this background. . . . Austria falls somewhere in between these two poles.

What is important here is not so much the validity of Therborn's interpretation of the Japanese case (which may have over-emphasized the non-economic motives of Japanese élites), but rather the fact that *alternative causalities*, firmly grounded in the diversities of national context and history, are admitted to the terrain of legitimate explanation.

The other central issue which comparative political economy has to confront in taking Japan seriously, is whether there is in fact some theoretically persuasive notion of corporatism which possesses empirical plausibility in the Japanese case. If so, corporatist theory might have an important role to play in exposing the underpinnings of what must, from the perspective of the late 1980s, be regarded as truly an economic miracle. We refer of course to Japan's exceptionally strong showing on virtually *every* dimension of macroeconomic performance, including growth, inflation, investment, and trade. And clearly, it is not merely coincidental that these achievements have been won against the backdrop of self-restraint by labour – although this is a form of discipline with no obvious links either to strategic political exchange from a position of working-class strength (Pizzorno, 1978) or the state's coercive use of its authority to steer the economy towards mass unemployment (as in Kalecki, 1943).

The comparative literature, we have discovered, contains two different applications of corporatism to Japan. One of these refers to class relations at the micro level (labour–management collaboration in the enterprise). The other is the more conventional idea of union élites undertaking to rein in worker militancy in return for negotiated policy concessions from the state. An intriguing question is whether the Japanese case is 'functionally equivalent' to the corporatist political economies in one or both

67

of these senses. To address this issue requires some discussion of the peculiarities of the evolution of labour markets, industrial relations and social policy in Japan, and how these are related to the distinctively Japanese pattern of labour quiescence and cooperation in the enterprise. Attempts to label this pattern 'corporatist' will be criticized as distortions of both the concept of corporatism and the dynamics of the Japanese case. I shall then turn to Japan's success in combatting wage inflation and productivity decline. The critical question is whether labour's cooperative behaviour should be attributed to a turn in the mid-1970s towards corporatist participation of labour in the negotiation and coordination of national economic and social policies (I argue that it cannot). My conclusion will be that underlying the Japanese enigma is a constellation of forces with powerful historical and logical coherence, and that aspects of this same constellation may also be discerned in some other countries.

Is the Japanese Employment System 'Corporatist'?

The distinctive features of labour organization and industrial relations in Japan are sufficiently well known to warrant only the briefest rehearsal here. In Dore's authoritative account, these features – 'factory and company based trade union and bargaining structures, enterprise welfare and security, greater stability of employment . . . and a cooperative or corporate ideology' – add up to *a system of welfare corporatism* (1973, p. 370). More recently, Lincoln and Kalleberg have also applied the concept of corporatism to the micro level in Japanese and other settings characterized by 'organizational structures and management practices aimed at fostering corporate loyalty, commitment, and dependence on the part of labour' (1985, p. 740). The task before us in this section is to evaluate whether such a conceptualization makes sense.

Japanese trade unionism did not emerge on a significant scale until after World War II, although it retained a core characteristic of pre-war and wartime precedents, namely organization on a firm-by-firm basis (outside the public services). The potentially class-based character of unionism is compromised in Japan not only by its decentralized structure, but equally by low and uneven coverage and keen internal divisions. With only about a third of the wage-earners organized (even less in the eighties) union penetration is modest by international standards. Membership is also unusually concentrated in the public sector (accounting for about a third of the total) and in large private enterprises. While Japan's smaller (under 100 employees) privately-owned firms generate more than half of GNP, they have never accounted for more than one tenth of the organized work-force. Moreover, while it is customary for big firms to employ large numbers of 'temporary' workers and indirectly to engage the services (both off-site and on) of workers who are on the payroll of subcontractors, as a rule only permanently employed staff are admitted to unions.

Although enterprise unions are affiliated to national associations, the latter are divided into federations with competing political loyalties. There is a component of collective bargaining which takes place on a supra-enterprise and multi-confederal basis. Nevertheless, the main instrument for this – the annual 'spring wage offensive' (*shunto*) – sets only a basic floor on which enterprise unions then build. (Another major form of multi-firm negotiation has emerged in association with the International Trade Union Secretariats, but it has paradoxically further divided the workers by involving only 'non-political' coordinating bodies, which negotiate with employers within specific industries.) While the 'offensive' and collective bargaining generally may be accompanied by quite dramatic forms of worker hostility towards management, stoppages of work have a primarily demonstrative cast. Most involve large numbers of workers participating in brief pre-scheduled actions in support of *shunto* demands. As a result, until the contemporary withering away of open disputation, Japan's comparative strike volume ranked a little below the median for the main OECD countries.

A historical perspective is essential for comprehending the meaning of this pattern of collective action by workers for the Japanese enigma of presumptively corporatist labour market and macroeconomic outcomes. Strong elements of continuity are evident in the strategic action of Japanese élites in politics, the bureaucracy and big business, who have sought since the beginnings of industrialization to protect the authority of state, family and employer against the bacillus of working-class mobilization and solidarity (Gordon, 1985; Pempel and Tsunekawa, 1979). In the pre-war period, the state intervened to prevent coercively the formation of unions and the emergence of worker suffrage and labour parties, while assisting and encouraging employers to develop labour policies with a strong enterprise-level orientation. Employers experimented with personnel practices which subsequently became associated with the post-war system of labour management – including division of the workforce into 'lifetime' and temporary employees, and the internalization (to the enterprise) of the supply of skilled labour. A good deal of modern scholarship (see also Dore, 1973; Jacoby, 1979; Taira, 1970) is agreed that such innovations need not be understood as a form of cultural particularism, but rather as economically rational employer responses to specific problems of recruiting and controlling labour.

Japan's military defeat in World War II and the radical reforms initially instituted by the American occupation authorities at first constituted a sharp break with the prior political supremacy of a conservative ruling coalition and the economic domination of the giant *zaibatsu* combines. In the space of only a few years, support for left-wing parties mushroomed (they even participated in the government for a brief period in 1947–8) and unionization spread to more than half of the work-force. Labour chose to organize for collective action in the first instance on an enterprise basis. This choice accorded with prior experience and also reflected an assumption that only by reviving their enterprises' economic capacity could workers hope to transcend their desperate economic plight. However, after only a few years of enthusiastic 'democratization', the United States began to throw its considerable weight behind employer and state offensives, which largely restored the traditional political exclusion and organizational weakness of the working class.[3] Inspired by a revised conception of global US interests, the Occupation moved sharply away from its initial objective of crushing Japan's military and economic might, adopting in its stead a Cold War inspired determination to create an economically robust and politically sympathetic Japan able to 'support herself and assume the role of a protective barrier against possible unrest in East Asia' (cited by Sumiya, 1974, p. 67).

A variety of interventions during the late 1940s had the effect of deterring labour militancy and of deepening left–right schisms in the labour movement. The Occupation effectively banned or broke a number of pivotal strikes, 'red purges' were carried out in the radical unions, and the legal framework was in significant ways de-liberalized. Particularly important was the offensive against labour during 1949, when state policies (mass lay-offs and the rescinding of union rights in the public sector, coupled with slashes in subsidies and unemployment pay) created conditions in which the major private employers were expected to reassert their authority. Management indeed succeeded in winning a series of showdowns with militant enterprise unions. At the same time, the big firms accepted union demands for job security and linking wages to worker need (age). In a context of economic revival, these could be awarded at relatively low cost, while yielding pronounced benefits – the loyalty of older workers (who if necessary were willing to support the formation of docile 'second unions') and acceptance of the highly constrained terms on which the large enterprises were willing to accommodate to collective bargaining: no negotiations with 'outsiders', and no unionization of temporary or subcontracting workers.[4]

The emergence of rapid economic growth and the transition from labour surplus to labour shortage might have shifted the balance of power yet again in favour of labour and had the effect of lowering workers' attachment to the enterprise and stimulating a more class-oriented form of organization. That this did not come about was by now (*circa* the mid 1950s onwards) the result mainly of employer initiative, rather than the role of the state. Firstly, extensive 'rationalization' (capital-intensification) was carried out with an eye to reinforcing managerial control in the workplace. Secondly, the unions' attempt at multi-employer wage bargaining – in the form of *shunto* – was accepted as a means of partially mitigating competition among the big firms, provided that more wage uniformity could be achieved without squeezing profits.[5] Thirdly, the big enterprises have structured their 'internal' labour markets in ways that heighten the dependence and loyalty of those workers who enjoy the privileges of job security and union membership. The relevant incentives include formidable barriers to upward mobility across firms,[6] the deferment of wages through such devices as seniority-based pay and large retirement grants, and the benefits provided by company welfare services and profit-sharing bonuses.

Under these circumstances, it is understandable that private sector trade unions have taken up a very limited adversarial role and have generally been cooperative towards managerial objectives. Indications of union co-optation by the firm abound – including company-provided union facilities and salaries, occupancy of union positions by supervisory employees, and the career line which runs from union office into management (Hanami, 1979). Nevertheless, collaborative unionism is not the result of co-optation *per se* but rather of the terms of the 'settlement' which ended labour's post-war struggles, and the compelling economic logic institutionalized in the Japanese employment system. It is clearly materially worthwhile for the permanent/unionized work-force to join efforts to improve the competitive position of the enterprise – especially since these efforts are supported by ramified forms of social control over would-be free-riders. The benefits for employers have included low turnover costs, a high probability of enjoying the fruits of investments in worker training, little or no disruption to production or challenge to managerial authority by unions, and the ability to mitigate the fixed costs of a permanent work-force by flexible job assignments and the elastic utilization of temporary and subcontracted labour.

Just as Japan's dual economy organically links the big oligopolistic firms at the core with their suppliers and subcontractors on the periphery, so too do the workers of the 'primary' and 'secondary' segments of the dual labour market perform complementary roles – the one exhibiting flexibility in adapting job content and level of remuneration to the needs of the firm, and the other accepting insecure employment as a condition of existence. That the workers of the secondary labour market have accommodated to their fate may be explained, firstly, by the not inconsiderable rewards that could nevertheless be obtained and, secondly, by the powerful social forces which legitimate the rationing of 'good jobs'.[7] As in other dual labour markets the lower tier of undesirable jobs is peopled mainly by socially marginal (that is, relatively powerless) groups. In Japan, these are not foreign guest-workers but principally women, complemented by older men in second careers, certain ethnic minorities, and rural seasonal workers. Social attitudes regarding gender roles, together with admission and streaming policies in the educational system and outright discrimination by employers, have combined even more effectively than in the West to support labour market inequalities (*Business Week*, March 4, 1985; Steven, 1982).

Is Enterprise Welfare Japan's Substitute Welfare State?

Before returning to the larger question of whether the specificities of workplace labour relations in the Japanese context may usefully be subsumed under the corporatist label, we should recall that in Dore's conceptualization the label of choice was *welfare* corporatist. The implication is that just as the corporatist mode of managing class conflict has been transferred in Japan to the micro level, so too have the functions of the welfare state. And if it is indeed the case that 'welfare corporatism' is a form of quasi social democracy transplanted to a different institutional domain, then the apparent paradox of full employment co-existing with meagre social expenditure and decentralized industrial relations would dissolve. The explication of the underdevelopment of the Japanese welfare state and the development of comprehensive company welfare in large enterprises is therefore essential for reaching a verdict on the applicability of the micro-corporatist model.

The size and significance of the state in the Japanese political economy presents a marked contrast to familiar patterns of the mainstream of Western experience, in that the state combines a role of great importance in steering and assisting the economic activity of (big) business with exceptionally modest intervention in the distribution of national income. Whether considered in terms of public provision of social services like health and education, or of public transfer payments under minimum income and social insurance schemes, Japan's welfare state has always stood out as an extreme 'laggard' (for example, Wilensky, 1975). It would, however, be mistaken to interpret this as no more than a particularistic artifact – either of Japan's cultural tradition or of the predilection of its ruling party for small government and balanced budgets. Instead, labour market dualism must be seen as a key to understanding Japan's conservative social policy. An elaborate system of employment-linked social protection simply excludes the employees of small enterprises, while at the other pole of the labour market, social security 'has been tied to a large extent to the employer's policy of personnel management' (Takahashi, 1974, pp. 482–3).

Health and pension provisions are the predominant components of public social expenditure in Japan. In both cases, as Maruo (1986, p. 68) comments, 'all Japanese people are covered. That coverage is unequal, though, because of the dualistic structure of the public and private sectors, and the separation of big business, small business, and the self-employed.' Among wage-earners in the private sector, one third of the labour-force is employed by enterprises with fewer than ten employees, where unions and collective bargaining are non-existent and, it may be safely assumed, employer-initiated welfare schemes are rare. It is these workers who appear to be the principal clientele of the government's scanty health insurance scheme and who are most reliant on minimum public pensions. On the other hand, firms with at least a thousand employees are permitted by statute to provide their own health and pension benefits, under conditions which allow for superior benefits at relatively little additional cost to employers (Lee, 1987; Pempel, 1982 and 1989). Retirement allowances and other fully autonomous forms of enterprise welfare are even more closely associated with the scale of the enterprise. Not surprisingly then, as Hall (1988; p. 13) has shown, the total welfare expenses of employers rise in very similar proportions to wages and the rate of unionization along the gradient of increasing enterprise size. The close association between economic dualism and employer-furnished social benefits is also evident from the far higher probability of finding specific programmes in very large firms (5,000 or more employees) in comparison with industry as a whole – in 1973, 74 per cent versus 8 per cent for medical clinics, and 94 per cent versus 19 per cent for housing loans (Katsumi, 1974, p. 64).

Japan's public welfare programmes experienced unprecedented expansion in the 1970s. On the face of it, this might be taken as evidence of erosion of the sharp split between state and enterprise welfare. Yet, if anything, the new reforms actually served to crystallize the dualism of social policy. While the much-vaunted breakthrough to a 'Japanese-style welfare state' was highly consequential for social security expenditure (which rose ten times in real terms in the course of the sixties and seventies), this growth was closely tied to a rapid aging of the population and rising unemployment (Maruo, 1986). The responsiveness of the state to increased need may in turn by plausibly interpreted as the regime's reaction to a dangerous erosion of support for the Liberal Democratic Party (LDP) among the mass public. Subsequent deep cuts in social spending in the 1980s, after the LDP had more than recovered its electoral losses, reveal that a good part of the political commitment to more generous public welfare was no more durable than the threat to the legitimacy of the ruling party (Pempel, 1989). From a more qualitative perspective, although Japan did finally converge on the Western model in terms of the range of publicly enacted social programmes offered, to its citizens, it made very little movement towards the Social Democratic norms of universality, 'decommodification' and generosity so antithetical to its traditional pattern of social policy (cf., Esping-Andersen, 1985). Indeed, enlargement of statutory health and pension programmes took the form of an explicitly two-tiered system of minimal public provision alongside generous company-run and company-tied schemes in the larger private enterprises and their equivalents for public employees.

While the resilience of 'enterprise welfare' in big Japanese firms thus cannot be doubted, the question remains of whether provision for employment-linked social protection in Japan is really very different from other countries. One obvious difference lies in the widely remarked diffuseness in Japan of the boundary between work and private life, which receives concrete expression in the pervasive role played by paternalistic large employers, from arranging marriages to helping to place their employees' children in advantageous schools (Hanami, 1979). However, international comparisons of *monetized* forms of assistance suggest that Japan's distinctiveness is to be found not in the overall magnitude of company-level 'welfare effort' (Hall, 1988; Taira and Levine, 1985) but rather in its implications – for labour relations on the one hand and for capital formation on the other (cf., Pempel, 1982). The only big ticket items are housing facilities or subsidies, and retirement schemes. Given Japan's extremely tight housing market, the former is a compelling incentive for employees to demonstrate loyalty and flexibility (including acceptance of relocations). Contributions to retirement benefits are a form of deferred pay which, in the case of lump-sum payments, have the added attraction to the firm of constituting a fully tax-exempt source of investment funds. Even when combined with pensions (as in the largest enterprises), the benefit payable upon a worker's typically premature retirement is low enough neither to burden the firm nor to free older workers from the necessity of returning to work – quite possibly for the same employer, but at reduced pay. Indeed, the low level of social security for the Japanese elderly has been a powerful incentive for high rates of savings and participation in insurance schemes, which have in turn been a major factor in Japan's high rate of private investment (Johnson, this volume).

The 'residual' character of Japan's (public) welfare accords with expectations deriving from social democratic theory. In a polity in which unions are relatively limited in scope and have divided political affiliations, and where the labour movement has been excluded from government (not only formally but for the most part also effectively), we would not expect either left-wing initiative or pre-emptive action from the right to drive the enhancement of citizens' rights to social protection (Korpi, 1980). Given also the enterprise context of trade unionism and collective bargaining, and the unions' concentration in firms with suffici-ently wide profit margins to afford company welfare schemes, it is hardly surprising that the organized workers who benefit from the public/private split in social policy are generally opposed to extended public provision, while the unorganized labour-force which is most reliant on the welfare state lacks the collective voice to demand such extension.

This makes clear the striking congruence between the Japanese pattern of modest public welfare co-existing with highly differen-tiated occupational welfare, and the logic of the dual labour market. The exposure to market forces, which is the hallmark of a residual welfare state, is a powerful incentive to the workers and small business-people of the 'peripheral' sector to perform the roles assigned to them in the economy – as 'flexible' workers and suppliers, and savers. At the other extreme, the double-stranded tie – of dependency and loyalty – which binds 'permanent' workers to their employers in the sheltered private sector labour market (i.e. the large corporations) is clearly reinforced by, and even conditional upon, the critical role played by company housing, health, and retirement schemes. In a world of high and portable universal pensions, free public health care and cheap and plentiful housing, Japan's industrial giants would be hard-pressed to maintain their paternalist authority, the

precedence among workers of enterprise over class consciousness, and the selflessness of workers' orientation to productivity
and profits.

So Are Japanese Labour Relations 'Welfare Corporatist'?

In his influential essay 'The End of Convergence', John
Goldthorpe (1984) portrays *corporatism* and *dualism* as distinct
and to a large extent incompatible models of political economy.
In Goldthorpe's view the most conspicuous differences between
these two models concern the organization, political status, and
power position of labour. Under corporatism, unions organize on
a national (class-wide) basis, trading off restraint in their
economic demands in return for participation in and benefits
from the making of public policies. In contrast, the dualist model
explicitly excludes large sections of the work-force from the
sphere of unionization and 'industrial citizenship', while confining
collective action by organized workers to purely sectional and
economic objectives. With its labour movement parties permanently beneath the pinnacles of parliamentary and bureaucratic
power, and its exclusionary forms of unionism and career mobility
in the market arena, Japan must be regarded in this context as a
quintessential instance of the dualist political economy. The
question is whether the coexistence within the large enterprise of
labour weakness and political exclusion with both labour-
management cooperation and an elaborate system of social protection justifies the characterization of Japanese industrial relations
as welfare corporatist.

In my view the dualist model is by far the most appropraite
prism through which to interpret the Japanese case. Dualism in
Japan has constituted a highly effective framework for organizing
production and controlling labour in accordance with the goals of
rapid economic growth and perpetuation of the twinned
dominance of big business and the Liberal Democratic Party. In
addition to material benefits, including a surprisingly diffuse
sharing of the fruits of prosperity, dualism has been effective
because the blue-collar working class was successfully split
between the less privileged and those securely employed men
fortunate enough to work for the government and other big

employers. It follows that overall outcomes like full employment and industrial peace result from the aggregation of two
distinct logics – a condition of linked subordination and
protection in the primary labour market, and quite different
but equally powerful economic and ideological constraints on
labour in the secondary market. In parallel, social policy has not
been managed by any wholesale delegation of the functions of
the welfare state to the firm. Instead, we again observe a split
system, of state-subsidized company welfare in the primary
labour market co-existing with a public safety net which
minimally shelters other wage-earners from economic insecurity.

Over and above the substantive grounds for preferring the
dualist to the corporatist paradigm in the Japanese case, the
representation of labour relations within the firm as corporatist
also suffers from a fatal methodological flaw. Notions of 'micro-
corporatism'[8] commit the error of confounding the causes and
consequences of corporatism in labour relations. The inference is
made that these relations are corporatist because they are accompanied by labour restraint, compensated by economic security and
welfare. Yet scientific enquiry can hardly proceed by defining
causal categories in relation to their presumed consequences;
corporatism should rather be conceived in terms of what it is that
brings about labour restraint/welfare in a corporatist context.

In this spirit, I would suggest that the essential features of
corporatist industrial relations must include labour's *comprehensive* organization, the *negotiated* basis of labour restraint, and the
role of the *state* in stimulating and facilitating concertation
between its distributional interventions and the actions of unions
and employers. Viewed in this light, the attempt to draw a
Japanese analogy at the level of the large enterprise is
unconvincing. As we have seen, labour organization in Japan
mirrors the splitting of the working class in the labour market;
unions play a subordinate rather than codetermining role in fixing
the *quid pro quo*s received by labour in return for the exercise of
restraint; and, above all, no parallel can be found within the firm
to the state as mediator between labour and capital and regulator
of distributional processes. This is not to argue that corporatism
should be treated as a unitary phenomenon. On the contrary, the
most fruitful applications of the concept have been those which
delineate alternative varieties of corporatism (for example,
Katzenstein, 1985; Pontusson, 1983; Regini, 1982). But such

diversity is appropriately sought in the different ways in which labour organizes as a class and the varying extent of its political power in different settings – that is to say, in variations within corporatism's 'essential' framework – rather than by transplanting the concept to a quite different locus of analysis.

Economic Adjustment in the Seventies: Has Japan Become Corporatist?

Irrespective of the adequacy of micro-corporatism as a conceptual metaphor for Japanese labour relations, there remains the quite different possibility that in recent decades the Japanese political economy has begun to evolve in the direction of 'real' macro-level corporatism. Several observers have singled out the 1975 spring wage round as a watershed which allegedly pioneered a Japanese variant of corporatism based on 'information sharing' and an 'implicit contract' between labour, capital and state élites (Shimada, 1983; Taira and Levine, 1985). At the same time, some political scientists (notably Harari, 1986) argue that Japanese labour's traditional exclusion from policy-making networks is now a thing of the past – and so, therefore, is the conception of state/society relations in Japan as 'corporatism without labour'. It is not possible here to evaluate these developments with any authority. Instead, relying only on readily available information – including that furnished by the proponents of the 'transition to corporatism' thesis – I shall point to some serious grounds for questioning the validity of this thesis. Specifically, it is necessary to address three developments which might be interpreted as a transition to neo-corporatist political exchange between labour leaders and the state. First, events after 1974 include outcomes – the maintenance of close to full employment and the state's expansion of its social expenditure – which presumably could have been rewards provided by the state in return for union moderation. Second, the 1975 wage round constitutes a genuine watershed, in which *shunto* militancy – the aggressiveness of both demands and tactics – declined dramatically, also a presumptive indication of a turn by labour to political exchange. Finally, we need to weigh the evidence that union leaders are no longer frozen out of official policy-making forums, and may have been transformed into corporatist 'social partners'.

Were there *quid pro quo*s?

The idea that welfare state expansion in the 1970s was a negotiated reward for labour restraint can be easily disposed of. This expansion was in full swing before 1975, and we have already had occasion to point out that it is best interpreted as the state's response to rising demographic need on the one hand and the increasing political vulnerability of the LDP on the other. More puzzling is the fact that despite the severe consequences for Japan of the oil crisis, and the subsequent decline in the economy's longterm growth rate, Japanese unemployment remained below the levels prevailing in all but a handful of the Western nations. This record is consistent with the view that organized labour became party to a job-preserving 'social contract'. However, there are important qualifications which surround 'full employment' in the Japanese context. Even before the 1970s recession, questions were raised about the quality and comparability of Japanese labour-force statistics. Official data on unemployment apparently failed to monitor a good deal of new labour market slack in the period following the first oil price shock, particularly that due to women's involuntary exit from the labour market or downgrading to part-time employment (Nishikawa and Shimada, 1980). To illustrate the import of these omissions, on the basis of labour-force data assembled by Ernst (1978), it may be estimated that in 1975 Japan's official unemployment rate of 1.9 per cent would have reached about 5 per cent (similar to the OECD average at the time) after the inclusion of 'discouraged workers' and corrections for under-counting.

It is true that similar criticisms have also been levelled at the statistics for other countries – including Social Democratic Sweden (for example, Haveman, 1978). Nevertheless, it matters greatly for the labour market strength of workers whether declining aggregate demand is compensated primarily by the forced withdrawal of weak sections of the labour-force – migrants in Switzerland and women in Japan – or by new jobs (or else the bridges to new jobs provided by 'active manpower policies'). An additional basis of Japanese labour market adjustment is evident in a variety of trends during the mid-seventies recession. In large private enterprises, employer responses included overtime cuts, temporary lay-offs, and job redefinitions or relocations for the 'permanent' work-force, while later there was a noticeable shift in favour of more 'flexible' forms of employment, notably subcontracting (Tokunaga, 1984; Koshiro, 1983). In other words, personnel policy closely followed the dynamics of a dual labour market. Initially workers without tenure were termined or cut back to part-time employment, recruitment of 'mid-career' workers from outside was frozen, and at the same time measures were adopted to ration work among tenured employees while also increasing their productivity. When the demand for labour recovered, employers had learned their lesson, and stepped up 'flexibility' within the internal labour market while relying mainly on secondary labour from external sources for expansion.

Not surprisingly, then, despite low measured rates of unemployment, the coming of the economic crisis threw workers in the primary labour market onto the defensive. This is rather dramatically attested by stagnating union membership, even after employment recovered; and by a dramatic decline in work stoppages. Indeed, in an 18-country comparison of trends in strikes and unemployment through the early 1980s, this author singled out Japan (along with the United States) as exemplifying 'a massive crisis-induced retrenchment of strike activity' (Shalev, 1983b, p. 438). From the mid-1970s, labour militancy became restricted primarily to declarations of disputation involving little or no loss of working time.

Was there a move to 'social contract' bargaining?

In 1975 and again in 1980, in the wake of the decade's two oil price shocks, union wage demands fell substantially below expectations derived from prevailing economic conditions and prior wage trends. Shimada (1983, pp. 198–9) has interpreted this as evidence of 'flexible wage moderation' grounded in the emergence of a 'functional equivalent' of corporatist 'information exchange and sharing among organized actors'. In a similar vein, Taira and Levine (1985, pp. 250 and 248) write that, beginning with the 1975 *shunto*,

There was an implicit contract between the government,

unions, and workers. If the government kept its promise to reduce the rate of increase in consumer prices and to maintain employment, workers would keep their promise not to demand a greater increase in money wages than could be justified by increases in productivity. . . . In addition, . . . government social and labour welfare measures were strengthened, and trilateral and bilateral consultation . . . seemed to flourish. . . . There was also a precipitous decline in industrial disputes. . . .

Nevertheless, from the accounts of the 1975 wage round offered by Shimada and Taira and Levine, it is doubtful that 'information sharing' and 'consultation' were the key to union wage and strike behaviour:

1 In the background, as Taira and Levine admirably demonstrate, a number of *structural changes* combined to alter profoundly the outlooks of both labour and management in large-scale private enterprises. For employers the problems of inflation and growing international competition brought to a head their accumulating unease with a decade-long rise in industrial conflict, the increasing scope and cost of *shunto* demands as labour markets had tightened, and the growing expense of paying seniority-based wages to an aging 'permanent' work-force. At the same time, on the labour side the threat of unemployment after 1973 joined other growing constraints on workers in the big export-oriented manufacturing firms. Earlier on the leading edge of economic expansion, these unions had become the *de facto* vanguard of the *shunto* movement. But soaring energy prices and other global economic changes, combined with a pronounced technological drift to automation, was paring the number of primary sector jobs in manufacturing and greatly increasing the vulnerability of 'vanguard' labour to employer pressure.

2 The notions of tripartite information sharing and social contract bargaining imply a status of equal partnership for labour which is at odds with what actually happened. As Shimada has detailed, between the 1974 and 1975 wage rounds there was a closing of ranks among employers and high government officials and close coordination between them, culminating in the adoption of specific targets.

Apart from displays of 'formal' and 'symbolic' tripartism, the government did not consult the major labour organization until after its wage targets were determined, and offered the unions only vague promises of 'preparing favourable environments' in return for wage moderation (Shimada, 1983, pp. 189 and 193).

3 Again relying on Shimada, it is clear that sticks substantially outweighed carrots in the state's behaviour towards the unions. Taking their lead from the government, and behaving with unprecedented formal and informal discipline and unity, the leading industrial companies issued rigid wage offers. As indicated, these companies' employees had every reason to fear declining employment – and the government's actions only reinforced employer pressure on the unions. First, a tight money policy imposed a steep wage–employment trade-off on the negotiators. Second, a revision of unemployment insurance legislation (Nishikawa and Shimada, 1980), introducing new employment subsidies for distressed employers while pruning benefits to the unemployed, transmitted a policy commitment to preserving the status quo in the primary labour market. Third, the government pursued an aggressive policy towards labour in the public sector, the traditional stronghold of union militancy, which might otherwise have been an embarrassment to the posture of self-restraint which suited labour in the privately owned export industries.

Shinkawa's (1987) comprehensive study of wage restraint in 1975, which also rejects the thesis of a transition to corporatism, throws additional light on the origins of contemporary union moderation in Japan. His account reveals a profound gap between the internal solidarity of capital and the state on the one hand, and labour on the other, and implies that this was a major factor behind the unions' acceptance of what appeared at the time to be a painful cut in real wages. For quite specific political reasons, the new government formed at the end of 1974 awarded a high degree of autonomy to Mr Fukuda, its austerity-minded economics minister. Fukuda succeeded in overcoming opposition from within the state and close to it (government ministries, small business, and important LDP circles) to a policy of cooling down the economy and pressing aggressively for wage restraint. As a result, by the spring of 1975 both managers and workers in key manufacturing sectors were feeling the chilling effects of deflationary policies. The business community also exhibited a remarkable degree of discipline. While divided in both its interests and its formal associational activity, Japanese business is loosely coordinated by the *Zakai* – an influential alliance of top industrial and financial leaders spanning all the key business organizations. In the inflationary crisis of 1974, the *Zakai* succeeded in forging a class strategy and lobbying for a tough and concerted management line on wages. In contrast, on the side of organized labour longstanding divisions between the major national groupings had been deepened in the early 1970s by the success of Sohyo's efforts to 'politicize' unionism and the *shunto*. A crucial motive on the part of the 'bread and butter' union groupings (and one wholeheartedly supported by both employers and the government) was their desire to isolate Sohyo. This they succeeded in doing by accepting the government/employer line on wages and thereby cultivating excellent public relations while leaving Sohyo to fight a losing battle with militant public employers.

Has labour become a partner in policy networks?

Union leaders in 1975 and thereafter did have grounds for hoping that big employers and the state would respect the norm of job security in the primary labour market, provided that labour exercised pronounced wage restraint.[9] But rather than representing a tripartite accommodation, the unions' readiness for concessins stemmed from the short- and longterm economic vulnerability of the principal players on the labour side, their determination to alter the balance of power within the labour movement, and concerted action against the unions by business and the government. These forces combined to vitiate the old *shunto* strategy of a highly visible national campaign for large real wage increases.

This at least is the scenario which I have deduced from the secondary evidence cited. Nevertheless, doubt would be cast on this scenario if it could be shown that, far from being simply the objects of employer and state initiatives, top union leaders had actually become policy-making partners in a setting of genuine tripartism. Some observers have indeed implied something along these lines. In particular, Ehud Harari (1986 and this volume) has argued that labour's exclusion from policy networks was exaggerated in past scholarship and has become untenable as a contemporary description. He contends that for a mix of ideological and instrumental reasons, union federations had themselves been at least partly responsible for their own past absence from consultative frameworks; but that in any event, this gap has to an important extent been corrected. Citing data on the composition of statutory advisory bodies, Harari shows that in the decade after 1973 union representation on such bodies experienced a major quantitative increase accompanied by penetration into hitherto closed circles. Moreover, it is shown that labour representatives have included the 'militant' as well as the 'moderate' stream of unionism, and that the delegates themselves do not regard their role as tokenistic.

Harari's findings, while an important corrective to simplistic notions of organized labour as a political pariah, nevertheless fall short of substantiating the kind of policy-making partnerships in which unions participate in the corporatist nations of Western Europe (see Katzenstein, 1985; Taira and Levine, 1985, p. 266). It remains the case in the 1980s that business interests are routinely represented on advisory bodies, whereas only a minority include representatives of labour. The latter in any case enjoy only limited participation, especially in the 'sensitive' areas from which unions were formerly excluded altogether. The major union confederations receive their weightiest representation on committees dealing with employment and welfare – areas in which state intervention is modest, to the satisfaction of organized workers, sheltered as they are by the primary labour market. In contrast, as Harari points out, union delegates have little or no influence where they need it most – on committees occupied with the formation of broader macroeconomic policies. In addition to these limitations, Itoh's (1986) independent study of the relationship between interest groups and state agencies reveals quite striking qualitative differences between labour and most other types of associations. On the one hand, many union officials involved in such contacts (although proportionately less than the representatives of business and most other groups) did perceive open channels of communication. But they were also far less likely to report stronger indications of interpenetration, such as receipt of direct state subsidies or so-called 'administrative guidance'.

In fact, as Shinkawa (1987) points out, the state's commitment to *partial* legitimation and incorporation of labour union élites dates from the late 1950s, when influential figures within the ruling Liberal Democratic Party came to believe that (a) the aggressive labour policies hitherto pursued by employers and the state had already succeeded in generating a 'settlement' consistent with economic growth; (b) this settlement could be upset by traumatic confrontations (such as the Mitsui coal-miner's strike of 1960); and (c) the continued political alienation of left-leaning unions could have politically embarrassing implications for the government (as in the bitter conflict over the US–Japan Security Treaty). This pre-emptive response was reinforced in the late 1960s and early 1970s by the perception on the part of an electorally declining LDP of growing *shunto* activism as signifying an 'ominous threat of a general strike . . . [which could] turn into a political challenge from the union-supported left-wing opposition parties' (Taira and Levine, 1985, p. 258). It was not until the glove of limited policy participation was backed up by the fist of economic uncertainty that the unions surrendered both their high-wage policy and the trend towards broader mobilization and demands in the framework of the 'spring offensive'. There are therefore no strong grounds for believing that expanded union inclusion in the policy network constituted a qualitative break with conditions prior to the economic crisis, when organized labour evidently saw no reason to abandon mass mobilizations for the lure of political exchange. The retreat from the labour militancy of the early 1970s is better explained as the product of damaging economic trends, a unified external opposition and disunity among the unions themselves, than as a transition to a new *bargained corporatism* (Crouch, 1977) rooted in political inclusion of the labour movement.

Conclusion

The management of distributional conflicts in the labour market rests on quite different bases in the Japanese context from those which underpin corporatist arrangements in the Social Democratic nations of Western Europe – even though in the last decade and a half these countries have shared with Japan the distinction of relatively favourable economic performance (particularly in relation to unemployment) achieved in a relatively consensual atmosphere. I have criticized each one of the routes along which scholars have attempted to bring Japan under the analytical umbrella of the corporatist model. At the outset it was shown that quantitative studies of corporatism from a cross-national perspective exhibit uncharacteristic disagreement over whether Japan is or is not 'corporatist'. This disagreement reflects not only the confused conceptual and methodological state of the art but also real ambiguities. Notions of corporatism which link it to powerful and solidaristic labour movements are clearly alien to Japanese realities, and so are those which single out the characteristic institutions of corporatist policy-making. Theoretically and methodologically, it is more fruitful to treat these difficulties as grounds for seeking an alternative model to corporatism for the Japanese case, than to constrain concept and case to converge.

If such a convergence is nevertheless to be achieved, it requires either that labour's position in the Japanese political economy (as evidenced in patterns of employment, labour relations, and social policy) can be shown to be in some sense the functional equivalent of European-style corporatism; or that Japan has actually been moving towards the European model of strategic class action by labour on the basis of political incorporation and exchange. This essay's critical reconsideration of the evidence for each of these propositions casts doubt on both. The 'welfare corporatism' said to characterize large private enterprises is best understood in terms of the dualism of the Japanese economy, labour market, and working class, and the linchpin role played by the private/public split in social welfare. On the macro-societal plane, the participation of Japanese labour associations in the making of domestic public policy remains severely bounded, and trade union élites are still far short of engaging in active social contract bargaining. Labour quiescence since the middle of the 1970s is better explained by the whip of market conditions, the pressure of unified opponents, and the reinvigoration of the dual labour market, than by the elevation of peak labour organizations to the status of guardians of public order.

All this suggests that, for comparativists interested in locating Japan on a cross-national map, greater attention to the context of distributional conflict is required, in place of continued attempts to impose a single-stranded conceptual model on Japan's empirically inhospitable environment. This certainly need not necessitate a retreat to the particularistic case-study approach. One country which shares with Japan a hegemony of big business and conservative politics co-existing side by side with full employment, labour–management collaboration and successful policies of economic adjustment, is Switzerland (Katzenstein, 1980). Like Japan, Switzerland is characterized by a comparatively low rate of labour organization in divided and decentralized trade unions, and a modest socialist vote. But the Swiss model of labour movement incorporation into institutions of state in effect signifies the upper limit to the Japanese trend towards ending labour's exclusion while perpetuating its inability to rule. No less important, the labour markets of both countries are deeply dualistic, with large strata of relatively powerless workers occupying undesirable job slots. The union movement, reflecting the concerns of primary sector workers and their employers, excludes secondary sector labour and consents to a dual welfare system which perpetuates residual social provision by the state and helps preserve harmony in the enterprise. The synthesis of co-optation in politics and dualism in the market arena common to Switzerland and Japan appears to offer a more enlightening model of labour in the Japanese political economy than attempts to constrain the corporatist model to fit Japanese realities, or vice versa.

Notes

1   Much of this chapter is in the nature of an incursion into terrain usually reserved for experienced Japanologists, by an author with little primary expertise on Japan. I am grateful to the editors of this volume for encouraging my audacity and to participants in seminars which they organized for helpful comments; to T.J. Pempel for pointing me to valuable sources; to Toshimitsu Shinkawa and Carl Le Grand for sharing their unpublished work with me; and to Walter Korpi and the Swedish Institute of Social Research for generous

hospitality while the paper was in preparation.

2 The Pearson correlation between the Cameron and Czada scores is 0.91 (n=17). (Note that here, as in all subsequent calculations, the original data series were transformed into a common scale ranging from −1 to +1.)

3 For a rich collection of sources relevant to the period, see Livingston, Moore and Oldfather (1976). Moore (1983) provides the definitive account of the period of labour resurgence early in the occupation period. I rely here on informative articles by Sumiya (1974) and Tokunaga (1983), and also on Armstrong, Glyn and Harrison's (1984, pp. 136–40) compilation of contemporary sources.

4 The claim that these constraints on worker solidarity have been the price exacted by management for its conditional acceptance of trade unionism is substantiated by Sumiya (1974, p. 63), Taira (1970, p. 180), Dore (1973, p. 325), and, regarding the imposition of a 'no unionization clause' on subcontractors, by Carl Le Grand of the Swedish Institute for Social Research, who kindly shared with me the results of his unpublished fieldwork on subcontracting.

5 Particularly revealing in this respect is that, according to Tokunaga (1983, p. 321), since 1965 the leading iron and steel firms have presented a single take-it-or-leave-it wage offer to unions in their industry, an offer which appears to have influenced the overall level of *shunto* settlements. This is not to argue that Japanese workers would have been just as well off without *shunto*. Koshiro's (1983, pp. 230–8) econometric evidence indicates that *shunto* militancy in the public and private sectors has raised wages – although he also shows that spring wage settlements have been consistent with the maintenance of profitability.

6 These barriers apply to all but the 'half-way workers' recruited in boom periods by large enterprises from smaller firms or the self-employed. But, tellingly, these mid-career recruits are penalized by lower pay unless they produce an impeccable performance record (Koshiro, 1983, p. 257).

7 Regarding rewards: (a) under the pressure of labour shortages, the gap between men's wages in firms of different sizes narrowed during the 1960s; (b) from a life-cycle perspective, primary labour market workers are not always advantaged – their starting salaries are low, and so is their income after retirement; (c) it is plausible to assume that *household* income in the long run is much more equal than the cross-sectional gap between *individual* workers at any given moment in time (Pempel, 1989) – this is presumably why income inequality between households is lower in Japan than in most OECD countries.

8 Goldthorpe himself (1984, p. 340) uses the term micro-corporatism in a brief reference to the Japanese case, while stressing that a Japan-

style adjustment to dualism necessarily results in 'the fundamental division and effective depoliticization of the working class'.

9 Unions in 1975 agreed to a nominal wage increase below the rate of inflation. The actual increase in real wages after 1973 remained under 3 per cent for the rest of the decade – whereas earlier in the decade it was consistently above 8 per cent (Taira and Levine, 1985, p. 248).

References

Armstrong, P., A. Glyn and J. Harrison (1984), *Capitalism since World War II: The Making and Breakup of the Great Boom*. London, Fontana.

Bruno, M. and J.D. Sachs (1985), *The Economics of Worldwide Stagflation*. Oxford, Basil Blackwell.

Cameron, D.R. (1984), 'Social democracy, corporatism, labour quiescence and the representation of economic interest in advanced capitalist society' in J.H. Goldthorpe (ed.), *Order and Conflict in Contemporary Capitalism*. Oxford, Oxford University Press, pp. 143–78.

Castles, F.G. (1978), *The Social Democratic Image of Society*. London, Routledge.

Crouch, C. (1977), *Class Conflict and the Industrial Relations Crisis: Compromise and Corporatism in the Policies of the British State*. London, Heinemann.

Crouch, C. (1980), 'The conditions for trade-union wage restraint', fifth draft of paper for Brookings Institution project on the Politics and Sociology of Global Inflation.

Czada, R. (1987), 'The impact of interest politics on flexible adjustment policies' in H. Keman, H. Paloheimo and P.F. Whiteley (eds.), *Coping with the Economic Crisis: Alternative Responses to Economic Recession in Advanced Industrial Societies*. London and Beverly Hills, Sage, pp. 20–53.

Dore, R. (1973), *British Factory – Japanese Factory: The Origins of National Diversity in Industrial Relations*. Berkeley and Los Angeles, University of California Press.

Ernst, A. (1978), 'Unemployment and underemployment in Japan: an outline of the state of empirical research' (in German), *Mitteilungen aus der Arbeitsmarket und Berufsforschung*, 1.

Esping-Andersen, G. (1985), 'Power and distributional regimes', *Politics and Society*, 14(2), pp. 223–56.

Goldthorpe, J.H. (1984), 'The end of convergence: corporatist and dualist tendencies in modern western societies' in J.H. Goldthorpe (ed.), *Order and Conflict in Contemporary Capitalism*. Oxford, Oxford University Press, pp. 315–43.

Goldthorpe, J.H. (1984), *idem* (ed.), *Order and Conflict in Contemporary Capitalism*. Oxford, Oxford University Press.

Gordon, A. (1985), *The Evolution of Labor Relations in Japan: Heavy Industry, 1853–1945*. Cambridge, Mass., Harvard University Press.

Hall, R. (1988), 'Enterprise welfare in Japan: its development and role', Welfare State Programme, Suntory-Toyota International Centre for Economics and Related Disciplines, London School of Economics, Discussion Paper No. WSP/31.

Hanami, T. (1979), *Labor Relations in Japan Today*. Tokyo, Kodansha.

Harari, E. *Policy Concertation in Japan*. Occasional Paper No. 58/59 of the East Asian Seminar, Free University of Berlin's Social and Economic Research on Modern Japan Series. Berlin: Verlag Ute Schiller, 1986.

Haveman, R.H. (1978), 'Unemployment in Western Europe and the United States: a problem of demand, structure, or measurement?', *American Economic Review*, 68(2), pp. 44–50.

Itoh, M. (1986), 'Labor unions as interest groups: the case of Japan', unpublished paper, Political Science Department, Nagoya State University.

Jacoby, S. (1979), 'The origins of internal labor markets in Japan', *Industrial Relations*, 18(2), pp. 184–96.

Kalecki, M. (1943), 'Political aspects of full employment', *Political Quarterly*, 14(4), pp. 322–31.

Katzenstein, P. (1980), *Capitalism in One Country? Switzerland in the International Economy*. Cornell University, Western Societies Program Occasional Paper No. 13.

Katzenstein, P. (1985), *Small States in World Markets: Industrial Policy in Europe*. Ithaca, NY, Cornell University Press.

Korpi, W. (1980), 'Social policy and distributional conflict in the capitalist democracies. A preliminary comparative framework', *West European Politics*, 3(3), pp. 296–316.

Korpi, W. and M. Shalev (1980), 'Strikes, power and politics in western nations, 1900–1976', *Political Power and Social Theory*, 1, pp. 301–34.

Koshiro, K. (1983), 'Development of collective bargaining in post-war Japan' in T. Shirai (ed.), *Contemporary Industrial Relations in Japan*. Madison, University of Wisconsin Press, pp. 205–57.

Lee, H.K. (1987), 'The Japanese welfare state in transition' in R.R. Friedman, N. Gilbert and M. Sherer (eds.), *Modern Welfare States: A Comparative View of Trends and Prospects*. New York, New York University Press, pp. 243–63.

Lehmbruch, G. and P.C. Schmitter (1982), *idem* (eds.), *Patterns of Corporatist Policy Making*. London and Beverly Hills, Sage.

Lehner, F. (1987), 'Interest intermediation, institutional structures and public policy' in H. Keman, H. Paloheimo and P.F. Whiteley (eds.), *Coping with the Economic Crisis: Alternative Responses to Economic Recession in Advanced Industrial Societies*. London and Beverly Hills, Sage, pp. 54–82.

Lincoln, J.R. and A. Kalleberg (1985), 'Work organization and workforce commitment: a study of plants and employees in the US and Japan', *American Sociological Review*, 50, pp. 738–60.

Livingston, J., J. Moore and F. Oldfather (1976), *idem* (eds.), *The Japan Reader: Volume Two – Post-war Japan, 1945 to the Present*. Harmondsworth, Penguin.

Maruo, N. (1986), 'The development of the welfare mix in Japan' in R. Rose and R. Shiratori (eds.), *The Welfare State: East and West*. New York and London, Oxford University Press, pp. 64–79.

Nishikawa, S. and H. Shimada (1980), 'Employment and unemployment' in S. Nishikawa (ed.), *The Labor Market in Japan: Selected Readings*. Tokyo, University of Tokyo Press, pp. 124–41.

Panitch, L. (1981), 'Trade unions and the capitalist state', *New Left Review*, 125, pp. 21–43.

Pempel, T.J. (1989), 'Japan's creative conservatism: continuity under challenge' in F.G. Castles (ed,), *The Comparative History of Public Policy*. Cambridge, Polity Press, pp. 149–91.

Pempel, T.J. (1982), *Policy and Politics in Japan: Creative Conservatism*. Philadelphia, Temple University Press.

Pempel, T.J. and K. Tsunekawa (1979), 'Corporatism without labor? The Japanese anomaly' in P.C. Schmitter and G. Lehmbruch (eds.), *Trends Toward Corporatist Intermediation*. Beverly Hills and London, Sage, pp. 231–70.

Pizzorno, A. (1978), 'Political exchange and collective identity in industrial relations' in C. Crouch and A. Pizzorno (eds.), *The Resurgence of Class Conflict in Western Europe since 1968* (Volume 2). London, Macmillan, pp. 277–98.

Pontusson, J. (1983), 'Comparative political economy of advanced capitalist states: Sweden and France', *Kapitalistate*, (10–11), pp. 43–73.

Regini, M. (1982), 'Changing relationships between labour and the state in Italy' in P.C. Schmitter and G. Lehmbruch (eds.), *Trends Towards Corporatist Intermediation*. Beverly Hills and London, Sage, pp. 109–32.

Schmidt, M.G. (1982), 'The role of parties in shaping economic policy' in F.G. Castles (ed.), *The Impact of Parties*. London and Beverly Hills, Sage, pp. 97–176.

Schmitter, P.C. (1974), 'Still the century of corporatism?', *The Review of Politics* 36(1), pp. 85–131.

Shalev, M. (1983a), 'The social democratic model and beyond: two "generations" of comparative research on the welfare state', *Comparative Social Research*, 6, pp. 315–51.

Shalev, M. (1983b), 'Strikes and the crisis: industrial conflict and unemployment in the western nations', *Economic and Industrial Democracy*, 4(4), pp. 417–60.

Shimada, H. (1983), 'Wage determination and information sharing: an alternative approach to incomes policy?', *Journal of Industrial Relations*, 25(2), pp. 177–200.

Shinkawa, T. (1987), 'A Japanese style incomes policy: the 1975 spring labor offensive', unpublished paper, Toronto University, Department of Political Science. (English version of an article published in H. Ohtake (ed.), *Nipponseiji no Soten*. Tokyo, Sanichi Sobo, 1984.)

Steven, R. (1982), *Classes in Contemporary Japan*. Cambridge, Cambridge University Press.

Sumiya, M. (1974), 'The emergence of modern Japan' in K. Okochi, B. Karsh and S.B. Levine (eds.), *Workers and Employers in Japan*. Princeton and Tokyo, Princeton University Press and University of Tokyo Press, pp. 15–48.

Taira, K. (1970), *Economic Development and the Labor Market in Japan*. New York and London, Columbia University Press.

Taira, K. and S.B. Levine (1985), 'Japan's industrial relations: a social compact emerges' in H. Juris, M. Thompson and W. Daniels (eds.), *Industrial Relations in a Decade of Economic Change*. Madison, Industrial Relations Research Association, pp. 247–300.

Takahashi, T. (1974), 'Social security for workers' in K. Okochi, B. Karsh, and S.B. Levine (eds.), *Workers and Employers in Japan*. Tokyo, University of Tokyo Press and Princeton University Press, pp. 441–84.

Tarantelli, E. (1986), 'The regulation of inflation and unemployment', *Industrial Relations*, 24(1), pp. 1–15.

Therborn, G. (1986), *Why Some Peoples are More Unemployed than Others*. London, Verso.

Tokunaga, S. (1983), 'A Marxist reinterpretation of Japanese industrial relations, with special reference to large private enterprises' in T. Shirai (ed.), *Contemporary Industrial Relations in Japan*. Madison, University of Wisconsin Press, pp. 313–29.

Tokunaga, S. (1984), 'The structure of the Japanese labour market' in S. Tokunaga and J. Bergmann (eds.), *Industrial Relations in Transition: The Cases of Japan and the Federal Republic of Germany*. Tokyo, University of Tokyo press, pp. 25–55.

Wilensky, H.L. (1975), *The Welfare State and Equality: Structural and Ideological Roots of Public Expenditure*. Berkeley and Los Angeles, University of California Press.

5 Ritual, Strikes, Ceremonial Slowdowns: Some Thoughts on the Management of Conflict in Large Japanese Enterprises[1]

E. Ben-Ari

Introduction

For the better part of the post-war period, the most influential image of Japan's large enterprises was one in which 'joint decision-making, consensus and tightly integrated groups predominate' (Cole, 1971, p. 165). Yet as Krauss, Rohlen and Steinhoff (1984a, p. 11) note, this image – which was both a derivative and an exemplification of the 'group model' of Japanese society (Nakane, 1973) – is essentially a rendering of certain cultural ideals or emphases. In other words, this image is related to the well-known Japanese notions of harmony and consensus, and to the idea that conflicts and outright expressions of discords are unnatural embarrassments to be avoided whenever possible (Lebra, 1984, p. 42). Since the mid-1970s, however, a growing number of scholars have been attempting to correct the rather facile acceptance of the 'consensus and harmony' portrayal of large firms. These scholars (for instance, Vogel, 1975, p. xxi; Sugimoto, 1978, 1981; Sugimoto and Mouer, 1980, p. 8) have sought to underline the existence and to draw out the theoretical implications of the frictions and strife which are an integral part of these companies.

The emerging picture of these enterprises is of a complex of patterns of conflict and cooperation, of tension and harmony. Uncovering these complex patterns, however, does not imply abandoning the 'cultural factor' as a variable that can explain the dynamics of large firms. Nor does it simply mean contrasting the 'real' with the 'ideal' (Krauss *et al.*, 1984a, p. 11). Rather, the challenge for analysis is to show how this ideal – a historically constituted model of and for action – both structures and regulates the disaccords and the struggles which are found in these organizations. More specifically, this means examining how definitions of conflict situations, mechanisms for expressing tensions, and devices for managing frictions all affect the actual dynamics of industrial friction. To echo Krauss, Rohlen and Steinhoff (1984a, p. 11), culture should be seen as part of the conflict process, and not just as a policeman preventing conflict from occurring.[2]

Most of the studies which have attempted to deal with the theme of 'culture and conflict' in large Japanese organizations have tended to focus on such phenomena as the formal machinery of negotiations, the procedures for arbitration and mediation, or (most of all) the structures of decision-making. I propose to look at this theme from what is perhaps a rather novel perspective. It is novel in two respects: the social and organizational forms which are singled out for study and the theoretical tools which are utilized in order to analyse them.

The social and organizational forms to which I refer are the well-known strikes which the unions of large enterprises 'stage' periodically. During these short and highly structured situations, workers often don special costumes, gather in large assemblies and publicly assert their support for the class struggle and the basic unity of the working class. Yet these strikes, which are apparently held in order to stress the basic conflict between labour and management, actually figure as part of the process through which union–management cooperation is effected. They form an important first stage from which negotiations – usually smoothly – proceed.

While these situations undeniably belong to the interstices of these organizations – that is, to the narrow time junctures between the 'regular' periods of work activities – they should not be viewed as residual to, as somehow unimportant aspects of, the dynamics of these firms. For these occasions are 'cultural performances': special social constructs which differ and are set apart from everyday relations and behaviour but which, at the same time, allow the people participating in them to comment upon, explore and redefine the ties which bind them together. As MacAloon (1984, p. 1) puts it, 'cultural performances are intricate congregations of processes: not only of entertainment, of persuasive formulations, or of cathartic indulgences. They are also occasions in which people reflect upon and define themselves, dramatize their collective myths (and distresses), present themselves with alternatives, and eventually change in some ways while remaining the same in others.'

These remarks suggest two sets of questions which seem to be of importance for understanding the role of 'staged' strikes in Japan's large enterprises. The first involves the internal dynamics through which these occasions are constructed: the interplay of group dynamics and individual experiences which contribute to the capacity of such situations to transform groups and individuals. The second set of questions is related to the tie between these special situations and the wider social contexts within which they occur: those peculiarities of the gatherings which promote or limit their contribution to the workings of the organizations in which the participants are employed and to the expression of tension and the management of conflicts within them.

A final point should be mentioned. Given the variety of organizations and firms in Japan, and given the limits of this volume, I focus exclusively on the activities of large commercial enterprises. An analysis of smaller enterprises or the public sector (Harari, 1984; Shinofuji, 1978; Watanabe, 1981, pp. 62ff.) would necessitate taking into account a different set of organizational and social factors, and, by implication, a different set of cultural performances.

Firm-as-Family: Dependence and Commitment

Welfare corporatism

A short examination of the organizational attributes of Japan's large enterprises will help to place the argument in context. Dore (1973, p. 370) has coined the term 'welfare corporatism' to denote the complex of characteristics which marks these companies: longterm security and stability of employment, integration of (permanent) manual workers as full members of the organization, welfare programmes, recreational facilities, a 'familial' or corporate ideology, and company-based unions and bargaining structures.

In its essentials, 'welfare corporatism' developed out of the scarcity of skilled craftsmen which marked Japan's major industries during the first two decades of this century. Mindful of this labour shortage, managements instituted a number of measures to secure a steady and dependable flow of workers. First, as a corollary to the simplification of job skills, in-house training programmes were instituted (Okochi *et al.*, 1974, pp. 487–91). Then, in place of the prevalent ranking of occupations by grade and skill, wage increases began to be determined according to length of service with the enterprise. Finally, company welfare amenities were gradually introduced: seasonal and yearly bonuses, housing, recreation facilities, medical care, and educational activities. Once such links were in effect, it was thought, workers' identification with, and loyalty to, the enterprise would develop to ensure their interest in the stability of the whole system.

On another level – the ideological one – managements actively searched for means with which to legitimate the emerging industrial relations system. In concrete terms, their challenge was one of finding a way to shift the 'personalized paternalism of the small-scale employer' to the 'administrative paternalism of the large firm' (Cole, 1979, pp. 21–2). Two elements formed the core of the new industrial ideology:[3] the nature and definition of 'familial' corporate groups and the character of authority relations. Both elements were derived from pre-industrial emphases on high in-group identification and exclusivity, and on material and affective dependence on those in authority.

It is in this light that the way in which the supply of material benefits by companies served to reinforce the strong ideological emphases on in-group solidarity should be seen. The wage system, for example, served at one and the same time both to emphasize the security found in the firm for permanent workers, and to differentiate them drastically from temporary workers or those employed in less fortunate enterprises. Along similar lines, the managements of many large firms also attempted to adopt the cultural ideals according to which the traditional employer–employee relationship involved a willingness to strive for mutual understanding and the reconciliation of differences. The adoption of such ideals, it was thought, would lead to an avoidance of the class-confrontation type of conflicts which characterized Europe.

The post-war period, during which Japan's industries were reorganized, was also one in which 'welfare corporatism' was fully institutionalized. Employees of the larger firms slowly began – and by the late 1960s were already – enjoying a plethora of services and programmes such as pensions and retirement pay, yearly bonuses and loans, help with purchasing housing or company accommodation, company cooperatives and stores, dining halls and subsidized meals, health insurance and care, educational facilities and day-care centres, hobby clubs and sports amenities, and sometimes even holiday sites.

It was also during this period that the 'familial' or corporate ideology was most forcefully propagated by management, and to a large extent also accepted by a majority of workers. Evidence of this propagation can be found in almost any sampling of statements by middle-level and high-level managers, or in company mottos which abound with such imagery as 'trees and saplings', 'the cycle of goodness', JAL's 'we are one', or the well-known 'harmony and strength' (Rohlen, 1974). The stress on a spiritually harmonious whole is further emphasized through such means as company songs and insignia, ceremonies marking 'birth' into the family or achievement of permanent status, or elaborate farewell parties signifying separation.

At the same time, however, it should be stressed that this ideology – and its accompanying rituals and regalia – applies exclusively to permanent workers: that is, those people who are recruited from high school or university and who are expected to stay with the firm until their retirement (between the ages of 55 and 65). It is these people – and not the temporary workers who sometimes make up to 20 per cent of a larger firms' labour force – who are also eligible for the myriad company benefits mentioned above.

Enterprise unionism[4]

It is against this background that the form of unionism found in large Japanese enterprises should be understood. In broad terms, the Japanese experience is similar to that of other industrialized nations both in terms of organizational ratio (the percentage of workers organized in unions) and in the fact that union organization has been most successful in the large and medium-sized enterprises (Dunlop, 1978, p. 6; Shirai and Shimada, 1978; Shirai, 1975, p. 168). Its peculiarity, however, lies in the type of union that has developed: in Japan, the craft or industry-wide union is the exception. Union power in this society is dispersed among thousands of separate enterprise unions.

In general, an enterprise union consists exclusively of permanently employed workers regardless of their specific occupation (Tsukamoto, 1967; Japan Institute of Labour, 1979, p. 8).[5] The most important implication of this is that identification with the union tends to reinforce identification with the enterprise. Indeed, ideally, the 'consciousness of union members is not distinguished from that of the workers' status as employee' (Okochi *et al.*, 1974, p. 502). When coupled with the tendency of employees of large firms to see themselves as labour élites (Levine, 1967, p. 269), this kind of identification leads to a distinct concern of unionists with the conditions of their own enterprise, and to an equally distinct lack of regard for outside matters. These tendencies are reinforced, moreover, by another feature of union membership.

In contrast to other industrialized countries, where white-collar workers have tended to shy away from union membership (Dunlop, 1978, p. 6), in Japan they have readily joined local unions. This trend has been facilitated by a relative egalitarianism *within* the firm, as expressed in the narrow wage dispersion for all workers of the same age and length of service, and in their self-identification as an élite work-force. This has resulted in the difficulty for any particular group of workers (clerks or technicians, for instance) of emphasizing their sectionally-specific interests (Shirai and Shimada, 1978, p. 260). Moreover, rather than contributing to a divisiveness within the labour camp (Koshiro, 1983, p. 152), white-collar workers in fact contribute to a united union. Thus, for instance, white-collar workers provide the bulk of union leadership (Koshiro, 1983, p. 152), information about the financial situation of the firm (Cole, 1971, pp. 227–8), and a sophisticated ability to formulate policy and to bargain (Shirai, 1975, p. 168). When coupled with the view held by some managements that a term as union official provides good training for managerial positions, it is not surprising that 'service as an officer is often considered a task which is undertaken for the benefit of the enterprise' (Glazer, 1976, p. 882).

Moreover, unions are very often dependent on privileges granted to them by management in the form of office space, meeting rooms, telephones, furniture, or photocopying services. As Hanami (1984, p. 15) astutely notes, these facilities symbolize an essential intimacy in the union–management tie. The union is thus seen as a cooperative body contributing with management to the morale and ultimately to the success of the firm (Rohlen, 1974, p. 189). In the words of Okochi and his associates (1974, p. 503), the union becomes an appendage of the firm to which its members belong.

While relations with management are based on mutuality, ties with rank-and-file members are based on solidarity. When compared to the activities of unions in other countries, it is apparent that a great deal of time and effort is invested in order to reach decisions on the basis of as wide a consensus as possible (Shirai, 1975, p. 177). Leaders often send out 'feelers' to the rank-and-file members, and union gatherings take on the character of plebiscites rather than of meetings for determining strategies and positions. Indeed,

> before a leader hands down a decision, he listens to the
> opinions of other leaders and members, tries to reconcile
> differences and gets as many others as possible to participate in
> the decision-making process. This is the 'mass line' or 'mass
> debate'. (Levine, 1967, p. 175)

The use of so many resources at these debates well reflects the union's basic role as an active articulator and propagator of in-group solidarity. The union and its leadership are embedded, in short, within the organizational and social structures of the enterprise: 'under these circumstances, it becomes difficult for the union to represent effectively the interests of its members, as distinct from the interests of the company' (Cole, 1971, p. 228).[6]

Management ideology, cultural analogy

Against the background of this portrayal, it may be justifiable to assert that it is in large Japanese firms that the 'firm-as-family' analogy has greatest currency today. This applies not only to the substantial material reliance of employees on their companies, nor just to the propagation of a familial ideology. Perhaps more importantly the appropriateness of this analogy is related – as a long line of scholars (Kiefer, 1980, p. 436; Cole, 1979, p. 253; Rohlen, 1974, p. 263) have noted – to the emotional and intellectual identification of workers with their workplace, and especially with their workmates. As Fruin (1980, p. 447; 1978) puts it:

> The Japanese display a cultural preference for affective as well as instrumental work commitment which large firms are more easily able to take advantage of through their considerable emphasis on corporate welfare and paternalism. In this cultural sense, therefore, the firm *as* a family, when used to describe the spirit or feeling of a firm has a certain validity in post-war Japan, (emphasis in original).

Reinforcing this holistic concept or analogy of 'corporation-as-extended-family', as Dore (1984, pp. xxxiv–xxxvii) well under-lines, are both a widespread sense of trust in the fairness of the whole system, and a sentiment of 'belonging to' (rather than 'working for') the company.

The strength of this analogy, however, should not be attributed solely to the successful inculcation of an external managerial ideology. Rather, it should be seen, along the lines of Murakami's (1985, p. 413) thesis, as the outcome of the successful adaption of certain cultural ideals to the circumstances of large modern enterprises. To put this differently, the 'firm-as-family' refers to the adaption of such cultural emphases as 'group orientedness', 'socio-centric personalities', and 'particularistic identities' (Kiefer, 1980, p. 436) to the organizational structures of large firms. As Kiefer (1970, p. 71) perceptively observes, managements have made use of the concepts and attitudes learned in primary and secondary (i.e. school) socialization – and which are themselves rooted in wider 'traditional' emphases – to create similar ones at the workplace.[7]

Questions, dilemmas, tensions

Thus the 'firm-as-family' analogy well encapsulates the major peculiarities of large Japanese enterprises: a strong coupling between commitment to and identification with workmates, and a high level of material dependence on the firm. Such a depiction, however, does not imply – as indeed a depiction of the 'traditional' extended family does not imply – an idyllic or untroubled existence for the employees of these companies. In the past few decades, these workers have increasingly come to recognize, to express openly, and to question, the strains and tensions and the coercive potentials that characterize relations within these firms.

On one level these problematic issues refer to the anxieties which are associated with large bureaucratic organizations and with small, highly cohesive work-groups. Dore (1984, p. xii) talks of the disquiet which many workers feel at the possibility of being arbitrarily 'posted' from one plant to another and having to uproot their family as a consequence. Rohlen (1974) mentions the often strong group pressures to conform, which some employees feel; while Plath (1980, ch.4), in an evocative essay, portrays some of the apprehensions associated with an office worker's stagnating career.[8]

Yet the difficulties which are associated with the workplace are related to another, deeper level. Since the beginnings of the Meiji era, there 'had been a fundamental national consensus about the importance of economic growth and of Japan achieving a favourable position in international trade' (Vogel, 1975, p. xv). This consensus lay beneath the willingness to undertake many personal and national sacrifices, and to constantly strive for the achievement of such goals. But now we are witness to 'a turning away from traditional or, more exactly, from *modern* traditional values. What is developing is a new set of expectations of public life' (Passin, 1975, p. 836). People are now turning to other goals – welfare, quality of life, personal fulfilment – in search of a new purposefulness. Such a search has been manifested in such causes as ecological groups or citizens' movements, but it has also increasingly spilled over into the area of worker concerns (Harari, 1978, p. 1025).

In the case of employees of the larger firms, this search is especially pertinent. For these people, the 'totality' of commitment imposed either through their dependence on company benefits, the great peer-group pressure to conform or their internal identification with their workmates, poses serious difficulties and dilemmas.[9] Two contradictory trends are evident in this regard. On the one hand, developments within the firm – higher wages and a decrease of working hours – and outside it – a growth of leisure facilities and amenities – have made it less able to command such a 'totality' of life concerns among workers. This is reflected in research which shows that workers have started to place greater value on leisure than on work, and have shifted the locus of leisure to the home at the expense of the company (Bennett and Levine, 1976, p. 477; Hazama, 1976, p. 49; Dore, 1984, p. xxiii).

On the other hand, however, these trends have not justified the failures to fulfil expectations at the workplace. Thus, for instance, in the face of demands for more free (and freer) time, many employees do not take all the vacation time available to them (Bennett and Levine, 1976, p. 481; Cole, 1979, p. 231). Furthermore, while younger workers see lunch and after work hours as their own, as they get older the orientation outside the firm decreases (Cole, 1971, pp. 160–79), and they more readily work on company concerns on their own. Hence, rather than signalling a clear trend away from the firm, these developments in fact point to emergence of certain dilemmas which workers now face.

These dilemmas, in turn, are compounded by the fact that for most employees personal fulfilment can only be achieved on the basis of their material dependence on the firms. Whether this fulfilment is defined in terms of popular entertainment or the participation in a variety of clubs, it is ultimately based on the firm's loans (i.e. for homes and cars), wages, overtime, bonuses, or other benefits. The worker is thus caught in a bind, in which only continued commitment to the firm can ensure activities outside it.

Over and above demands for greater material rewards, workers are also increasingly calling for such things as job choices and job enrichment programmes (Takahashi, 1974), meaning in work (*hatarakigai*) (Takeuchi, 1982, pp. 54–63), and more fulfilling work experiences (Bennett and Levine, 1976, pp. 481). As in the case of the search for private fulfilment, here again the trend is not one in which workers are clearly turning away from work, but one in which uncertainty and confusion are found. As Cole (1971, p. 174) aptly puts it, it is 'not a matter of tradition simply fading away, rather a process of competition goes on inside each individual'. Yet this 'competition' is not phrased in class terms. While there 'is always a vague, but real sense of resentment over being manipulated and being forgotten' (Rohlen, 1974, p. 179), this sense is interpreted in personal terms. It is the membership of the enterprise – and the duties implied in such membership – that forms the core of resentment. To provide an example:

The oppression the workers feel – and undoubtedly they do feel it – is not the oppression of coercive external authority. It comes from the inner compulsion bred from submission to the norms and targets which the organization has set for them. (Dore, 1984, p. xxi)

The question thus becomes one of the special social forms through which the tension and resentments generated by the workplace can be released – that is, mitigated, expressed and sometimes resolved.

In this respect, however, workers in Japan's large firms are placed in a special situation. Cole (1979, p. 244) following Hirschmann (1970) identifies two principal modes of protest within organizations. The first – 'exit' – refers to a departure from one's organization in order to better one's conditions. As is evident from the literature, this alternative is rather limited in the context of larger Japanese companies (Dore, 1973, p. 100). The high identification with and commitment to workmates, employees' expectations of future security and steady growth of income, and the prospect of being compelled to enter smaller (i.e. less prestigious and less successful firms) upon leaving, well underline this situation. In general terms then, while labour mobility is slowly increasing, it is still a somewhat limited trend (Hanami, 1979, p. 43).

The second outlet for protest – 'voice' – refers to the articulation of grievances within the organization. Yet, here again, possibilities within bigger enterprises seem to be rather limited. The reasons given above for staying with the company, when reinforced by the nature of union–management coopera-tion, the cultural penchant for indirect expression of conflict, and the lack of union independence all work to effect such a limitation. Clearly other types of voices, tempered ones, are needed within these contexts: 'rituals of rebellion'.

Strike Action, Ritual Protest

Staged subversion and tangible collusion

Of the public modes of protest which can be utilized by workers, the strike is surely the most obvious. Ideally, its aim is to threaten the very basis of a firm's existence: production. Following World War II, Japan's workers gained not only the legal right to strike but also, no less importantly, political recognition of the basic legitimacy of such action (Tomazu, 1981, p. 48). Indeed, when compared with the pre-war era, the post-war period is marked by a sharp increase in all indices of strike activity (Shirai and Shimada, 1978). A closer examination of these trends, however, reveals that, with the exception of the early 1960s (which centred on a number of long strikes at modernizing coal-mines), two divergent patterns are evident: while the number of strikes and strikers has steadily increased since the early sixties, the number of days lost (a more accurate indication of effect on productivity) has remained generally steady (Shirai, 1984, p. 307). These patterns reflect the growing prevalence of the 'set strike', of which the *shunto* – or annual 'spring offensive' – is the prime example.

Around October, the national federations of unions initiate the activities related to *shunto* (Linhart, 1979, pp. 33ff; Shimada, 1980, p. 11). First a 'struggle committee' is appointed and it soon publishes a '*Shunto* White Paper', which contains a general schedule for 'offensive actions (on the basis of consultations with company managements), union wage demands (which are based on past and projected growth), and a list of the wider political aims of the campaign (for example, the implementation of social welfare programmes).[10] By February, individual enterprise unions put their claims before their managements, and proceed to secure their members' support for strike action. Then a detailed timetable of half-day, full-day, and two-day strikes is drawn up, with the unions with the strongest bargaining power at the beginning (Dore, 1987, p. 71). The struggle itself lasts from March through to May, and at its beginning both managements and union representatives evince militant posturing, present very rigid demands, and vow not to capitulate. It is during these times that workers castigate big business, the United States and the ruling élite, as well as emphasize the country-wide solidarity and militancy of the workers.

Soon a pace-setter – a large union representing an industry with a high growth rate – is chosen. Once this union reaches an agreement, a base for all other settlements exists. The actual bargaining is usually carried out on the enterprise level, with the top companies in all industries serving as a model for the smaller firms[11] (Dore, 1987, p. 71). Once the big firms have made their settlements, others follow in quick succession. By now the ceremonial castigation of the ruling party and the United States, as well as th demands for social programmes, are conveniently forgotten. As Dore (1987, p. 72) puts it, 'all is quiet and the union leaders and personnel managers can afford to go out golfing together again.' And, as Linhart (1979, p. 36) perceptively suggests, the militant posturing and expression of political demands 'bestow on *shunto* an element of ritual.'

Many similar features are found in what Hanami (1979, pp. 83–4) calls 'nominated' or 'designated' strikes. As in *shunto*, the strikes are held for short durations and as 'walk-ins' rather than 'walk-outs': that is, unionists do not consider it proper form to leave the workplace as a means of expressing grievances. Accordingly, at strike times workers converge on the enterprise and hold what Hanami (1979, p. 56) aptly names, 'staged performances'. Rohlen (1974, p. 186) vividly describes union meetings at 'his' bank:

> Union meetings are a special context where it is possible for the full flavor and rhetoric of unionism, Japanese style, to emerge, however briefly. General meetings are accompanied by a succession of aggressive postures and rolling cries precisely in the stereotype of the union image presented in the Japanese national press. Brave slogans, colorful banners, everyone in shirtsleeves, and poses before the camera with locked arms, all stylistic borrowings from the public displays of Japan's largest unions, are strictly observed. Nor are these things taken with much skepticism. The union leaders do take the identity of their union, as a union, seriously, and they try to act in public as union people should.

Other symbolic means which are used include the wearing of special insignia, such as arm- or headbands (*hachimaki*) (Hanami, 1984, pp. 109–10), or special ribbons which bear the union's demands (Linhart, 1979, p. 36); the use and display of specially prepared pennants; the posting up of posters and placards; singing of worker songs or shouting set slogans; or the holding of mass meetings in which management is abused (Hanami, 1979, pp. 129–30). Throughout these performances, universal demands – much like the ones published in the '*Shunto* White Paper' – are expressed vividly. A recurrent theme is the importance of working-class consciousness and the need for a united labour front against management. It is as though these performances originate in a basic view in which workers' and management interests are irrevocably divergent.

Yet, as in the case of *shunto*-related negotiations – and in contrast to the extremism of the staged performance – bargaining (which is carried out on the enterprise level) is marked by close cooperation (Shirai, 1984, p. 308). Here again workers and management share a basic understanding about the aim of furthering the good of the company. Rather than viewing the bargaining process as a zero-sum game, both unions and management tend to see it as one which is guided by mutual contributions to the success of a joint venture.[12] Accordingly, union leaders are not averse to fraternizing with management (as, for instance, in the custom of drinking together), or to sharing information with them. Indeed, in recent years, managements have increasingly provided their employees' representatives with detailed and often confidential information on management policies and objectives: for instance, investment programmes, production plans, staff planning and adjustment, training and retraining schemes, or measures for dealing with redundancies (Shirai, 1984, pp. 313–14). Moreover, during the actual bargaining process, the two parties tend to avoid the public expression of differences and to collude in wide-ranging behind-the-scenes negotiations on their way to wage settlements. Here again, Hanami (1979, p. 109; see also Ishida, 1984, p. 30) notes, 'as soon as wage problems are settled, the unions usually call off a strike and forget all about their solemn and noble causes . . . [staged performances] are no more than a ritual.

The recurrent insistence on the 'ritual' character of the *shunto*-related and 'staged' strikes suggests a recognition on the part of a number of scholars that such activities are marked by an essential quality that differentiates them from what is usually meant by strike action. Yet the mere designation of these strikes are rituals does not by itself suffice as an explanation for their internal dynamics or their relations to the social order within which they occur.

Steam-valves and masks

Gluckman's (1963, 1955) analysis of 'rituals of rebellion' – that is, rites which emphasize conflicts in certain ranges of relationships, yet which establish cohesion within the wider social order or over a longer period of time – may serve as a useful theoretical framework for tackling these issues. These rituals, he states (1963, p. 114), are instances of institutionalized protest 'which is seemingly against the established order, yet which arises to bless that order to achieve prosperity.' The strength of his analysis lies in illuminating the interrelationships between participants' commitment to and dependence on a social system, and the type of protest that emerges within it. More specifically (Gluckman, 1963, p. 126), his assertion is that 'rituals of rebellion' arise in social systems which are marked by a basic tension: a tension which emerges out of the concurrent existence of (a) material arrangements marked by the dependence of one group on another, (b) a high acceptance of the basic legitimacy of this system by the participating groups, *and* (c) the lack of alternatives for articulating this tension.

My assertion is that similar conditions are found in Japan's large firms: given the institutional dependence of permanent workers on their companies, given their relatively high commitment to their workmates and workplace, and given their lack of options for leaving their firms or openly voicing their dissatisfactions, 'rituals of rebellion' are a principal, logical (in the systemic sense) mode of protest in these contexts.

But how do these rituals work? Gluckman's answer is essentially a functionalist, steam-valve explanation (Babcock, 1978, p. 22). His stress is on the contribution to the social system of a kind of cathartic experience which the participating individuals undergo (Gluckman, 1955, p. 125). Workers who are in a position of inferiority, to illustrate our case, find relief in the public expression of their hidden resentments and feelings about the conflict that exists between themselves and management. Once they have temporarily disburdened themselves of their grievances they are once more ready to carry out the roles within a system they basically accept. These ritual rebellions, in other words, allow the discharge of repressed emotions which stem from recurring sources of collective and individual distress: tensions at work, a sense of inequality, or feeling of being manipulated and exploited. This is basically a steam-valve explanation because it underscores the temporary release of pressures and tensions which nevertheless continue to exist.

Such an explanation is similar to the interpretation given to a related set of occasions: the 'ritual inversions' found in group sports. Rohlen (1974, p. 111) provides the following account:

> During the warmer months interoffice softball tournaments are held. An astute observer of bank social relations commented that the inversion of the usual hierarchy during sports events created by the athletic superiority of the younger men makes such recreation a useful means for reducing office tensions. That every strike-out by a normally demanding boss is a home run for relations sounds funny, but certainly such recreation does intensify office solidarity.

In both cases – in rites of rebellion and in rituals of inversion – the circumscribed change of normal behavioural codes is subject to group life. This is because both kinds of situations imply a return to normal life – albeit in a refreshed state – and to the fulfilment of (work) group expectations.

Formulated in this manner, the explanation still remains at too general a level: it begs a more specific set of questions about the relationship between the *actual dynamics* of the staged performances and the wider backdrop of dependence and mutual commitment between workers and management. More specifically, these are questions about the role of 'emotion work' – i.e. the means employed in order to summon emotions (Scheff, 1979, p. 8) – and 'mobilized attention' – i.e. the medium through which affective means of behaviour are communicated (MacAloon, 1984, p. 10) – within the rituals of rebellion. They are questions, in other words, about the ways in which feelings and ideas unfold within these situations and bear upon the social order of the companies.

Hanami's (1984, p. 117) perceptive insight provides a first step towards an answer to these questions:

> . . . within the enterprise 'family', one in which employees hesitate to ask even for what they are entitled to, it takes great courage to ask for a wage increase or better working conditions

that are not contractually promised. Just to raise demands and gain attention in some firms, workers need to destroy the daily personal relationships and normal atmosphere within the company.

What are the means, then, by which this (temporary) process of destruction occur? In a word, these are the special symbolic devices that workers utilize during strikes: insignia and uniforms, songs and slogans, and marches and 'untoward' behaviours.[13] As Hanami (1984, p. 113) graphically puts it:

In order to destroy the day-to-day harmonious relationship of the enterprise family, union leaders assume a rude, inhuman, and even violent attitude and go on to stage unnecessarily wreckless actions: wearing armbands and headbands, hoisting flags, pasting up posters, attacking management people personally.

What workers do through these actions, to put this explicitly, is to don masks, to use special mediums which disjoin their personal identity from the behaviour being enacted (Honigmann, 1977, p. 275). They are thus in a position – for the duration of these performances – to express their hostility with impunity because they are 'not themselves' (Honigmann, 1977, p. 278). For a limited time then, they are not the normally identified, circumscribed, constrained members of their firms, concerned about how they are regarded. This is borne out by the reaction of many employers, who often complain that 'the employees who enter union activities used to be very polite "nice guys" but suddenly changed in character and became rude after they started participating in union activities' (Hanami, 1979, p. 106).

These staged performances, then, are not unlike other ritual contexts such as Christmas mumming (Firestone, 1978, p. 106), in which non-strangers temporarily become strangers. In these social contexts, which are marked by a basic social inequality, such rituals provide a legitimate licence through which members of disprivileged classes can abuse more established, more powerful members. It is in this light, then, that the ways in which certain Japanese cultural ideals – i.e. certain historically emergent models of and for action – structure the workplace and its attendant modes of conflict management, should be seen. For while other rites of rebellion (like Christmas mumming) usually occur at the periphery of industrialized societies (Manning, 1983), in Japan they take place in one of the most central of this society's social spheres. My suggestion is that the 'firm-as-family' analogy provides an interesting way to conceptualize not only how Japanese cultural ideals are related to the structural and 'sentimental' conditions of large enterprises, but also how they are part of the ways in which conflict is constantly limited and played out. Yet the existence – to borrow again from Gluckman – of such 'tribal' elements of ritual rebellion in a highly complex society raises a much deeper problem.

In rituals of rebellion, the stress is on the abuse of powerful incumbents rather than on a challenge to or questioning of the validity of the roles themselves (Handelman, 1982, p. 173). This realization thus raises the following question: what is it that limits these kinds of occasions – like their African counterparts (Gluckman, 1955, p. 122) – to being rituals of rebellion and not of revolution? This is no mean question because it touches directly upon the issue of what kind of potential marks Japanese society – or at least its industrial relations system – for change.

Gluckman (1955, pp. 125–6) hints at an understanding of these potentials and limits for social change when he states that rites of rebellion appear to express simultaneously two kinds of messages: while on one level such rituals state that in virtue of their position social inferiors hate their superiors, on another level they state that they support them. An answer to this question, then, leads the analysis towards an explanation of Japan's industrial rituals as communicative forms, as meta-social commentaries (Geertz, 1972).

Messages and meta-messages

Any act of communication involves (at least) two levels of transmission of information. The first level – that of communication – includes the actual messages which are being transferred. The second level – that of meta-communication, or communication about communication – entails information about how the actual messages are to be understood (Bateson, 1972). Meta-communications (or meta-messages) define how the actual statements and expressions which are found within a social context are to be understood, to be interpreted. Thus, for instance, in order to understand that the action taking place within a certain situation is play, it must be framed by the meta-message 'this is play'.

In a nutshell, my argument is as follows: the meta-messages which are transmitted during the 'staged performances' of the workers, not only diverge but, more importantly, transcend (or, more strongly, negate) the actual messages being expressed. On one level, workers communicate messages about such things as worker solidarity, class conflict or the need to castigate big business and its allies. At the same time, however, on another level, these same workers communicate (meta-) messages which emphasize the essential unity of the firms where they are employed, and the importance of these companies' smooth operation.

Important information about how actions within social frames are to be understood is often carried by meta-messages which involve the timing (the 'when') and the manner (the 'how') by which these situations are constructed (Paine, 1976, pp. 73–4). Thus, for example, the fact that many of the 'staged strikes' are coordinated ahead of time attests to how labour's representatives actually share a definition of timing with the very groups (managements) they are purportedly struggling with. In such cases, an ostensibly 'independent' act by the union is subordinated to the dependency tie with the firm. Similarly, the fact that strike action, rather than signalling the breakdown of negotiations, usually signals the beginning of talks (Levine, 1967, p. 268), and the fact that workers' 'struggles' have become expected annual occurrences (Dore, 1987, p. 70), bestow an element of conventionality to these situations. Such peculiarities, then, actually signal a continuity of normal relations despite the stated messages of militancy and opposition.

The manner, the 'how', by which the strikes are carried out serves to reinforce this meta-message of a basic continuity of normal relations. This is because messages about working-class solidarity are carried by the very groups that the messages are rejecting: the labour élites. Along the same lines, while shouting about class-consciousness, workers march and demonstrate in close-knit, highly exclusive enterprise-union groups. Moreover, the discipline exerted by local union leaders on their members to act as well-defined, well-regulated groups tends to intensify this oneness. These marches, in other words, are ritual gestures which can actualize a sense of a group that is beyond the sum of its parts, but being circumscribed to enterprise unions, they *in effect* actualize a sense of a limited, exclusive collectivity.[14]

The complexity of the situation, however, does not end here. The recognition by workers, of the need to 'transform' themselves during the struggles, and the seriousness with which they and others perceive themselves (Hanami, 1979, p. 47; Rohlen, 1974, p. 186) raise the following problem: how do the conscious interpretations of workers' behaviours square with the overall logic of these social frames?

From managements' point of view, employees' behaviour during the performances is seen as consistent with the overall nature of relations within the enterprise. The demonstrations are thus seen as an example of 'within-the-firm solutions to conflict situations. They are part of a loose gentleman's agreement (Fridell, 1972, p. 268) in which, within a certain margin, subordinates can 'do their own thing'. This margin is allowed so long as it does not seriously interfere with the smooth functioning of the enterprise. In this context, the weakness of the unions and the high commitment of workers is well recognized by management, which is then willing to accept these actions as 'childish tantrums' (Hanami, 1979, p. 106). The 'firm-as-family' analogy, in other words, is employed in this context as an ideological account of not only workers' behaviour, but also of their mis-behaviour, of this misconduct.

Labour's interpretation of these situations differs at the local enterprise and national levels. On the national level, the struggles serve as a basic justification for the organizational existence of labour federations (Cole *et al.*, 1966, p. 316). Being limited to only political activity, these organizations have evolved into bodies whose main aim is to make sure that in the enterprise struggles the universal messages of working-class solidarity and rejection of the conservative forces are made. That these messages are delivered through an expressive show of militancy is interpreted as an earnest accomplishment of the national centres' aims. On the enterprise level, one finds that such actions are interpreted within the framework of a vaguely defined ideal of union leadership. By fulfilling the 'expressive' aspects of this role, union leaders can both keep up their sense of meeting the more 'radical expectations of them, while at the same time facilitating their participation in, and contribution towards, the smooth functioning of their firms. Each leadership group, then, 'strives to manifest its power to impress not only the other but also its followers and inside and outside rivals' (Levin, 1967, p. 266). Thus, these 'struggles' are usually understood by the actors to be circumscribed roles undertaken for a short while, at the end of which a return to 'normal' is expected.

Conclusion

While briefly recapitulating the main points of this analysis, I shall try and draw out some of its wider implications. The 'firm-as-family' analogy well captures the organizational and structural peculiarities of Japan's large firms: the heavy material dependence of workers on their companies, and their high acceptance of, identification with, and commitment to their work groups. The appropriateness of this analogy does not imply the idyll which is often portrayed by the group model of Japanese society with its emphasis on hierarchical and exclusive groups, benevolent and magnanimous leadership, or consensus and harmony (see Moeran, 1984, pp. 107–8; Smith, 1983, p. 94). Rather these emphases reflect certain cultural ideals that exist side-by-side with competition, conflict, interpersonal friction, personal anxieties, and a growing search for individual fulfilment at work and outside it. The challenge, from a theoretical point of view, is thus not of contrasting the 'ideal' with the 'real', but of developing analytical tools for delineating just how these ideals influence the concrete dynamics by which the strains and struggles are played out.

Following the works of Max Gluckman and Gregory Bateson, I have proposed that a fruitful approach to this problem may be to focus on the special social situations which are set apart from, yet which are related in a unique way to, the social order and relations of these firms. The primary examples which formed the case of the analysis were the staged strikes which unions hold and which allow both emotional catharsis and the simultaneous transmission of messages about basic conflict and (paradoxically) cooperation within these firms.

Such an approach offers a way to relate specific interactions and encounters – like strikes, walk-ins, or slowdowns – to the limits imposed by historically contingent power relations and symbolic structures. Thus, for instance, take the patterns of dependence on and commitment to the workplace, which themselves are properties that emerged out of the pre-war history of negotiations between labour, management, and government (Gordon, 1985, pp. 413–16). These social and organizational patterns serve both to constrain the ability of workers to exit their companies and to limit the type of voice they can use to carry their protest. Similarly, the cultural preference for non-confrontational means of conflict management restricts the manner by which discontent can be exhibited. These patterns, in other words, form the social, structural, and cultural background or preconditions against which ritual strikes emerge.

Symbolic structures, however, do not only constrain action (or, more correctly, action alternatives). They also provide more concrete 'scripts', 'loose associative chains' (Rosaldo, 1980) that guide behaviour in the specially constructed frames. Cultural structures, in other words, provide templates of ways in which perceptions, feelings, and thoughts are fused into patterns for action (Bruner, 1986, p. 69). It is in this light that the relative 'ease' with which workers don their masks of tenacious and aggressive representatives of the working class should be seen. This is because they have ready-made cultural 'texts', towards which they can orient themselves and within the outlines of which they can interact with little of the difficulties that occur in less structured situations.

Stages strikes, however, do not occur in a cultural 'vacuum'. It is on the level of symbolic structures – or, to use another term with caution, tradition – that an affinity or connection between these situations and other Japanese cultural occasions can be found. Thus, for example, the rites of rebellion found in the large firms, it may be suggested, are related symbolically to many Shinto rites. In both kinds of occasions one can find similar patterns of temporary metamorphoses, inversion and relaxation of rules, the use of uniforms and insignia, and at times violence and aggression (Linhart, 1986, p. 207; Honda, 1984).

For all this, however, there is still something about the situations which have been described here which cannot be reduced simplistically to their being mere reflections of certain power structures and relations. They are not 'just' functional prerequisites for the continued and smooth operation of the large firms. They are also special, liminal events with their own special potential. As MacAloon (1984, p. 3) puts it, when entering 'the state of liminality, all manner of unexpected, dangerous, or potentially creative things may happen.' We may thus ask about the potential of staged strikes to decrease, diffuse, or defuse reflexivity (MacAloon, 1984, p. 13; Errington, 1987, p. 655): the capacity of people to distance themselves from their experience and to stand apart from and comment upon this experience.

In stages strikes, one finds the creation – through the donning of masks, for example – of special 'times' during which the reality of ordinary work-a-day life can be handled and discussed from a distance. Yet these occurrences do not involve a simple inversion of mundane reality, but – to use Turner's (1977, p. 73) metaphor of lenses – a special kind of magnification and distortion of it.

In a word, in the labour-related rituals of rebellion there appears to be a margin – albeit a highly complex margin – for collective reflexivity. In these cases the use of masks does not signify a descent into a situation of basic human similarity, but rather the creation of an otherness which is essential for any serious reflection about a social order. While this reflection does, admittedly, take place within a framework which emphasizes cooperation and mutual interests, the conduct of the workers during the strikes still carries a certain 'subversive' potential. This is because the hints and allusions, the expressions of scorn and the inversions, which are found in these situations, carry the possibility of questioning the legitimacy of the system.[15]

It must quickly be added, however, that this questioning does not, in itself, lead to the establishment of a clear and coherent body of alternative thought with its own internal logic and structure. Rather, like many other cultural performances which raise doubts about the social order (Turner, 1978, p. 294), these occasions do little more than provide hints and suggestions in regard to the possibilities of a different kind of social order. The allusion found in the 'rites of rebellion' which take place in Japan's large firms is to what Robert Bellah (1971) has termed Japan's 'tradition of submerged transcendence': to the possibilities, in other words, of universalism, of conflict, and of the breaking of group boundaries. Yet whether this kind of tradition, or parts of it, will eventually emerge and be actualized within the framework of the large firms is again dependent on other factors: on the political and economic situation of these companies, and on the general climate of public debate and expectations in the country.[16]

Notes

1 Data on which the paper for this chapter is based was gathered in Japan while the author was supported by an Otsuki Peace Fellowship (1981–3). Thanks are due to Uri Almagor, S.N. Eisenstadt, Reuven Kahane and Adam Seligman for comments on an earlier version of the paper and to the Harry S. Truman Institute of the Hebrew University of Jerusalem and the Koret Foundation for aid in completing it.

2 This theoretical point is also made by Lebra (1984, p. 57). She has suggested that harmony and conflict in this society should not be seen as bipolarities, but rather as mutually related characteristics: the more harmony-oriented, the more conflict-sensitive. This is because, as the Japanese place more value:

> upon social interdependence, cooperation, solidarity or harmony, than, say, the Americans, they are more likely to interfere with one another's actions. The norm of harmony may be precisely what makes people more aware of conflicts with others, conflicts between their self-interest and obligations, and so forth. (Lebra, 1984, p. 56)

Thus, the harmony which one can find in many, but of course not all, sectors of Japanese society may best be understood as the outcome of constant efforts to avoid and manage very real conflicts within and between groups (Krauss *et al.*, 1984b, p. 378). Thus, cultural values which emphasize harmony and the avoidance of conflict may actually intensify conflicts and therefore 'require' special efforts to handle them.

3 The formulation of the new ideology was facilitated by the activity of such ideologues as Uno Riemon. Reflecting a wide consensus around the aim of building a strong Japan in order to counter the threat of the West, he believed that 'educating workers to strive for the development of modern industry, with labor–management cooperation, took precedence over participation in a labor movement that produced domestic confrontations between labor and management.' (Hazama and Kaminski, 1979, p. 80). The concrete measures he urged for are interesting: periodic salary increases at fixed intervals, life-time employment, and retirement stipends.

117

4 Good overviews of the pre-war history of unionism in Japan can be found in Nishioka (1968, ch.3) and Gordon (1985).

5 Indeed, despite proclamations from national labour bodies to the contrary, since the end of the war, enterprise unions have not seriously sought to widen their numbers. Because permanent status is a precondition for union membership, and because life-time employment underlies this status, the very exclusion of temporary workers serves to symbolize the permanency of the unionists. This facilitates the definition of clear boundaries around permanent workers, leaving all outsiders literally 'on their own' (Levine, 1967, pp. 260–1).

6 With few exceptions, national union organizations are federations of enterprise unions within specific industries (railways or textiles, for instance). Within these bodies, enterprise unions are highly autonomous: they make or change their own constitutions; control vital decisions; elect their own officials; initiate and stop industrial action (Japan Institute of Labor, 1979, p, 69; Levin, 1967, p. 267), decide independently on union dues; and are virtually autonomous in allocating funds to the national union (Shirai and Shimada, 1978, p. 257). Hence, on the national level, the enterprise union is 'not simply an administrative unit . . . a strong industrial union as the United Auto Workers in the US, but tends to be a self-contained autonomous unit' (Cole, 1971, p. 200). On the local level, then, it is not surprising to learn that workers tend to attach more importance to their enterprise union than to industry-based federations (Koshiro, 1983, p. 143).

7 Moreover, the picture of managers cynically manipulating workers by pulling at some hidden cultural principles is but a caricature. As De Vos (1975), Hanami (1979) and Dore (1984, p. xxxi) note, management feels internal commitment to keeping up their side of dependency relationships. Whether this be expressed in a readiness to 'hear-out' workers or to provide them with many of the necessities of life, this is recognized by workers and at times used by them for instrumental gains.

8 Skinner (1979, p. 148; see also Schodt, 1983, p. 111–14) notes how employees recognize their own frustrations and disaffections in the scenes and characters depicted in *sarariiman manga* (salaryman comics), a humorous and often biting genre enjoyed by many workers of large firms: preoccupation with status, bootlicking and careering, frustrations at inequalities at the workplace, threatening and debasing relations with superiors, and the necessity of working with imperious and often pretentious managers.

9 A fascinating illustration of the dilemma posed for workers in deciding between the values of the public (i.e. work) and private

(i.e. home) realms is found in Tada's (1978) essay on 'My-homism'. This attitude – and its emphasis on material amenities within the home – has been treated at times with more than a bit of sarcasm. But as Tada (1978, p. 210) observes, beyond 'the snow-white image of washing machines, electric rice-cookers, refrigerators, and the like' lies the deeper search for personal fulfilment. Especially for younger people:

> it is a symbol of one way to protect their individuality and personal integrity. . . . The reason that young men enjoy the environment of the kitchen and laundry is not so much because they have a burning desire to help their wives but because, to risk exaggeration, they seek to restore in the home the consistency and unity of work and play. (Tada, 1978, p. 211)

10   Intense media activity – reviews, projections, interviews, criticisms – also surrounds the annual 'spring offensive'. The articles and notices published yearly by the *Rodo Shiryo Sokuho* (Labor Data Bulletin) or the *Nihon Rodo Zasshi* (Journal of the Japan Institute of Labor) offer good examples of this activity.

11   The following are examples of the concrete issues which are dealt with during bargaining: the annual across-the-board base-up increase; annual and semi-annual bonuses; periodic increases every worker is entitled to; and the guarantee of permanent employment for the enterprise's regular workers.

12   Sugimoto (1978, p. 286), in a wide-ranging article, underscores this point by showing how unionization in Japan has tended to confine unionists' attention to their particular milieu and has prevented them from effectively protesting issues outside it.

13   Hanami (1979, p. 219) relates an incident that exemplifies such behaviour: during one strike, union members stood at the entrance of a supermarket and shouted to the customers that the food that day was rotten.

14   This is what Turner (1986, p. 140) seems to refer to when he discusses how some 'social events are contained in multiple frames, hierarchically arranged, frame within frame, with the ultimate "meaning" of the event shaped by the dominant "encompassing" frame'.

15   A word of caution: the types of encounters that I have been discussing should not be understood simplistically as being typical of all situations marked by conflict and tension in Japan. As Krauss, Rohlen and Steinhoff (1984a, p. 12) caution us, in the same society, conflict may be managed differently in different contexts. As conflict takes place in different contexts:

it must be transformed, often in complex ways. Its character and intensity must be shaped to the new environment, and this change in turn introduces new limits and avenues for resolution. (Krauss *et al.*, 1984, pp. 9–13)

As I have tried to show, the character and intensity of expressing tension or managing conflicts in Japan's large firms are shaped by the limits and potentials – i.e. the internal order or logic – of staged strikes.

16 Along these lines, it may be hypothesized that as the structural characteristics of Japan's large firms will change – the microelectronics industry being a case in point (Kuwahara and Umezawa, 1982) – so too will the limits on 'exist' and 'voice' within these companies.

References

Babcock, B.A. (1978), Introduction, in *idem* (ed.), *The Reversible World: Symbolic Inversion in Art and Society*. Ithaca, Cornell University Press, pp. 13–36.

Bateson, G. (1972), *Steps to an Ecology of Mind*. New York, Ballantine.

Bellah, R.N. (1971), 'Continuity and change in Japanese society' in B. Barber and A. Inkeles (eds.), *Stability and Social Change*. Boston, Little Brown, pp. 377–404.

Bennett, J. and S.B. Levine (1976), 'Industrialization and social deprivation: welfare, environment, and the post-industrial society in Japan' in H. Patrick (ed.), *Japanese Industrialization and its Social Consequences*. Berkeley, University of California Press, p. 439–92.

Bruner, J. (1986), *Actual Minds, Possible Worlds*. Cambridge, Mass., Harvard University Press.

Cole, A.B., C. Totten and C.H. Uyehara (1966), *Socialist Parties in Postwar Japan*. New Haven, Yale University Press.

Cole, R.E. (1971), *Japanese Blue Collar: The Changing Tradition*. Berkeley, University of California Press.

Cole, R.E. (1979), *Work, Mobility and Participation*. Berkeley, University of California Press.

De Vos, G.A. (1975), 'Apprenticeship and paternalism' in E.F. Vogel (ed.), *Modern Japanese Organization and Decision-Making*. Tokyo, Tuttle, pp. 210–17.

Dore, R. (1973), *British Factory, Japanese Factory. The Origins of National Diversity in Industrial Relations*. London, George Allen.

Dore, R. (1984), Introduction to S. Kamata, *Japan in the Passing Lane*. London, Unwin, pp. ix–xi.

Dore, R. (1987), *Taking Japan Seriously: A Confucian Perspective on Leading Economic Issues*. London, Athlone.

Dunlop, J.T. (1978), Introduction, in *idem* and W. Galenson (eds.), *Labor in the Twentieth Century*. New York, Academic.

Errington, F. (1987) 'Reflexivity deflected: the festival of nations as an American cultural performance', *American Ethnologist*, 14(4), pp. 654–67.

Firestone, M. (1978) 'Christmas mumming and symbolic interactionism', *Ethos*, 6, pp. 92–113.

Fridell, W.M. (1972), 'Notes on Japanese tolerance', *Monumenta Nipponia*, 27, pp. 253–71.

Fruin, W.M. (1978), 'The Japanese company controversy: ideology and organization in a historical perspective', *Journal of Japanese Studies*, 4(2), pp. 267–300.

Fruin, W.M. (1980), 'The family as a firm and the firm as a family in Japan: the case of Kikkoman Shoyu Company Limited', *Journal of Family History*, 5, pp. 432–49.

Geertz, C. (1972), 'Deep play: notes on a Balinese cockfight', *Daedalus*, 101, pp. 1–38.

Glazer, N. (1976), 'Social and cultural factors in Japanese economic growth' in H. Patrick and H. Rosovsky (eds.), *Asia's New Giant*. Washington, D.C., Brookings, pp.813–96.

Gluckman, M. (1955), *Customs and Conflict in Africa*. Blackwell, Oxford.

Gluckman, M. (1963), *Order and Rebellion in Tribal Africa*. London, Coles and West.

Gordon, A. (1985), *The Evolution of Labor Relations in Japan: Heavy Industry – 1853–1955*. Cambridge, Mass., Harvard University Press.

Hanami, T. (1979), *Labor Relations in Japan Today*. Tokyo, Kodansha.

Hanami, T. (1984), 'Conflict and its resolution in industrial relations and labor law' in E.S. Krauss *et al.* (eds.), *Conflict in Japan*. Honolulu, University of Hawaii Press, pp. 107–35.

Handelman, D. (1982), 'Reflexivity in festival and other cultural events' in M. Douglas (ed.), *Essays in the Sociology of Perception*. London, Routledge, pp. 162-90.

Harari, E. (1978), 'Unemployment in Japan: policy and politics', *Asian Survey*, 18(10), pp. 1013–28.

Harari, E. (1984), 'The public sector in Japan: industrial relations and politics', *Asian and African Studies*, 18(1), pp. 87–109.

Hazama, H. (1976), 'Historical changes in the life style of industrial workers' in H. Patrick (ed.), *Japanese Industrialization and its Social Consequences*. Berkeley, University of California Press, pp. 21–51.

Hazama, H. with J. Kaminski (1979), 'Japanese labor–management relations and Uno Riemon', *Journal of Japanese Studies*, 5(1), pp. 71–106.

Hirschman, A. (1970), *Exit, Voice, and Loyalty*. Cambridge, Mass., Harvard University Press.

Honda, S. (1984), 'Shinto in Japanese culture' *Bulletin of the Nanzan Institute for Religion and Culture*, 8, pp. 24–30.

Honigmann, J.J. (1977), 'The masked face', *Ethos*, 5, pp. 262–80.

Japan Institute of Labor (1979), *Labor Unions and Labor–Management Relations*. Japan Institute of Labor, Tokyo.

Kamata, S. (1984), *Japan in the Passing Lane*. London, Unwin.

Kiefer, C.W. (1970), 'The psychological interdependence of family, school, and bureaucracy in Japan', *American Anthropologist*, 72, pp. 66–75.

Kiefer, C.W. (1980), 'Loneliness and Japanese social structure' in J. Hartog *et al.* (eds.), *The Anatomy of Loneliness*. New York, International Universities Press, pp. 425–50.

Koshiro, K. (1983), 'Japan's labor unions: the meeting of white and blue collar' in M. Hyoe and J. Hirschmeier (eds.), *Politics and Economics in Contemporary Japan*. Tokyo, Kodansha, pp. 143–56.

Krauss, E.S., T.P. Rohlen and P.G. Steinhoff (1984a), 'Conflict: an approach to the study of Japan' in *idem* (eds.), *Conflict in Japan*. Honolulu, University of Hawaii Press, pp. 3–15.

Krauss, E.S., T.P. Rohlen and P.G. Steinhoff (1984b), 'Conflict and its resolution in post-war Japan' in *idem* (eds.), *Conflict in Japan*. Honolulu, University of Hawaii Press, pp. 377–97.

Kuwahara, Y. and T. Umezawa (1982), 'Saikin no gijitsu shinpo to rodo mondai: Maikuroerekutoronikusu no koyo rodo e no eikyo to hyoka', *Nihon Rodo Kyokai Zasshi*, 24(1), pp. 39–55.

Lebra, T.S. (1984), 'Nonconfrontational strategies for management of interpersonal conflicts' in E.S. Krauss *et al.* (eds.), *Conflict in Japan*. Honolulu, University of Hawaii Press, pp. 41–60.

Levine, S.B. (1967), 'Post-war trade unionism, collective bargaining, and Japanese social structure' in R.P. Dore (ed.), *Aspects of Social Change in Modern Japan*. Princeton, Princeton University Press, pp. 245–85.

Linhart, S. (1979), 'Aspects of social conflict in Japan: the annual spring wage offensive of the trade unions' in I. Nish and C. Dunn (eds.), *European Studies on Japan*. Keel, Norburg, pp. 30–8.

Linhart, S. (1986), 'Sakariba: zone of "evaporation" between work and home?' in J. Hendry and J. Webber (eds.), *Interpreting Japanese Society: Anthropological Approaches*. Oxford, JASO Occasional Papers, Number 5, pp. 198–210.

MacAloon, J.J. (1984), Introduction: Cultural performances, cultural theory, in *idem* (ed.), *Rite, Drama, Festival, Spectacle: Rehearsals Toward a Theory of Cultural Performance*. Philadelphia, ISHI, pp. 1–15.

Manning, F.E. (1983), 'Cosmos and chaos: celebration in the modern world, in *idem* (ed.), *The Celebration of Society: Perspectives on Contemporary Cultural Performance*. Bowling Green, Bowling Green University Popular Press, pp. 3–30.

Moeran, B. (1984), 'Individual, group and *seishin*: Japan's internal cultural debate', *Man*, 19(2), pp. 252–66.

Murakami, Y. (1985), '*Ie* society as a pattern of civilization: response to criticism', *Journal of Japanese Studies*, 11(2), pp. 401–21.

Nakane, C. (1973), *Japanese Society*. Harmondsworth, Penguin.

Nishioka, T. (1968), *Nihon no Rodo Kumiai Soshiki*. Tokyo, Nihon Rodo Kyokai.

Okochi, R. *et al.* (1974), 'The Japanese industrial relations system: a summary' in *idem* (eds.), *Workers and Employers in Japan*. Princeton, Princeton University Press, pp.485–516.

Paine, R. (1976), 'Two modes of exchange and mediation' in B. Kapferer (ed.), *Transaction and Meaning*. Philadelphia, ISHI, pp. 63–86.

Passin, H. (1975), 'Changing values: work and growth in Japan', *Asian Survey*, 15(10), pp. 821–50.

Plath, D.W. (1980), *Long Engagements*. Stanford, Stanford University Press.

Rohlen, T.P. (1974), *For Harmony and Strength: Japanese White-Collar Organization in Anthropological Perspective*. Berkeley, University of California Press.

Rosaldo, M. (1980), *Knowledge and Passion*. Stanford, Stanford University Press.

Scheff, T.J. (1979), *Catharsis in Healing, Ritual, and Drama*. Berkeley, University of California Press.

Schodt, F.L. (1983), *Manga! Manga! The World of Japanese Comics*. New York, Kodansha.

Shimada, H. (1980), *The Japanese Employment System*. Japan Institute of Labor, Tokyo.

Shinofuji, H. (1978), *Kokutesu Rodosha no Soshiki to Undo*. Tokyo, Rodo Junposha.

Shirai, T. (1975), 'Decision making in the Japanese labor unions' in E.F. Vogel (ed.), *Modern Japanese Organizations and Decision Making*. Berkeley, University of California Press, pp. 167–84.

Shirai, T. (1984), 'Recent developments in collective bargaining in Japan', *International Labor Review*, 123(3), pp. 307–18.

Shirai, T. and H. Shimada (1978), 'Japan' in J.T. Dunlop and W.

Galenson (eds.), *Labor in the Twentieth Century*. New York, Academic, pp. 241–322.

Skinner, K.A. (1979), 'Salaryman comics in Japan: images and self-perception', *Journal of Popular Culture*, 13(1), pp. 141–53.

Smith, R.J. (1983), *Japanese Society: Tradition, Self and the Social Order*. Cambridge, Cambridge University Press.

Sugimoto, Y. (1978), 'Quantitative characteristics of popular disturbances in post-occupation Japan (1952–1960)', Journal of Asian Studies, 37(2), pp. 273–91.

Sugimoto, Y. and R. Mouer (1980), 'Reappraising images of Japanese society', *Social Analysis*, 5/6, pp. 5–19.

Tada, M. (1978), 'The glory and misery of "My Home"' in J.V. Koschmann (ed.), *Authority and the Individual in Japan*. Tokyo, Tokyo University Press, pp. 207–17.

Takahashi, T. (1974), 'Yoka to rodo', *Nihon Rodo Kyokai Zasshi*, 16(10), pp. 22–31.

Takeuchi, S. (1982), *Rodo Seinen Hakusho*. Tokyo, Rodosha Seiiku Kai.

Tomazu, K. (1981), 'Rodo Kumiai to ho', *Ho to Seisaku*', 1, pp. 48–51.

Tsukamoto, T. (1967), 'Kigyo rodo kumiai to Nihonteki roshi kankei', *Nihon Rodo Kyokai Zasshi*, 9(7), pp. 112–13.

Turner, V. (1977), 'Process, system, and symbol: a new anthropological synthesis', *Daedalus*, 106, pp. 61–80.

Turner, V. (1986), *The Anthropology of Performance*. New York, PAJ Publications.

Vogel, E.F. (1975), Introduction: toward more accurate concepts, in *idem* (ed.), *Modern Japanese Organization and Decision Making*. Berkeley, University of California Press, pp. xiii–xxv.

Watanabe, Y. (1981), *Gondai Nihonho Nyumon*. Tokyo, Iwanami Shinsho.

Part Three
CONFLICT RESOLUTION IN THE POLITICAL AND CULTURAL SPHERES

6 Victors without Vanquished: A Japanese Model of Conflict Resolution

B. Shillony

Introduction

Although the existence of conflicts is universal, the nature of conflicts and the way in which they tend to be resolved differ from one society to another. As Japan developed a political tradition that was in many ways different from those of other nations, the way in which the Japanese have viewed their conflicts and the strategies that they have employed to resolve them are also different from those of other societies.

The political tradition of Japan emphasized the primacy of harmony and the importance of consensual decision. The ideal solution of a conflict was not a total victory for one side and a humiliating defeat for the other, but an accommodation by which both winner and loser could co-exist without too much loss of face.

Such solutions were ideologically possible, because, contrary to the West, Japan never possessed a dogmatic religion which makes a sharp distinction between right and wrong or urges its believers to fight the infidels. Shinto, Confucianism and Buddhism in Japan were all tolerant religions that did not object to other cults and did not preach sacred wars. None of these religions had a stern, omnipotent God that commands his people and scrutinizes their behaviour. In a situation where no one fought for God or against Satan, it was easy to reach an accommodation once the fighting was over.

The Western ideal of winning, as exemplified in boxing, is that of a knock-out. Victory is pronounced as the winner raises his hand and the loser lies flat on his back. In Japan, victory, as exemplified in *sumo*, is achieved by unbalancing the opponent and pushing him out of the ring. The excruciating gap between winner and loser in Japan is thus more muted.

The near absence of foreign enemies, due to Japan's insularity, meant that most of the wars that the Japanese fought until modern times were internal struggles, in which all sides shared the same political culture, beliefs, codes of behaviour and language. It was therefore feasible for winners to co-opt their former enemies, as it was possible for losers to join the camp of their erstwhile foes. From the winner's point of view, it was often wiser to permit the defeated enemy to keep some of his strength and honour, and in this way to assure his loyalty, than to subjugate him harshly and risk a future revenge. As no side attempted to impose its beliefs on the other, it was possible for the losers to join the winners in good faith.

Japanese history has its share of winners and losers, but it does not have many vanquished. Defeat in battle or losing a contest did not spell extinction. Losers were given a chance to maintain their status and follow the 'trend of times' by joining the winners. This pattern repeated itself time and again, despite the vast differences between one period and another and one conflict and another.

Ancient Japan

The first great political struggle in what was to become the state of Japan occurred sometime in the first centuries of the Christian era, when the clan of the Yamato kings overcame the other clans and united the country under its leadership. Although there are no records of that struggle, its outcome was epoch-making, as the victorious dynasty of the Yamato kings is still the reigning imperial family of Japan. That victory had also religious ramifications, as the deity of the Yamato clan, the sun goddess Amaterasu Omikami, became the chief Shinto deity.

What happened to the losers? The defeated clans were not suppressed, but continued to assert power while acknowledging the sovereignty of the imperial line. Their deities continued to be venerated, and the main rival of the sun goddess, her brother Susano-O, was merely banished to western Japan. The Izumo

Shrine, where his son Okuninushi is still worshipped, is the second holiest shrine of Shinto.

The next crucial conflict, which took place in the sixth century and is recorded in the ancient chronicle *Nihongi*, was about the question of whether to adopt the new religion, Buddhism, that had been introduced from Korea. Alien in its origin and concepts, the new religion threatened the vested interests of the Shinto shrines and their clergy. It might have also undermined the authority of the Emperor, who was himself a living Shinto god and the high priest of the sun goddess.

The confrontation that developed was a contest of power between the Soga clan, which wanted to control the imperial court through the patronage of the new religion, and the Nakatomi and Mononobe clans, which wished to thwart that plan. The Soga clan emerged victorious in the struggle and Buddhism was adopted as a state religion. This was a crucial victory, as Buddhism is still the main religion of the Japanese people (*Nihongi*, 1972, books XIX, XX).

But what happened to the defeated religion? Unlike the pagan religions of Europe and the Middle East, which were obliterated with the advent of the monotheistic religions, Shinto continued to prosper as one of the two religions of the realm. The emperors became patrons of Buddhism, while retaining their status as living Shinto gods and high priests of Amaterasu Omikami. Victory for one side did not mean extinction for the other. For a millennium and a half, until the middle of the nineteenth century, the two religions co-existed peacefully, mixing with each other in many ways, and keeping their separate identities in other ways. In time, Buddhism was Japanized to such an extent that in the long run Shinto may seem to be the winner rather than the loser in the contest between the two. Today most Japanese regard themselves as both Shintoist and Buddhist.

The following great clash occurred in the seventh century, when a group of royal princes tried to introduce the centralized government system of China, in order to strengthen the authority of the Emperor. This new system, based on Confucian ideology, undermined the position of the semi-autonomous clans. In 645, this group of princes carried out a successful *coup d'état* and reorganized the government on the Chinese model. A few decades later, a capital was constructed in Nara, where all power, wealth and culture were concentrated.

The Chinese system of centralized authority won, but the old aristocracy was not vanquished. Residing in the imperial capital, it continued to wield power by monopolizing the new posts and by marrying its daughters to the imperial family. Gradually, the emperors became puppets in the hands of the aristocracy (Sansom, 1958, vol. I).

Feudal Japan

In the twelfth century, after a long period of central government, a new challenge emerged. The restless samurai became so independent, that they were fighting among themselves and invading the capital. In the middle of that century, a warrior of the Taira clan, Kiyomori, assumed the highest government post in the capital; and at the end of that century another chieftain, Minamoto Yoritomo, after routing the Taira, took control over the whole country and established his feudal capital in Kamakura in eastern Japan, from where he ruled as Shogun. Within a century, the political regime had changed from centralized monarchy to decentralized feudalism.

What happened to the losers? In Europe, the Roman emperors were gone before feudalism was established, but in Japan the old imperial dynasty and its court aristocracy continued to exist and to function under the new regime. They lost power to the warriors, but they did not vanish. The emperors and aristocrats adapted to the new circumstances and provided the new government with the legitimacy, titles, and artistic accomplishments that it needed. Kyoto lost to Kamakura in political and military terms, but continued to be the Emperor's capital and to lead in religious and cultural terms (Mass, 1974).

Feudalism bred disintegration and internal wars. These wars intensified in the fifteenth and sixteenth centuries, until the whole country sank into political chaos. In these long-drawn struggles over territory and income, *bushido*, the code of the samurai, developed. According to *bushido*, the warrior should prefer a noble death to defeat or surrender. Honour could not be compromised, so conflicts had to be resolved by victory or death. This fanatic attitude of *bushido*, antithetic to the tradition of compromise, resulted in the brutal treatment of opponents and the cult of self-disembowelment (*seppuku*).

But this code of behaviour applied more to individuals than to groups, and more to junior warriors than to senior commanders. While individual samurai were expected to fight to death and commit suicide if unable to win, their lords often changed sides, leading their armies from a losing camp to a victorious one. Thus these wars produced a new type of samurai chieftain, one who was a shrewd politician no less than a commander of troops. From among this new breed of politician–warriors emerged the three great unifiers of Japan in the second half of the sixteenth century. In 1600, Tokugawa Ieyasu, defeating a coalition of opponents, reunited the country under his control and established a dynasty of shoguns which ruled Japan for the following two and half centuries (Duus, 1969).

Unlike the absolute monarchs of Europe at that time, Ieyasu did not remove the feudal lords from power, but incorporated them into his new state apparatus. About two thirds of the country was entrusted to these lords, as Ieyasu's vassals, and the largest domains remained in the hands of his former rivals, the so-called 'outer lords' (*tozama*). By allowing these 'outer lords' to keep their domains, Ieyasu gained their loyalty for more than ten generations (Hall and Jansen, 1968).

Imperial Japan

In 1868, Japan went through one of the greatest revolutions in its history. Within a few years, the Tokugawa regime, the feudal domains, and the whole ruling samurai class were abolished. After reinstating the Emperor as the head of state, the new leadership carried out far-reaching reforms that turned Japan once again into a centralized state, although this time on the Western and not the Chinese model. This was the famous Meiji Restoration.

A major difference between the Meiji Restoration and similar revolutions in other countries was the fate of the losers. The old regime was defeated and discarded, but its people were not punished. They were invited to join the new government and most of them did so. One of them, Katsu Kaishu, who had commanded the shogunal forces defending Edo (now Tokyo), became the builder of the new navy. The Shogun himself was retired with a large estate, and the great feudal lords were compensated with handsome amounts of money. As a result of this leniency towards the defeated regime, no attempt was ever made to restore it to power. The Meiji Restoration had its winners and losers, but it had no vanquished (Totman, 1980; Beasley, 1972).

In 1877, nine years after the Restoration, a great rebellion shook the country, when 15,000 ex-samurai of the former domain of Satsuma rose in arms against the new government. They did not intend to restore the old regime, but wanted a more conservative internal policy and a more aggressive external policy. The civil war that resulted lasted for eight months and cost the lives of 11,000 soldiers from both sides. The rebellion was suppressed and its leader, Saigo Takamori, committed suicide. It was the greatest rebellion in the modern history of Japan.

The punishment meted out to the rebel leaders were severe: twenty-two of them were sentenced to death and executed and 220 were sentenced to various prison terms. But the dead Saigo was not discredited. He was described as a misguided patriot, and eleven years after his death a big statue of Saigo was erected in the Ueno Park of Tokyo, to commemorate the peaceful capture of the capital under his command during the Meiji Restoration. Saigo is the only leader who has such a prominent public statue in Tokyo. He is also the only modern figure to be referred to, after his death, as 'great': the 'Great Saigo'. Saigo's son, Kikujiro, who had fought on the rebels' side and lost a leg in the campaign, was later appointed mayor of Kyoto.

Imperial Japan knew many political conflicts: the confrontation between the oligarchs and the elected politicians of the Diet, the clash between the state and its intellectual critics, the contest between the military and the civilian bureaucracy, and the rivalries within the military. Although these were all serious disputes, the outcome of which shaped the future course of Japan, none of them was clearly decided (Jansen and Rozman, 1986).

In the confrontation between the oligarchs and the elected politicians that took place in the last decades of the nineteenth century and the first decades of the twentieth century, the oligarchs maintained the upper hand. But the elected politicians gradually enhanced their influence until, in the mid-twenties, they began forming party cabinets. By accepting cabinet posts, the politicians were co-opted by the oligarchic establishment. The oligarchs discovered that it was more prudent to share power with the representatives of the people than to exclude them and turn them into revolutionaries (Akita, 1967; Najita, 1967; Duus, 1968).

In the clash between the state and its intellectual critics, the state won. In the 1930s, many liberal and left-wing intellectuals were dismissed from office and imprisoned. But, unlike in the totalitarian countries, these critics were not killed. Most of the hard-core communists survived the war in jail. Many of the left-wingers recanted in prison and their sentences were reduced (Shillony, 1981).

In the contest between the military and the civilian bureaucrats, the military achieved supremacy, leading Japan to war first against China and then against the United States and Britain. But although the military won, the bureaucrats were not vanquished. In internal affairs they held out against the pressures of the army, retaining their power over the civilian population. Thus, ironically, it was the undemocratic bureaucracy of pre-war and wartime Japan that blocked, more than anyone else, the establishment of a military dictatorship (Spaulding, 1971).

The factional strife within the military exploded in the 1930s in the form of assassinations and attempted *coups d'état*. In this conflict, the conservative faction won and the radicals were defeated. The rebels and assassins were arrested and punished. In the case of the abortive February 1936 revolt, seventeen of the rebel leaders were sentenced to death and executed. But the high-ranking officers who had sympathized with the rebels and encouraged them were not punished. In the following years, many of the rebels' demands, such as economic reforms and military expansion, were adhered to by the wartime authorities (Shillony, 1973).

In 1940, on the eve of the Pacific War, the political parties of Japan were disbanded and they did not reappear until after the war. But although the parties disappeared, the party politicians remained in their positions and continued to exert influence through the Diet. Most of these politicians were re-elected during the wartime elections of 1942. Neither the military nor the

133

bureaucracy succeeded in breaking the local power of these politicians (Berger, 1977; Drea, 1979).

The pattern of victory without vanquished, which helped smooth conflicts inside Japan, was not employed in Japan's dealings with foreign countries. The assumption was that foreigners behaved according to different principles and therefore could not be expected to react in the same way as the Japanese. Nothing of the magnanimity and generosity that was shown towards defeated rivals at home was displayed towards the subjugated peoples abroad. It is difficult to predict what might have happened had the Japanese treated the Koreans, the Chinese and the South-East Asians in a more humane way, but the harshness that they manifested gained them enormous animosity, of the kind which they had succeeded in avoiding at home.

The same Japanese, who had refined the techniques of conflict resolution inside the country, were very awkward in trying to prevent or resolve conflicts with other nations. The behaviour of foreigners seemed to them suspicious, while their own behaviour often looked menacing to other countries. The misunderstandings and misjudgements that led to the Pacific War were glaring examples of Japan's incompetence in resolving international conflicts.

Post-War Japan

Ironically, the most successful application of the Japanese formula of victors without vanquished towards a foreign nation occurred when the Americans occupied Japan in 1945. The leniency with which the United States treated its erstwhile enemy was totally different from what the Japanese had expected from a foreign occupier. By exhibiting magnanimity and goodwill towards the losers, the Americans achieved the same results that the Japanese had achieved by using this formula in the past (Kawai, 1960).

Post-war Japan has witnessed less political violence and more prosperity and stability than imperial Japan, yet conflicts and confrontations remained common. There were clashes between left and right, employers and employees, students and the establishment, industry and environmentalists. These confrontations ended usually with one side winning and the other side losing, but the victors were not vindictive and the losers were left with their honour intact.

In the confrontations between left and right, the right has had the upper hand in the ballot box, and government has remained securely in the hands of the conservatives. But the left was often successful in local elections and is still influential in academia and among intellectuals (Stockwin, 1974).

In the conflicts between management and labour, the former has come out victorious and the voice of business in Japan is today louder than that of labour. Yet, labour is far from being vanquished. It is still strong on the enterprise level, and it is often consulted in formulating industrial policies (Vogel, 1979).

In the long-drawn clashes between students and the authorities, the latter have triumphed. The student riots were suppressed and the public turned against them. The demonstrations gained little and the student movement was split by factional feuds. But many former student rebels made careers in establishment enterprises. Their stamina and experience in organization made them attractive to business recruiters (Steinhoff, 1984).

The clash, at times bitter, between industry and environmentalists has lost its intensity as the government, once supportive of industry, took up the side of the environmentalists. Yet, this change of policy did not mean the defeat of industry. The business leaders, often themselves residents of affected areas, became convinced that a clean environment was better for the economy than a polluted one (Pempel, 1982).

The tendency of winners to accommodate losers in order to restore harmony is evident in Japan not only in politics, but also in daily life. Except for sports, where competition is open and winning is all-important, most Japanese are still reluctant to score a victory that would disgrace the opponent. Although Japan possesses a Western-style legal system, the people shrink from litigation and prefer mediation. Even when suits are brought before a court, the judges prefer to use conciliation in order to avoid humiliating the loser. The ratio of lawyers to population in Japan is the lowest among industrial capitalist states. In 1988, there were only 16,500 judges and lawyers in Japan, as against 655,000 in the USA (*Japan 1989*, 1989, p. 90).

Conclusion

The model of victors without vanquished has often been applied in Japanese history. Although it did not prevent clashes and confrontations, it cushioned their consequences. By minimizing humiliation and animosity, it enabled the losers to integrate into the camp of the winners. The victors' concessions in the short run were compensated in the long run, by gaining a sense of commitment from the former losers.

As confrontations were not between believers and infidels, but between feuding interests, morality meant establishing harmony rather than enforcing justice. Fighting and conflicts always existed, but they were considered immoral because they disturbed harmony. As there was no sharp difference between right and wrong, it was easier to forgive a former enemy and gain his loyalty.

The lack of dogmatic and militant religions can explain the ideological flexibility in the recent past. The Japanese liberals who turned nationalists in the 1930s and 1940s and then turned again into pacifists in the 1950s were not necessarily opportunists. Most of them were following a long tradition of accommodation to the changing trends. They were the losers invited to join the winning camp, and they did so with great enthusiasm.

Yet, this formula which worked well in Japan, where a cultural homogeneity existed for a long time, was not applied in Japan's foreign relations or its colonial policies. It was in these two fields that the greatest failures of conflict resolution occurred.

References

Akita, G. (1967), *Foundations of Constitutional Government in Modern Japan, 1868–1900*. Cambridge, Mass., Harvard University Press.

Beasley, W.G. (1972), *The Meiji Restoration*. Stanford, Stanford University Press.

Berger, G.M. (1977), *Parties out of Power in Japan, 1931–1941*. Princeton, Princeton University Press.

Drea, E.J. (1979), *The 1942 Japanese General Election*. University of Kansas.

Duus, P. (1968), *Party Rivalry and Political Change in Taisho Japan.* Cambridge, Mass., Harvard University Press.

Duus, P. (1969), *Feudalism in Japan.* New York, Knopf.

Hall, J.W. and M.B. Jansen (eds.) (1968), *Studies in the Institutional History of Early Modern Japan.* Princeton, Princeton University Press.

Jansen, M.G. and G. Rozman (eds.) (1986), *Japan in Transition.* Princeton, Princeton University Press.

Japan 1989, An International Comparison. Tokyo, Keizai Koho Center, 1989.

Kawai, K. (1960), *Japan's American Interlude.* Chicago, The University of Chicago Press.

Mass, J.P. (1974), *Warrior Government in Early Medieval Japan.* New Haven, Yale University Press.

Najita, T. (1967), *Hara Kei in the Politics of Compromise, 1905–1915.* Cambridge, Mass., Harvard University Press.

Nihongi, Chronicles of Japan from the Earliest Times to AD 697. Tokyo, Tuttle, 1972, vols. XIX, XX.

Pempel, T.J. (1982), *Policy and Politics in Japan.* Philadelphia, Temple University Press.

Sansom, G. (1958), *A History of Japan.* Stanford, Stanford University Press, vol. I.

Shillony, B. (1973), *Revolt in Japan.* Princeton, Princeton University Press.

Shillony, B. (1981), *Politics and Culture in Wartime Japan.* Oxford, Clarendon Press.

Spaulding, R.M. (1971), 'The bureaucracy as a political force' in J.W. Morley (ed.), *Dilemmas of Growth in Prewar Japan.* Princeton, Princeton University Press, pp. 33–80.

Steinhoff, P.G. (1984), 'Student conflict' in E.S. Krauss, T.P. Rohlen and P.G. Steinhoff (eds.), *Conflict in Japan.* Honolulu, University of Hawaii Press, pp. 174–213.

Stockwin, J.A.A. (1974), *Japan: Divided Politics in a Growth Economy.* London, Weidenfeld and Nicolson.

Totman, C. (1980), *The Collapse of the Tokugawa Bakufu, 1862–1868.* Honolulu, The University of Hawaii Press.

Vogel, E.F. (1979), *Japan as Number One.* Cambridge, Mass., Harvard University Press.

7 Resolving and Managing Policy Conflict: Advisory Bodies

E. Harari

Recent studies of the policy process in Japan have revealed widespread conflict not only over issues based on class differences (the left–right ideological cleavage), or on 'cultural' differences (the modernity–tradition ideological cleavage), [1] but also in areas where such cleavages were not readily salient, or where those involved in conflict were on the same side of the ideological divide (Donnelly, 1977; Campbell, 1977; Ōtake, 1979; Johnson, 1982; Cusumano, 1985; Samuels, 1987). Moreover, although the class-based, and to a somewhat lesser extent the culture-based, ideological cleavages have in recent years appeared to have lost their potency (Richardson and Flanagan, 1984; Krauss *et al.*, 1984, p. 392; Pempel, 1987; Curtis, 1988; Hayashi 1988, p. 11), non-ideological policy conflict has not abated; on the contrary, in some areas it appears to have intensified. Examples are jurisdictional conflicts among units of the national bureaucracy, and conflicts among constituent members of so-called 'sub-governments' or 'iron triangles', namely groupings of some ruling Liberal Democratic Party (LDP) politicians, certain interest group organizations, and respective units of the national bureaucracy (Ōtake (ed.), 1984; Horne, 1985; Johnson, 1986; Nakano (ed.), 1986; Satō and Matsuzaki, 1986, pp. 99–100; Pempel, 1987).

The realization of the pervasiveness of policy conflict has prompted several systematic analyses of *institutions* of policy conflict resolution and management in Japan (Mochizuki, 1982; Krauss *et al.*, 1984, p. 385–6; Campbell, 1984; Baerwald, 1986; Clemons, 1987; Upham, 1987). These studies, as well as other studies of the policy process in Japan, have either neglected, given scant attention to, or played down the role of an important institution of Japanese government – the advisory bodies. In this chapter, I offer a different view, throwing the role of Japanese advisory bodies in policy conflict resolution and management into sharper relief.[2]

The Japanese government has established an extensive and variegated system of statutory and non-statutory advisory bodies, composed either exclusively or partially of persons not currently in regular government service. Statutory advisory bodies (hereafter SABs) are established by various laws or, since 1983, by cabinet ordinances. They are commonly referred to as *shingikai*. Non-statutory advisory bodies (NSABs) are informally established by the Prime Minister, cabinet members, non-cabinet heads of government agencies, or high-ranking government officials, and are collectively referred to as the 'private advisory bodies' (*shiteki shimon kikan*). In recent years, over 200 SABs and over 200 NSABs have been in existence at the national level.[3] They have been assigned to deal with practically every policy area and operate in the various stages of the policy process.

Broadly speaking, references to Japanese advisory bodies playing down their role tend either to allege or to imply that they are either *irrelevant* to policy conflict or *incapable* of resolving or managing conflict.

To begin with, their irrelevance is implied in official pronouncements. Only a minute number of SABs (four in 1986) have explicitly been established to 'resolve conflict', and these have rarely met to deal with concrete cases.

This official view may reflect the tendency, said to be characteristic of Japanese official pronouncements, to down-play the existence of policy conflicts. References (Rinji Gyōsei Chōsakai, 1964, p. 87; Muramatsu, 1981, p. 125; Komiya, Ōkuno and Suzumura, 1984, pp. 18–21) to advisory bodies' function of 'adjusting interests' (*rigai chōsei*) also pose a semantic difficulty because they may be interpreted to mean various things, including conflict resolution or management.[4] But irrelevance is also implied in the argument critics tend to make to the effect that by controlling their membership, agenda, sources of information, etc., the authorities establishing them assure that the advisory bodies inevitably ratify, and thus legitimate, the authorities' policy positions.

At the other extreme, advisory bodies are said to be incapable of resolving and managing conflict because at least part of their members represent organizations such as government ministries (Johnson, 1975, p. 8; Shindo, 1978, p. 18; Campbell, 1984, p. 315) or interest organizations (Satō, A., 1978, p. 5) with conflicting, firm, and unbridgeable positions, implying that these members perform the representational role of instructed delegates rather than free agents.

The allegations and implications that Japanese advisory bodies are irrelevant to policy conflict, or that they are incapable of resolving or managing policy conflict, suffer from one or several of the following shortcomings: generalizing from one or a small number of cases; relying on anecdotal evidence; and focusing exclusively on either the SABs or the NSABs. To avoid these shortcomings, I have studied both SABs and NSABs, employing several complementary research methods, such as case studies and survey research. In addition, I have compared the case of advisory bodies in Japan with findings about advisory bodies in 'Western' countries in order to determine whether Japanese advisory bodies are unique.

The validity of arguments regarding the role of Japanese advisory bodies in policy conflict resolution or management partly rests on what is meant by 'conflict resolution' and 'conflict management'. I shall therefore present my definition of these terms before clarifying how advisory bodies are related to public policy conflict and analysing advisory bodies' role in conflict resolution and management in Japan.

Definitions

As Pharr points out (1984, in reference to Coleman, 1957; Coser, 1967; and Kriesberg, 1972), the prevailing tendency has been to define conflict in terms of incompatibility of goals, and to distinguish among three facets of conflict: (a) the objective reality of parties pursuing goals which are incompatible (*latent* conflict); (b) the realization of the parties concerned that their objectives are incompatible (*manifest* conflict); and (c) the *behaviour* of the parties concerned in their pursuit of the respective goals. And as

Pharr further points out (1984, p. 219, in reference to Di Palma, 1973), 'conflict latent in the objective situation may or may not become manifest.' Similarly, Campbell (1984, p. 311), applying to Japanese society March and Simon's (1958) hypothesis regarding the effect of goal-sharing on conflict resolution, observes that, '. . . the *subjective* sense of sharing a goal may be more important in determining the mode of conflict resolution than whether or not the participants objectively (as perceived from outside) have common interest.' To these I would add that while the parties concerned may *perceive* their respective goals as being incompatible, there are cases where in reality these goals are not necessarily incompatible; and thus conflict behaviour at times is an outcome of the parties concerned *perceiving* their goals as being incompatible, regardless of whether or not these goals are in fact incompatible. The issue of protective legislation for working women, such as prohibiting night work, is an example. Employers want it abolished to gain more flexibility and save costs. Some womens' organizations oppose it on the grounds that it is a regressive rather than a progressive measure. But a case can be made that abolishing such protective legislation is an indispensable step in the direction of equal employment opportunity (Shinoda 1986; Hanami 1986; Upham 1987).

By conflict behaviour, I refer to one or more of the parties concerned employing means to induce their rival or rivals to change their behaviour in the direction of facilitating the achievement of the goals of those employing the respective means. Conflict behaviour varies in intensity according to the types of means employed: reasoned persuasion, promise of reward, threats, and infliction of various degrees of damage. And the intensity of conflict behaviour tends to vary by the degree of incompatibility of the goals and the perceptions of the sides involved of the possible effectiveness of the respective means.[5]

Thus conflict resolution refers to purposive action or inaction designed to: (a) erase the perceptions of incompatibility of goals – either by one or both sides redefining their goals, and/or by the sides involved having realized that their goals are not necessarily incompatible, through access to new information, data, and scientific knowledge (i.e. empirically tested hypotheses); and (b) make one or more of the participants realize the ineffectiveness of mobilizing for conflict the resources at their disposal as a means to achieving their respective goals. In the same vein,

141

conflict management refers to purposive action or inaction designed to mitigate the perception of incompatibility of goals and persuade one or more of the participants of the benefits of de-escalating conflict behaviour or at least of the ineffectiveness of escalating it.[6]

'Public policy' conflict involves purposive government action or inaction under one or two circumstances: (a) the parties concerned are two or more government units (such as two ministries or two bureaux in a given ministry) and their purposive action or inaction affects persons or groups inside and outside government, such as two ministries making claims for jurisdiction over a certain policy area; and (b) the parties concerned include one or more government units as well as persons or groups outside government.

Advisory Bodies and Policy Conflict

Official pronouncements (Administrative Management Agency, 1982, p. 5) describe Japanese SABs as: (a) introducing new expertise into government; (b) reflecting views and ideas of interests concerned in public policies; (c) promoting fair and equitable implementation of public policies; and (d) helping to coordinate related programmes of various government organizations. In fact, every one of these harbours perceptions of incompatibility of at least some of the goals of those concerned.

This is probably more readily evident in the case of SABs ostensibly designed to reflect views and ideas of interests, and/or promote fair and equitable implementation, and/or coordinate related government programmes, than it is in the case of SABs ostensibly designed to introduce new expertise. To be sure, the interests whose views and ideas are to be reflected vary from one advisory body to another, depending on the scope of the policy problems the advisory body is entrusted with; and the perceptions of incompatibility of goals are reflected more in the views and ideas of some interests than in those of other interests; but perceptions of incompatibility of some goals are present even among constituent members of 'sub-governments' or 'iron triangles', who generally share the common overarching goals of promoting and dominating a given policy area. Perceptions also differ as to what constitutes fair and equitable implementation. And related government programmes often manifest incompatibility of goals with respect not only to 'substantive' matters of policy, but also to organizational jurisdiction and spheres of influence (*nawabari*).

Perceptions of incompatibility of goals even emerge where advisory bodies are ostensibly designed to introduce expertise into government. Expertise is not necessarily identical with neutrality – not only in the obvious case where certain representatives of interest organizations are justifiably reputable for their expertise in the field related in the concern of the respective advisory bodies, but also where non-affiliated experts are concerned. Certain types of expertise not only affect perceptions of how policy problems should be *resolved*, but also – and not less importantly – affect (if not determine) the way policy problems are *defined*; and the way policy problems are defined affects (if not determines) how policy problems are resolved or managed. (This view of problem definition and problem solving is more generally developed in Dery, 1984; and Cairns, 1986, p. 20, referring to the research staff of the MacDonald Commission in Canada, expresses a similar view when he writes: 'Members of the different disciplines did not see the same world.')

Referring to presidential advisory commissions in the United States, Merton (1975) argues that each member has a 'constituency' he or she has to take into account. Even the genuinely un-affiliated experts have a constituency: their professional or scientific reference group (Merton, 1975, p. 165; Gianos, 1974, p. 420). That Merton's concept of constituency is applicable to Japanese advisory bodies is demonstrated by the composition of their memberships.

The charter of many SABs prescribes specific categories from which members are to be chosen – either exclusively, or in addition to, persons broadly referred to as 'persons of learning and experience' (*gakushiki keikensha*). The categories in question are cabinet members, Diet members, government bureaucrats representing their respective organizations, and representatives of interest organizations, including governments at sub-national levels. In recent years, such SABs with formally prescribed memberships have been close to 50 per cent of all SABs in existence (Sone Yasunori Kenkyūkai, 1985, p. 11). The charters of seven of these SABs not only prescribe that their memberships consist of representatives of specific interest groups, but also of persons of learning and experience as *'representatives of the public interest'*.

SAB membership lists published by the government (*Shingikai sōran*, intermittently; *Shokuinroku*, annually) identify the large majority of members, including the persons of learning and experience, by their current organizational affiliation; some by their former organizational affiliations or by their occupations. Many of the organizations and occupations can easily be associated with certain readily identifiable interests concerned with the policies considered by the respective SABs. These interests include not only economic sectors, such as business, agriculture, and labour, but also governments at sub-national levels (prefectures, metropolitan areas, cities, towns, villages); professions (law, medicine); public corporations, national enterprises, and other organizations with 'special juridical status' (*tokushu hōjin*); women; and environmental protection. Other organizations are not readily identifiable as being associated with particular interests: universities, mass-media organizations, and 'research organizations'. Members affiliated to these organizations are highly salient among the 'representatives of the public interest', notably less so among persons of learning and experience not specifically designated as representatives of the public interest.

A closer scrutiny of these research organizations reveals that many of them have been established by government ministries or interest organizations, or have been directly or indirectly supported by government ministries or interest organizations. The members from universities and the mass media tend to have had close contacts with certain government bureaucracies or certain interest organizations, or both, and to have been considered by the bureaucracies and interest organizations to have demonstrated sound and fair judgement.

While members are formally appointed by the Prime Minister, ministers, and heads of government agencies, the actual selection is usually carried out by higher-level bureaucrats. In interviews, bureaucrats admit, sometimes brag about, having formed or used such bodies as instruments of control, legitimation, mobilization of public consent, etc. However, they have increasingly operated within various constraints, such as pressures from Diet members and interest groups, as well as from rival government bureaucracies, constraints which limit bureaucrats' leeway in appointments – not only of interest group representatives, but also of persons of learning and experience (Tachi, 1983, pp. 186–7).

Complete lists of the 'private' advisory bodies (NSABs), let alone of their members, have not been made public. In fact, my enquiries suggest that such lists have never been compiled (also Tsujinaka, 1985). The information sifted from newspaper reports, case studies of various policy areas, unpublished reports of several NSABs, and responses from several government ministries to my enquiries indicates that, even though these bodies are formed informally, the constraints the authorities face in appointing members are similar to the constraints they face in appointing SAB members, though less often and less intensely. NSAB members also tend to be associated with various organizations, occupations, and disciplines concerned with the respective policy problems; thus they also have their own constituency to take into account while participating in the work of their respective NSABs.

Certain interest groups are either excluded from or under-represented in both SAB and NSABs. The persistent exclusion of Nikkyōso (Japan Teachers' Union) from advisory bodies attached to the Ministry of Education, and the temporary exclusion of interest group representatives from the Beika Shingikai (Rice Price Council) attached to the Ministry of Agriculture, Forestry and Fisheries are notable examples of the former; the under-representation of labour and consumer group representatives in SABs attached to the Ministry of International Trade and Industry (MITI), and of citizens' (*jūmin*) and environmental protection groups in the Chūō Kogai Taisaku Shingikai (Anti-Pollution Measures Council) attached to the Environmental Protection Agency are examples of the latter. With the exception of the case of Nikkyōso, the tendency in recent years has been to make SABs more widely inclusive and to somewhat increase the representation of the under-represented (Harari, 1986; Tsujinaka, 1986). By and large, exclusions are determined by the authorities; but certain individuals, especially certain university professors and certain intellectuals outside academia, have persistently excluded themselves from membership of govern-mental advisory bodies: either because on ideological grounds they generally refuse to cooperate with the authorities, or out of conviction that advisory bodies in Japan are simply manipulative tools of the authorities.

Conflict Resolution and Management

In a large majority of cases, SABs are presented by the appointing authority with a policy proposal, which they are requested either to approve, propose revisions to, or reject. There are cases where policy proposals presented by the authority are rejected by the respective SAB; for example, MITI's attempt in 1975 to bring about a recommendation by the Advisory Committee for Energy for upstream consolidation of the oil industry (Samuels, 1987, pp. 211–2); but such cases are relatively infrequent. Often, the proposals are approved either as presented by the authority or after revisions have been introduced. Less often, SABs are presented with several policy alternatives and are requested to approve one of them; or they are presented with a policy problem and are requested to examine it and present recommendations for policy. In the case of some SABs, such as the Local Government System Investigation Council (Ōgita, 1979, p. 43), the latter practice is more common than in others. Finally, in a relatively few cases, SABs take up a policy problem at their own initiative.

Where the authority presents one policy proposal, the deliberation of the advisory body is often conflict-free and short; the advisory body approves the proposal – either without revisions, or after minor revisions have been introduced. On the surface, such practice may be taken to signify that relations in the policy areas in question are harmonious and free of conflict; alternatively, it invites suspicions that the advisory bodies are controlled by the authorities, and are used, even abused, to legitimate the authority's own policy positions by creating the impression that its policies have been examined by an advisory body.

Further probing, however, tends to reveal that some of these policy proposals are not identical with the authority's initial position, but rather products of conflict of various degrees of intensity between the authority presenting the proposals and at least some of the organizations or groups represented on the advisory body. In such instances, conflict resolution has been carried out in other forums prior to the SAB deliberation – not in isolation from but rather *in anticipation of* the SAB deliberation (Sone Kenkyūkai, 1985). By law or by practice, it has become expected that in certain matters of policy the respective authorities obtain the opinion of – though not necessarily the approval of – a SAB (Kataoka, 1985, pp. 353–4).[7] Thus, even where a SAB expeditiously and unanimously approves a policy proposal presented to it by the authority, the SAB often plays an anticipatory role in conflict resolution or management. One of the forums used in this anticipatory process are non-statutory advisory bodies.

Where anticipatory conflict resolution or management fails, the authority either drops its initiative, keeps it dormant until circumstances have become more propitious, or presents its policy proposal to the SAB. Where it does the latter, conflict is carried over into the SAB deliberations.

SABs respond to the authority's request for advice in the following ways: (a) by presenting a report of one position, adopted either by consensus or by majority vote; (b) by presenting a report containing more than one position; and (c) by failing to agree to present a report. Responses to a questionnaire I mailed in 1974 to SAB members[8] suggest that the most common response is a report adopted by consensus. Seventy-four per cent of the respondents recalled that the most common practice in the SABs they were members of was presenting a report containing one position adopted unanimously; 16 per cent – a report by majority vote; 5 per cent – a report enumerating more than one position; and less than 1 per cent recalled failing to present a report as the most common practice.[9]

This distribution is of individual members' recollection of the experience of SABs in which they participated; it is not a distribution of the prevailing practices of individual SABs. Comprehensive and authoritative information regarding this aspect of the behaviour of all SABs is not available. The fact that the respondents were members of advisory bodies in various policy areas (with the exception of foreign and defense policies, narrowly defined) suggests that the two types of distributions would be similar. Moreover, that SAB behaviour in this regard may have varied by policy area can be indirectly inferred from the fact that, while the majority of the representatives of all types of interest groups – except for 'non-established' consumers, women, and 'citizens and residents' – recalled consensus as the dominant practice,[10] these majorities were markedly higher in the case of labour (78 per cent) and of business and agriculture (72 per cent) than in the case of professionals (56 per cent; especially the medical profession).

Presumably, the answer to the question 'What contributes to the prevalence of consensus decision-making in Japanese SABs?' should be simple: the Japanese are widely believed to make decisions by consensus. Two things, however, are worth noting. First, when asked about their own preferences, only 7 per cent of my respondents said that no report should be adopted unless the members could reach a consensus on it. In contrast, a majority of 70 per cent responded that, while consensus should be attempted, where consensus cannot be reached a report ought to be adopted by majority vote. Fourteen per cent preferred to have the SAB enumerate divergent positions; and, as could have been expected, only 1 per cent indicated that decisions should be made only by majority vote. In other words, most members seemed to feel that, having agreed to participate, they should strive to present a report – preferably, though not exclusively, by consensus.

The second thing worth noting regarding consensus decision-making in advisory bodies is that Japan is not unique in this respect. Studies conducted in countries where consensus decision-making is not considered to be the norm also reveal a similar tendency of advisory bodies to reach decisions by consensus – often following a process of bargaining.[11] The studies attribute this to members' wishes to make their mark in the policy process and to members' convictions that reports adopted by consensus are more likely to be taken seriously and implemented than are reports adopted in other manners.

Two authors (Merton, 1975; Wolanin, 1985), who focus their analysis on presidential commissions in the United States, which in most cases are temporary, attribute the proclivity of advisory bodies to adopt reports by consensus also to certain social dynamics generated by their finite lifespan and short life-expectancy perspective. I shall outline Wolanin's argument, which is the more comprehensive.

According to Wolanin, presidential commissions share significant characteristics with 'temporary systems', as conceptualized
by Miles (1964, pp. 437–92). Most relevant here are temporary
systems' time perspective and participants' isolation from their
normal work environment. These characteristics contribute to the
creation of an atmosphere of personal security, mutual trust, and
openness, that facilitates cooperation, rapid performance and
freedom to innovate. Participants tend to become less encum-
bered by ossifying traditions or by hesitation to make bold,
unconventional recommendations for change, the implementation of which lies beyond the expected lifespan of the commission.

Wolanin recognizes that presidential commissions differ from
Miles' temporary systems in that, unlike the former which
operate in isolation from their normal work environment,
presidential commissions are highly visible and their participants
continue their regular work while serving on the commission.
This double commitment can restrain development of the
intense, open, and cooperative interaction between participants
that occurred in the temporary systems studies by Miles. On the
other hand, the continued involvement in their normal tasks
keeps their feet on the ground and checks the tendency,
characeristic of other temporary systems, to set overly ambitious,
unrealistic goals and to become overconfident in their ability to
have their recommendations implemented.

Some of Japan's most famous advisory bodies have been
temporary ones; entrusted with a policy problem when they were
established, they were disbanded once they had completed their
task or reached their deadline. The SAB on educational reform
and the NSAB known as the Maekawa Group are recent
examples. Most SABs and some NSABs, however, have been
continuous (hereafter 'permanent'); and although members of
Japanese SABs are appointed for fixed terms (two years in 75 per
cent of SABs), memberships are renewable, and in fact have
often been renewed.[12] Exceptions have been in such cases as
death and illness, or where by law or custom membership is
reserved for officers of specific organizations (for example, the
Japan Medical Association or the Textile Workers Union):
leadership turnover within these organizations is followed by the
new officers replacing their predecessors as members of the
respective SABs. Permament advisory bodies from time to time

examine policy proposals or policy problems, usually at the initiative of the authority in question; in some cases, at chairmen's or members' initiative.

While there are certain differences between Japanese permanent and temporary advisory bodies, there are also certain similarities between them which are relevant here. Temporary advisory bodies tend to be more 'permanent' than their designation suggests: (a) in that there is some overlap in their memberships with those of permanent advisory bodies in the respective policy areas; and (b) in that, in some cases, such as those mentioned, the time they spend studying and deliberating tends to be as long, or even longer, than the time some permanent advisory bodies spend studying and deliberating new subjects the authorities assign them. And permanent advisory bodies tend to be more 'temporary' than their lifespan suggests: (a) because of some turnover in their memberships, and (b) because some of the authorities' requests for advice set deadlines for submitting reports.

I do not have sufficient information to evaluate the effect of approaching deadlines for submitting reports on the behaviour of members. There is some evidence that members' temporary social isolation from their 'normal' environments – such as being closeted together for several days in a hotel (Ishii, 1987, p. 15), or travelling together in Europe on a 'study tour' (Upham, 1987, p. 196) – tend to have the effect referred to by Miles and Wolanin. However, what in the Japanese case seems to be more significant is the continuity of the relationships among the participants which tends to affect their perceptions of their representational role *vis-à-vis* their respective constituencies.

It is widely held that a relatively high internal homogeneity, on the one hand (Krauss, Rohlen and Steinhoff, 1984, pp. 385–6), and a highly complex, and often protracted, consensual decision-making process in Japanese organizations (*nemawashi*), on the other, leaves their representatives with extremely limited leeway in their relations with representatives of other organizations. These representatives are thus bound by certain fixed positions which they can ignore or modify only at the risk of antagonizing at least some elements within their organizations, or not before another intra-organizational *nemawashi* has successfully been concluded. This constraint is indeed powerful. But the behaviour of representatives of Japanese organizations is also influenced by their 'membership' of what Adams (1976) calls 'boundary transaction system'. I find this concept, developed as a model for the study of inter-organizational negotiations in the field of industrial relations in the 'West', as well as several related ones from the general literature of the social psychology of bargaining, to be especially suitable for the study of advisory bodies in Japan.

Boundary transaction systems are open social systems whose members are 'boundary role persons'. A boundary role person is a member of an organization whose role entails interacting both with other members of his or her own organization and with members of other organizations whose role similarly entails interacting both with members of their own organizations and with members of other organizations. 'The boundary role person of a given organization', says Adams (1976, p. 1181), 'is subject to the influence of constituents, as individuals and as a group . . . and to the influence of his counterparts . . .' and '. . . he may also be influenced by third party interventionist[s].' Let me elaborate briefly, starting with the influence of counterparts.

The more continuous the relationship among members of a boundary transaction system, the better able they become to learn not only of each other's goals and related 'objective' and 'technical' matters, but also, in the words of Brown and Terry (1975, p. 8), 'of the constraints under which they operate and the likely reactions by one organization to actions by the others.' Donnelly (1984, p. 366) captures this tendency in Japan in specific reference to the policy area of land diversion, emphasizing the important contribution of the 'political empathy' generated by long-range relationships 'for the creation of a workable consensus about the outer limits of feasible actions, even if it did not guarantee ultimate unanimity.' The more continuous the relationship, say Morley and Stephenson (1977, pp. 258ff.), the higher the likelihood that bargainers will move from 'collective bargaining' where they tend to represent the views of their groups or organizations to 'interpersonal bargaining' where they are more prone to take into account their own view as well as the views of their counterparts. This is practically what Krauss, Rohlen and Steinhoff (1984, p. 389) mean when they refer to the Japanese preference for 'personalizing' conflict management in face-to-face settings. What facilitates this kind of conflict management is the continuity in the relationship of the participants. And the more continuous the relationship of the boundary role persons, says

Adams (1976, p. 1182), the more they tend to develop an optimizing perspective rather than a maximizing perspective. 'Maximizing transaction outcomes implies a short-term point of view – single transactions are considered to the exclusion of possible future ones. Optimizing, on the other hand, suggests a perspective which comprehends transaction outcomes within a set of expected transactions over a period of time.' Studies reported by Ouchi (1984) of policy-making concerning business in Japan, including the work of advisory bodies, reveal a negotiation practice whereby a concession by one side at one point in time is reciprocated by a counterpart's concession at a later point in time.

These propositions regarding the dynamics generated by longterm relationships and their referents in the Japanese experience put the concept of constituency into perspective. Members of advisory bodies tend to have a constituency, but their perceptions of their constituencies' interests and policy positions do not reflect an instructed delegate type of representational role. This is also suggested by the findings of my survey. The respondents were asked to indicate to whom they felt most responsible. Fourteen per cent indicated 'the interest group they belonged to or the organization that recommended that they be appointed to the SAB'; 19 per cent indicated 'the appointing authority'; around 50 per cent indicated either 'those affected by the policies concerned' (45 per cent) or 'no one in particular' (8 per cent).[13] The responses of the public interest members were slightly different in that they scored somewhat higher (14 per cent) on 'no one in particular' and somewhat lower (13 per cent) on 'the appointing authority'. And while the combined rate of the public interest members feeling mostly responsible to either the group concerned or the authority (27 per cent) was not negligible, the overall distribution of their responses suggests that they tend to view themselves as instructed delegates even less than do other members.

Learning and empathy are enhanced by the tendency to divide advisory bodies into sub-committees and sub-sub-committees whose number of participants is small and in which the interaction between participants is more intensive and informal. When deemed necessary, sub-committees are assisted by groups of consultants. Advisory bodies ordinarily do not have independent research staff; officials of the respective authorities, at times belonging to more than one bureaucratic unit, provide staff support on a part-time basis. With several notable exceptions, such as the Natural Resources Investigative Council (Shigen Chōsakai) at the Environment Agency, and the Economic Council (Keizai Shingikai), advisory bodies in Japan, like advisory bodies in other countries, tend to initiate little research of the scientific variety. And where it finds it both advisable and feasible, the respective authority will screen the information it presents to the advisory body, either at its own initiative or at members' request. However, while the government bureaucracy has been *the* major source of policy-related information in the country, it has not had a monopoly in this respect; and the sources of information at the disposal of other participants have increasingly improved. Deliberations in sub-committees tend to be earnest and thoughtful and, more often than not, advisory councils' recommendations are drafted by the respective sub-committees and are approved by the plenary session, at times after minor revisions have been introduced. Where sub-committee recommendations are not approved, the chairmen tend to appoint a drafting committee consisting of representatives of the major contenders, or consisting exclusively of those persons of learning and experience whose partiality in a given conflict is less salient than of other members, and who are in a better position to project an image of independence of judgement. To facilitate consensus, the drafting committees often formulate a report couched in general, sometimes abstract, terms: pointing in a general direction the members can support, rather than spelling out specific recommendations. (Recent examples are cited by Elliot, 1983, pp. 773–4; Kumon, 1984, p. 161; Kuroha, 1987, p. 4; Calder, 1988, p. 526.)

The chairmen and these 'neutral' persons of learning and experience tend to be Adams' 'third party interventionist(s)'. They play two major roles. One is of *conciliators* and *mediators*: helping contenders reach an understanding. The other role is of *lightning rods*: where reports signify concessions on the part of certain groups or organizations, these highly respectable chairmen and persons of learning and experience are publicly identified as the authors or sponsors of the given recommendations, thus sheltering members representing the groups or organizations concerned from allegations by their constituencies or segments thereof of incompetence, 'selling out', or both.

Members who genuinely support or acquiesce in a report requiring concessions on the part of their groups and organizations can argue 'in their defense' that they have had no choice but to show respect for the third party interventionists, the ostensible authors or sponsors of the position in question, and avoid the latter's losing face. Thus third party interventionists act as both catalyzers and legitimizers in conflict resolution and management. A thorough study by Muramatsu and Krauss (n.d., p. 47) reveals that Japanese interest group leaders prefer to resolve conflict with other interest groups directly, rather than through a third party such as SABs. Certain conflicts, however, especially those in which government is involved, are taken up by, or emerge in, advisory bodies, where the third party interventionists' role of catalyzers and and legitimizers is taken advantage of both by the authorities and by interest group representatives.

At this point, the relationship to conflict resolution and management of the various manners of advisory body decision-making has to be clarified. I shall start with consensus.

While, as noted, the presentation of a report adopted by consensus does not necessarily signify the non-existence of conflict, neither does it necessarily signify that conflict has been resolved. It can mean that conflict has been managed, in that the participants have to a certain extent changed their perceptions of the incompatibility of their goals or part of their goals, and/or realized the futility of escalating their conflict behaviour and the possible benefits of de-escalating it. The participants still have to persuade their constituencies of the desirability, or inevitability, of supporting or acquiescing in the report; and although the lightning rods are helpful in this respect, success is not guaranteed.

A report adopted by consensus can actually intensify conflict behaviour under two different sets of circumstances. One is where groups and organizations, notwithstanding their representatives' support or acquiescence, feel that the report falls far short of their initial expectations. Another is where more than one advisory body – each operating within the sphere of influence of, though not necessarily controlled by, a different government authority, and each consisting of members with different constituencies – issue conflicting reports. In such instances, the advisory bodies in question are referred to as the 'cheering party' (*ōendan*) of their respective government authorities. Instances of reports adopted by consensus – not to mention the other types of reports – failing to resolve conflict, or even contributing to its intensification, are widely reported. Such outcomes of the work of advisory bodies are the ones the mass media and academic researchers tend to pay attention to.

Reports adopted by majority vote – with or without spelling out minority positions – and reports enumerating more than one position, without the advisory body indicating a preference, both tend to signify that conflict has not been resolved. The mere fact that reports have been adopted and submitted, however, signifies that conflict has been managed, because members have the option of walking out and boycotting the proceedings. This is especially clear where, by law or custom, the authority cannot act without first having a report issued by a SAB. A well-known, though rare, *court ruling* to this effect concerns the Central Council for Social Health Insurance (Chūō Shakai Iryō Kyōgikai). The Minister of Health and Welfare, in 1964, presented to the council a proposal to have the insurance premium raised by 9.5 per cent. Both sides (insurers and insured) refused to have a formal report (*tōshin*) adopted. The public interest members decided to issue their own report in the less formal form of *hōkoku*, supporting the Minister's proposal. The Tokyo District Court ruled that, because the tripartite structure of the council implied that it was formed to conciliate conflicting interests and to protect the respective interests, the insurance premium rise could not come into effect before a *tōshin* was issued by the council (Satō 1969, pp. 115–17).

Matters left unsettled or even sharpened by an advisory body report tend to be referred to: (a) the same body at a later date, following a change in circumstances and/or in the membership of the given body, or both; (b) a different advisory body with a more comprehensive membership; (c) a SAB or an NSAB formed specifically to deal with the unsettled matter; where advisory bodies have issued conficting reports, the *ad hoc* advisory body tends to consist of 'representatives' of the advisory bodies in question. The work of these bodies takes place either concomitantly with, or at intervals between, attempts at conflict resolution and management carried out in other forums: direct talks, cabinet level committees, Diet committees, etc. Various complex issues have been dealt with by a *series* of advisory bodies of the varieties just described. Some remain unresolved –

especially those with ideological connotations, such as the issue of government employees' right to strike (Harari, 1973, 1974, 1984), and the revision of the criminal code (Hōmushō, 1976: Keiho Kaisei, 1978), but also issues where jurisdictional and other interests seem to prevail, such as reorganizing the prefectures (Samuels, 1983).

Conclusions

Advisory bodies in Japan manifest considerable diversity: in the degree of their formality; in their time-frame; in the comprehensiveness of their memberships; in the types and forms of formally and semi-formally assigned tasks; in the ways they operate and respond to government requests for advice. While only a negligible number of SABs have been established explicitly to resolve conflict, conflict is inherent in some facet of practically every advisory body. Japanese advisory bodies have been engaged in resolving and managing conflict, albeit with varying degrees of success as well as notable failures. And Japanese SABs and NSABs constitute a system with a recurrent and patterned structure, albeit with varying degrees of integration of its constituent parts, which has become, among other things, an institutionalized mechanism for conflict resolution or management – largely supplementing, at times supplanting, two types of mechanisms: on the one hand, non-structured mechanisms for conflict resolution and management, such as informal direct talks by the sides involved, and, on the other hand, institutions explicitly formed to resolve or manage policy conflict, such as Diet committees and the courts.

In comparative perspective, the widely publicized Japanese cultural traits of preferring consensus over other manners of decision-making and of personalizing conflict management only partly accounts for Japanese advisory bodies' role in conflict resolution and management. Just as important is a structural factor, i.e. the notable degree of continuity in the relationship of the participants, on the one hand, and the exclusion from membership of certain public policy contenders, on the other.

Finally, the contribution of advisory bodies not only to conflict resolution and management but also to conflict intensification, supports Krauss' argument (1984, p. 281) that, 'Cultural styles may help create conflict *or* accommodation, depending on how they are integrated with the institutional, ideological, and power context.'

Notes

1 For elaboration of this distinction between ideological differences in Japan, see Watanuki, 1967.
2 This chapter is a partial result of my long-term project on advisory bodies and the policy process in Japan in comparative perspective which I have carried out at the following institutions: Institute of Social Sciences, University of Tokyo; Truman Institute, the Hebrew University of Jerusalem; Center for Japanese Studies, University of California, Berkeley; Netherlands Institute for Advanced Study in the Humanities and Social Sciences, Holland; St Anthony's College and Nissan Institute of Japanese Studies, Oxford University; and Woodrow Wilson International Center for Scholars. The support of these institutions and of the Ford Foundation through the Israel Foundations Trustees is gratefully acknowledged.
3 Advisory bodies have also been established at lower levels of government, but they are not included in the present analysis.
4 On the various interpretations of *chōsei*, see Johnson, 1980. In Sone Yasunori Kenkyukai's study (1985), however, it clearly means conflict resolution and management.
5 This is a simplified variation on Korpi's (1974) model.
6 Unlike Lebra (1984, pp. 41–2), I do not include 'aggravation of conflict' as one aspect of conflict management.
7 As Pempel points out (1977), Sweden is another country where such practice has been institutionalized.
8 Respondents: 693; response rate: 35 per cent.
9 Two per cent did not answer this question and 3 per cent provided various variations on the responses reported here.
10 44 per cent of the latter.
11 For Britain: Baker, 1972, p. 107; Cartwright, 1975, p. 184; for the United States: Wolanin, 1975, p. 118; for Sweden: Meijer, 1969, p. 115; Premfors 1983, p. 628; and for Australia: Singleton, 1985, p. 21.
12 While rates of members' continuity vary, my comparison of two terms revealed an average membership continuity of 56 per cent.

13   The remaining indicated another alternative, or more than one
     object of responsibility, or did not answer the question.

References

Adams, J.S. (1976), 'The structure and dynamics of behaviour in
   organizational boundary poles' in M.D. Dunnette (ed.), *Handbook of
   Industrial and Organizational Psychology*. Chicago, Rand McNally,
   pp. 1175–99.
Administrative Management Agency (1982), *Administrative Reform in
   Japan*. Tokyo, Administrative Management Agency.
Baerwald, H.H. (1986), *Party Politics in Japan*. London, Allen and
   Unwin.
Baker, R.J.S. (1972), *Administrative Theory and Public Administration*.
   London, Hutchinson University Library.
Brown, W. and M. Terry (1975), 'The importance of continuity to the
   understanding of bargaining'. Paper presented at a symposium on
   Psychology and Industrial Relations. Nottingham, Annual Conference
   of the British Psychological Society.
Cairns, A.C. (1986), 'The MacDonald and other royal commissions: their
   role in public policy'. The 1986 David Alexander Lecture at Memorial
   University.
Calder, K.E. (1988), 'Japanese foreign economic policy formation:
   explaining the reactive state', *World Politics*, XL, pp. 517–41.
Campbell, J.C. (1977), 'Compensation for repatriates: a case study of
   interest group politics and party-government negotiations in Japan' in
   T.J. Pempel (ed.), *Policymaking in Contemporary Japan*. Ithaca,
   Cornell University Press, pp. 103–42.
Campbell, J.C. (1984), 'Policy conflict and its resolution' in E.S. Krauss,
   T.P. Rohlen and P.G. Steinhoff (eds.), *Conflict in Japan*. Honolulu,
   University of Hawaii press, pp. 294–334.
Cartwright, T.J. (1975), *Royal Commissions and Departmental Com-
   mittees in Britain*. London, Hodder and Stoughton.
Clemons, S.C. (1987), 'The committee system of Japan's national diet:
   sound and fury signifying something?', *Journal of North East Asian
   Studies*, 6, pp. 46–61.
Coleman, J.S. (1957), *Community Conflict*. New York, Free Press.
Coser, L.A. (1967), *Continuities in the Study of Social Conflict*. New
   York, Free Press.
Curtis, G.L. (1988), *The Japanese Way of Politics*. New York, Columbia
   University.

Cusumano, M.A. (1985), *The Japanese Automobile Industry: Technology and Management at Nissan and Toyota*. Cambridge, Mass., Harvard University.

Dery, D. (1984), *Problem Definition in Policy Analysis*. Lawrence, University of Kansas.

Di Palma, G. (1973), *The Study of Conflict in Western Society*. Morristown, General Learning.

Donnelly, M.W. (1977), 'Setting the price of rice: a study in political decisionmaking' in T.J. Pempel (ed.), *Policymaking in Contemporary Japan*. Ithaca, Cornell University Press, pp. 143–200.

Donnelly, M.W. (1984), 'Conflict over government authority and markets' in E.S. Krauss, T.P. Rohlen and P.G. Steinhoff (eds.), *Conflict in Japan*. Honolulu, University of Hawaii Press, pp. 335–74.

Elliot, J. (1983), 'The 1981 administrative reform in Japan', *Asian Survey*, 23, pp. 765–79.

Gianos, P.L. (1974), 'Scientists as policy advisers: the context of influence', *The Western Political Science Quarterly*, 26, pp. 329–456.

Hanami, T. (1986), 'Koyo kikai kinto ho no seiritsu – shiko to kongo no kadai', *Nihon Rodo Kyokai Zassi*, 322, pp. 2–13.

Harari, E. (1974), 'Japanese politics of advice in comparative perspective: a framework for analysis and a case study', *Public Policy*, 22, pp. 537–77.

Harari, E. (1984), 'The public sector in Japan: industrial relations and politics', *Asian and African Studies*, 18, pp. 87–109.

Harari, E. (1986), *Policy Concertation in Japan*. Berlin, Verlag Ute Schiller.

Hayashi, C. (1988), 'The national character in transition', *Japan Echo*, 15, pp. 7–11.

Homusho (1976), *Keiho Zenmen Kaisei ni tsuite no Kento Kekka to Sono Kaisetsu*. Tokyo, Homusho.

Horne, J. (1985), *Japan's Financial Markets: Conflict and Consensus in Policymaking*. London, Allen and Unwin.

Ishii, T. (1987), 'Rinkyoshin no sannenkan o furikaette', *Rinkyoshin Dayori*, 32, pp. 12–20.

Johnson, C. (1975), 'Japan – who governs: an essay on official bureaucracy', *Journal of Japanese Studies*, pp. 21–8.

Johnson, C. (1980), '*Omote* (explicit) and *Ura* (implicit): translating Japanese political terms', *The Journal of Asian Studies*, 6, pp. 89–116.

Johnson, C. (1982), *MITI and the Japanese Miracle*. Stanford, Stanford University.

Johnson, C. (1986), 'MITI, MPT, and the Telecom wars: how Japan makes policy for high technology'. Berkeley, BRIE Working paper, No. 21.

Kataoka, H. (1985), 'Shingikai no seijiryoku gaku', *Shakai Kagaku Tokyu*, 89, pp. 343–67.

Keiho Kaisei Hoan Shobun ni Hantai suru Hyakunin Iinkai (1978), *idem* (ed.), *Keiho Kaisei o Do Kangaeruka*. Tokyo, Sanichi Shobo.

Komiya, R., M. Okuno and T. Suzumura (1984), *Nihon no Sangyo Seisaku*. Tokyo, Tokyo Daigaku Shuppankai.

Korpi, W. (1974), 'Conflict, power and relative deprivation', *American Political Science Review*, 68, pp. 1569–78.

Krauss, E., T.P. Rohlen and P.G. Steinhoff (eds.) (1984), *Conflict in Japan*. Honolulu, University of Hawaii Press.

Kriesberg, L. (1973), *The Sociology of Social Conflicts*. Englewood Cliffs, Prentice Hall.

Kumon, S. (1984), 'Japan faces its future: the political economics of administrative reform', *Journal of Japanese Studies*, 10, pp. 143–65.

Kuroha, R. (1987), 'Iwayuru Kyoiku no kohai', *Rinkyoshin Dayori*, 32, p. 28.

Lebra, T.S. (1984), 'Nonconfrontational strategies for management in interpersonal conflicts' in E.S. Krauss, T.P. Rohlen and P.G. Steinhoff (eds.), *Conflict in Japan*. Honolulu, University of Hawaii Press.

March, J.G. and H.A. Simon (1958), *Organizations*. New York, Wiley.

Meijer, H. (1969), 'Bureaucracy and policy formulation in Sweden', *Scandinavian Political Studies*, 4, pp. 103–16.

Merton, R.K. (1975), 'Social knowledge and public policy: sociological perspectives on four presidential commissions' in M. Komarovsky (ed.), *Sociology and Public Policy*. New York, Elsevier, pp. 153–77.

Miles, M.B. (1964), 'On temporary systems' in *idem* (ed.), *Innovation in Education*. New York, Columbia University, pp. 437–92.

Mochizuki, M. (1982), 'Managing and influencing the Japanese legislative process: the role of parties and the national diet'. Ph.D. Harvard University.

Morley, I. and G. Stephenson (1977), *The Social Psychology of Bargaining*. London, George Allen and Unwin.

Nakano, M. (1986), *idem* (ed.), *Nihongata Seisaku Kettei no Henyo*. Tokyo, Toyo Keizai Shimposha.

Ogita, T. (1979), 'Chiho seido chosakai no ayumi', *Nihon Gyosei Gakkai*, 14, pp. 39–81.

Otake, H. (1979), *Gendai Nihon no Seiji Kenryoku Keizai Kenryoku*. Tokyo, Sanichi Shobo.

Otake, H. (1984), *idem* (ed.), *Nihon Seiji no Soten*. Tokyo, Sanichi Shobo.

Ouchi, W.G. (1984), *The M-Form Society*. Reading, Addison Wesley.

Pempel, T.J. (1977), *Policymaking in Contemporary Japan*. Ithaca, Cornell University Press.

Pempel, T.J. (1987), 'The unbundling of "Japan Inc.": the changing dynamics of Japanese policy formation', *Journal of Japanese Studies*, 13, pp. 271–306.

Pharr, S.J. (1984), 'Status conflict: the rebellion of the tea pourers' in E.S. Krauss, T.P. Rohlen and P.G. Steinhoff (eds.), *Conflict in Japan*. Honolulu, University of Hawaii Press, pp. 214–40.

Premfors, R. (1983), 'Governmental commissions in Sweden', *American Behavioral Scientist*, 26, pp. 623–42.

Richardson, B.M. and S.C. Flanagan (1984), *Politics in Japan*. Boston, Little Brown.

Rinji, G.C. (1964), 'Toshin', *Jichi kenkyu*, 40, pp. 87–92.

Samuels, R.J. (1983), *The Politics of Regional Policy in Japan: Localities Incorporated?*. Princeton, Princeton University Press.

Samuels, R.J. (1987), *The Business of the Japanese State: Energy Markets in Comparative and Historical Perspective*. Ithaca, Cornell University Press.

Sato, A. (1978), 'Shingikai no yakuwari', *Chiiki Kaihatsu*, 160, pp. 2–7.

Sato, S. and T. Matsuzaki (1986), *Jiminto Seiken*. Tokyo, Chuo Koronsha.

Sato, T. (1969), 'Shingikai', *Gyosei Kenkyu* 7, pp. 97–117.

Shindo, M. (1978), 'Shingikai toshin no sakusei to riyo keitai', *Chiiki Kaihatsu*, 160, pp. 15–20.

Shinoda, T. (1986), 'Shingikai: danjo koyo kikai kinto ho o meguru ishi kettei' in M. Nakano (ed.), *Nihongata Seisaku Kettei no Henyo*. Tokyo, Toyo Keizai Shimposha, pp. 79–110.

Singleton, G. (1985), 'The economic planning advisory council: the reality of consensus', *Politics*, 20, pp. 12–25.

Sone Yasunori Kenkyukai (1985), *idem* (ed.), *Shingikai no Kiso Kenkyu*. Tokyo, Keio University.

Tachi, R. (1983), 'Kanryo to Shingikai to Seito', *Hogaku semina*, 23, pp. 186–7.

Tsujinaka,Y. (1985), 'Shakai henyo to seisaku katei no taio', *Kita Kyushu Daigaku Hosei Ronshu*, 13, pp. 20–63.

Tsujinaka, Y. (1986), 'Rodo dantai: kyuchi ni tatsu (Rodo) no seisaku kettei' in M. Nakano (ed.), *Nihongata Seisaku Kettei no Henyo*. Tokyo, Toyo Keizai Shimposha, pp. 267–300.

Upham, F.K. (1987), *Law and Social Change in Japan*. Cambridge, Mass., Harvard University Press.

Watanuki, J. (1967), 'Patterns of politics in present-day Japan' in S.M. Lipset and S. Rokkan (eds.), *Party Systems and Voter Alignments: Cross-National Perspectives*. New York, Free Press, pp. 447–66.

Wolanin, T.R. (1975), *Presidential Advisory Commissions: Truman to Nixon*. Madison, University of Wisconsin Press.

8 Conflict and Non-Weberian Bureaucracy in Japan[1]

H. Befu

Introduction

Max Weber's social theory is so wide-ranging, so powerful, and so well constructed, that sociology since his time is often said to be nothing but footnotes to Max Weber. As we know, Weber's theory was constructed on the basis of his intimate knowledge of Europe, the Near East, India, and China, but not that of Japan, which hardly figures in any of his writings. Thus consideration of the Japanese case potentially throws a new light on Weber's social theory, and can suggest its revision.

For example, Ito (1980), in his analysis of Japanese government bureaucracy, has suggested that Japanese bureaucrats do not define their goals strictly in terms of the organization they belong to, such as the Ministry of Finance or the Ministry of Foreign Affairs, or in terms of the sub-units thereof to which they belong. Instead, their goal orientation is very much coloured by the satisfaction they feel in their awareness that they are working for Japan, that they are at the helm of the nation. Ito has also suggested that Japanese bureaucracy is organized for the purpose of promoting its members through the ranks and thus to provide a means of promoting them internally, irrespective of competence and talent. Of course this does not mean that an organization can survive without any competent member, but he argues that, while most bureaucrats are competent, many of them are not, and yet that such incompetent bureaucrats are also rewarded with higher status from time to time according to the seniority system. An important point is that bureaucracy in Japan, based on permanent employment and seniority, is predicated upon keeping workers and promoting them through the ranks. Indeed, every Japanese organization of fair size, which means one with a well-entrenched seniority system, has a number of incompetent managers who carry important-sounding titles, who draw corresponding salaries and yet are assigned to trivial tasks because of their incompetence.

What we seem to see here in short is that rationality and instrumentality of bureaucracy as conceptualized by Weber are 'compromised' by other principles – permanent employment and the seniority system – of Japanese bureaucracy. Yet experience has shown that Japanese bureaucracy – whether economic or political – is at least as efficient as any Western bureaucracy. Thus the Weberian notion of bureaucratic rationality perhaps needs another look. Yet the reason why the Weberian bureaucracy is legal–rational should not be taken lightly. In instituting, as we shall see, particularistic and functionally diffuse elements in Japanese bureaucracy, danger was inplanted for possible misuse of the office by the office holder. While Japan's 'cultural genius' has created a bureaucratic structure enabling Japan to avoid this pitfall, none the less, the danger is ever-present. Indeed, a small number of Japanese office holders do fall victim. Herein lies a conflict inherent in the Japanese bureaucracy precisely because it did away with the structural safeguard which Weber stipulated in bureaucracy in the form of legal rationality, i.e. functional specificity and universalism. This chapter is basically a discussion of the nature of Japanese bureaucracy, particularly in comparison with the received Weberian bureaucracy; but it will make references to the locus of structural conflict arising because of the special character of Japanese bureaucracy.

In reference to bureaucratic rationality, Weber (1947, p. 330) maintains that a bureaucrat 'is subject to an impersonal order', that he obeys authority 'only in his capacity as a "single member" of the corporate group, what he obeys is only "the law",' and that he does not owe 'obedience to him [a person in authority] as an individual, but to the impersonal order.' Weber (1946, p. 199) reiterates this point in another context:

It is decisive for the specific nature of modern loyalty to an office that, in the pure type, it does not establish a relationship to *a person*, like the vassal's or disciple's faith in fear or in patrimonial relations of authority. Modern loyalty is devoted to impersonal and functional purposes. (original emphasis)

What will be questioned in this chapter is whether the organizational rationality which Weber describes necessarily leads to efficiency, or, to put it in another way, whether organizational rationality is the only means leading to efficiency. The Japanese case may suggest an organization of bureaucracy which is not purely 'rational' in Weber's sense and yet is just as efficient.

This chapter examines the control system of Japanese bureaucracy and questions in the light of Japanese data specifically the Weberian conception of bureaucratic rule, which is defined in terms of functional specificity and universalistic criteria. This critical examination of Weber's theory will be done in the framework of social exchange theory. Thus the chapter will begin with a rudimentary introduction to the theory of social exchange to the extent that it bears relevance to the subject of exercise of power and control in bureaucratic setting.

Social Exchange – Basic Concepts

Resources

Theory of social exchange as developed here is predicated on the assumption that every member of a society possesses at least some resource which can be used or 'exchanged' for obtaining other resources which he or she needs or wants.[2] Resources for exchange may be 'instrumental' or 'expressive'. 'Instrumental' resources are material things, knowledge, skills, labour and other resources which enhance one's opportunity for achieving a goal or goals. 'Expressive' resources, on the other hand, are affection, respect, love and other expressions of one's feelings and attitudes, whose value is immediately expended upon being presented.

Resource value

Exchange resources, whether instrumental or expressive, have certain values attached to them. How the value of a given resource is determined is a complex issue. Only a rudimentary discussion can be entertained here. First of all, the value of a resource is generally determined through social consensus. A dinner offered at a friend's home, or even a seat offered on a train, has an exchange value, which again is generally agreed upon in a given society, so that it would not randomly fluctuate from one extreme to another, but rather remain within a narrowly circumscribed range. Within this range, however, it is the individual's personal assessment of the situation which would fix a specific value.

Expressive resources generally do not have a market value. No one would imagine maternal love to have a monetary value attached to it. This does not mean that members of a society do not have, do not agree in some general sense, relative values attached to expressive actions. Maternal love certainly has a greater value than casual friendship. The extent to which Americans try to think of expressivity in absolute monetary values is illustrated in law suits (concerning, for example, medical malpractice or divorce), in which the plaintiff might sue the defendant for 'psychological damage', attaching a specific monetary amount to the damage.

Balance

Moving closer to the heart of exchange theory, we assume that exchange of resources can result in a more or less balanced relationship, whereby both parties to exchange are satisfied that what they each gave is by and large equivalent to what they each received. This assessment of balance is calculated on the basis of the culturally agreed, as well as individually determined value of a resource as discussed above.[3]

'Balanced' versus 'generalized' exchange

While exchanges are more or less balanced under normal circumstances, some exchanges involve predominantly instrumental resources with a clear cut assessment of their values, while some others involve the opposite, namely, expressive resources, which are generally less amenable to precise value assessment. Marshal Sahlins (1965, p. 148) has called the former 'balanced exchange', and defined it thus: 'The reciprocation is the customary equivalent of the thing received and is without delay. . . . Balanced reciprocity may be more loosely applied to transactions which stipulate returns of commensurate worth or utility within a finite and narrow period.'

This is a characterization of balanced exchange as a social *event*. Looking at this from a social *relations* point of view, there are social relationships which are characterized by balanced exchange, where only those resources whose values are clearly definable in objective terms are exchanged. Market exchange serves as an archetypical example, where a buyer obtains merchandise by transferring a sum of money identical to the price indicated on the tag. Such a relationship is short-lived, and balance is acheived and completed through one simultaneous transaction of give-and-take. In this sort of exchange, exchange of resources is the primary or even sole objective of entering into social relationship; you approach a salesperson because you want the merchandise. You do not buy the merchandise in order to establish a lasting social relationship with the seller.

This 'balanced exchange' contrasts with 'generalized exchange' in Sahlins' terminology. This terminology is unfortunate in that, as a contrastive term to 'balanced' exchange, it suggests lack of balance. That no such absence of balance is implied in the concept should be clear from the discussion below, and is evident in Sahlins' own exposition of the concept. In generalized exchange, the value of exchange resources is relatively vague and imprecise. To put it another way, resources exchanged in the generalized mode tend not to have values that can be objectively assessed. Even when resources with rather precise market values are exchanged, expressive values, which are necessarily imprecise, are often added to the 'objective' value of the resources. This is precisely because an archetypical generalized exchange takes place between persons of close relationship, such as intimate friends or members of the immediate family, where social relationship is there to begin with, rather than being created through the exchange of resources, and the exchange of resources serves as a symbolic vehicle to transmit expressive values from one individual to another. There is another reason why, in generalized exchange, precise balance is hard to strike. In a relation of generalized exchange, many qualitatively different kinds of resources, instrumental and expressive, traffic back and forth. This makes even a rough calculation of balance between the 'give' and the 'take' a rather tricky affair.

This does not mean that in generalized exchange, balance is conceptually not part of the definition. A subjective sense of balance exists as much as in balanced exchange. The difference, however, is in the greater degree of 'play' allowed on striking a balance in generalized exchange. If a dinner for close friends, A and B, paid for by A, cost 10 per cent more than a reciprocal dinner for them paid by B, then the two may still regard the reciprocation to have struck a balance. Also, balancing in a generalized exchange is often struck over an extended period of time, and imbalance over a short period does not result in animosity or restructuring of the relationship.

In short, human relations in generalized exchange are functionally diffuse, long-lasting and characterized by expressivity overlaying instrumental exchange. In balanced exchange, in contrast, relationship is functionally specific, short-lived, and tends to involve primarily instrumental give-and-take.

Social Control in Exchange Framework

In social exchange, as noted above, it is assumed that parties to a transaction enter into, or maintain, a social relationship because they each have resources that the other party desires or needs. In this situation the resources needed may be given to the other party either with or without the expectation of compliance as part of the condition for receiving the resources. Lack of expectation of compliance does not, none the less, imply that the resource was given 'free'. Customary expectations of return in order to restore balance in the give-and-take still prevail; but in such a case it violates customary, and sometimes also legal, expectations if the giver demands a return for the resources given.

In another case, the receiver accepts resources provided by the giver in exchange for the giver's right to control or constrain the receivers's action. Employer–employee relationship is a typical example. The employer needs workers' labour, skill, knowledge, and other resources. Workers, on the other hand, need wage for sustenance. The worker agrees to give up some of his or her freedom to allow the employer to dictate his or her action in exchange for the wage received.

Parenthetically, control in exchange framework is a two-way process. Since both parties to an exchange need resources from each other, both can stipulate conditions of compliance for obtaining the needed resources. Trade negotiations which take place between Japan and the United States are a good example of mutual control. Both Japan and the United States wish to extract compliance from each other; for example, Japan wishing the United States to lower its expectation of Japan's arms build-up and the United States wanting Japan to liberalize beef importation. Each would offer its resources only to the extent that the other would comply with its wish. Each is willing to give its resource only if the other does. Control and compliance in such a case as this are mutual, and not one-sided.

A similar mutual control is often seen between politicians and industrialists. What politicians most want from industrialists is money, especially for electoral campaigning. What industries want from politicians are political favours, for example, the passage of bills favouring the industry, or influencing bureaucrats – through politicians – who have administrative control over industry. In these cases, too, providing resources which the other needs is contingent upon the other giving return resources. It is a 'give-and-take' conditional to 'take-and-give'.

However, most ordinary cases of 'control' involve one-sided control. For example, the employer controls, or has the right to give command to, employees, but not vice versa. This situation may be conceptualized as striking a balance in the following way. Namely, a combination of the employer's rewards as positive resource to an employee and his control over him as negative resource – both in kind and degree – is equivalent to the sum of the employee's time, skills, etc., provided for the employer. That is to say, the employer's reward to the worker is in fact in excess of the worker's resource given to the employer; but the excess portion is equivalent to the extent and kind of control the worker is subjected to.

This notion of control deviates from Max Weber's, which is defined as a probability of one's will (or command) influencing the action of the controlled, despite the resistance of the latter. Weber here is referring to 'power (*Mach*)' as control, and control as emanating from 'authority'. There is no denying that this type of control, operative only with the backing of coercive force to extract obedience, does exist in a society, as seen in the use of military or police forces. However, this is a very expensive means of extracting compliance in terms of the amount of time, resources and human power needed to realize a given unit of compliance. It is said, for example, that it costs $75,000 a year to keep one inmate in a medium-security prison in the United States. This amount is equivalent to the salary of a middle-level business executive in the United Sttes. The only difference is that one – the inmate – is totally non-productive, whereas the other – the company executive – is performing productive activities. The United States spends $26 billion on correctional facilities, presumably to keep inmates from causing further destruction (i.e. negative productivity) to the society – thus, in effect, merely to keep them non-productive. Defense build-up is another example of the costliness of coercive control. Hundreds of billions of dollars are spent each year merely to destroy, or to be ready to destroy, life and property.

According to Etzioni (1961, p. 5), there are two other means of
achieving compliance besides coercion: normative and renumerative. Normative means, depending on the actor's inner commitment to action, is the least expensive, of course, since, in its purest form, the only reward needed is satisfaction derived from following one's normative commitment. Remunerative means, where one receives material reward for compliance, is in an intermediate position between the normative and the coercive as regards 'cost' of compliance. It should be obvious by now that in exchange context, we are concerned with the 'remunerative' type of compliance, except that rewards in exchange terms include expressive rewards as well as material or instrumental rewards.[4]

Control in Generalized and Balanced Exchange

Control in generalized exchange

If control can be conceptualized in exchange context, we should be able to conceptualize in the framework of generalized and balanced exchange. For generalized exchange, one might think of the main household–branch–household relationship in the classic *dozoku* organization, of the sort reported by Aruga Kizaemon

(1943), as an empirical case approaching the ideal type. In the *dozoku*, system, the main household is morally responsible for the material and spiritual well-being of its branch members. The sense of 'well-being' encompasses all aspects of life from ancestral rites and economic welfare to social sphere. Branches, on the other hand, are morally obligated to provide whatever assistance the main household needs, be it agricultural labour, domestic help, assistance at various rites of passage, such as weddings, funerals, and memorial services. In this exchange, affective elements, which in English would be termed 'benevolence', 'appreciation', 'grace', etc., make up the expressive side of the coin.

As can be readily understood, while the main and branch-households engage in exchange of goods and services, and while there is a sense of balance in this give-and-take, true to the nature of generalized exchange, balance is measured over years and sometimes decades, and affective components of the exchange form crucial ingredients in the relationship.

Although I used the *dozoku* organization as an archetypical example of control in generalized exchange in Japan, other examples are abundant. The traditional master–disciple relationship (*totei seido*) in arts and crafts, where apprentices live with their master, and also the traditional *oyabun–kobun* relationship in organized underworld gangs (*yakuza*), are examples which, though not as close to the ideal type as the classical *dozoku* system, still retain a great deal of the elements of generalized exchange in the master–follower relationship. Moving still farther away from the ideal type and closer to the balanced exchange end of the continuum, though still more generalized than balanced, one finds such examples in Japan as the professor–student relationship, the master–disciple relationship in the *iemoto* system of traditional arts and crafts, and also the superordinate–subordinate relationship in modern bureaucratic organization.[5]

The extent to which exchange is generalized between supervisor and subordinate in a bureaucracy is certainly more limited than that in a *dozoku* system between the main household and its branches; but, as we shall see, the same general orientation towards generalized exchange among workers is unmistakably there in a corporate setting. While in generalized exchange the authority of the power holder is not clearly specified and certainly not codified, it is by no means unlimited. Conventions and expectations define what is regarded as 'appropriate' or 'reasonable' exercise of authority, beyond which critical comments are likely to be heard. In English, 'exploitation' would be an apt description of such an 'arbitrary' exercise of authority.

At the same time, the nature and extent of compliance by the subordinate in generalized exchange are also undefined and uncodified. The subordinate is at the 'beck and call' of the superior, but again within conventionally understood limits, voluntary compliance beyond which would attract attention as 'exceptionally praiseworthy', 'extremely devoted', 'exceedingly loyal', etc.

Control in balanced exchange

An archetypical case in point for control in balanced exchange is Weberian bureaucracy in its ideal-typical form. Here, the three elements in the equation of authority, reward, and compliance, are all clearly specified. Rewards of the subordinate in terms of salary and fringe benefits are fixed prior to the employment. The authority of the superior is also predetermined and specified in the position in which the superior exercises authority. That is, the authority is defined, not as his, but as being ascribed to the position and circumscribed by a set of well-defined rules and regulations. The person occupying the position exercises authority only because he or she happens to occupy that position. The parameters of authority are defined in terms of the position, and not in terms of the person occupying it. Lastly, the nature and extent of compliance by the subordinate, too, are defined in the contract that a person signs at the time of employment; they are inherent in the position that the person occupies and are often referred to as 'job description'.

In addition to the nature of the definition of authority and compliance, one important difference between generalized and balanced exchange has to do with the source of rewards in relation to the locus of authority. In the archetypical generalized exchange of the *dozoku* sort, the two are combined in one person: the holder of authority is the same person who dispenses rewards to his subordinates, and the rewards dispensed are his own personal resources. In balanced exchange, as in bureaucracy, these two are separated, although ultimately it is the

171

organization, the corporate body, which both holds authority and is the source of rewards. In reality, however, the corporation's authority is entrusted in and delegated to an individual in a supervisory position, and is exercised by him or her. Rewards, on the other hand, are dispensed through another channel, such as the payroll office. This arrangement symbolizes the separation of corporate organization and its agent for authority. It also demonstrates the difference between authority in balanced exchange, as in bureaucracy, and personalistic authority in generalized exchange.

It is worth emphasizing that in generalized exchange, the authority position is an 'achieved' status in the total sense of the word, and resources for exercising authority, i.e. for securing compliance, are generally obtained by the authority holder through individual effort. On the other hand, in bureaucracy, while the position of authority is 'achieved', the resources to be dispensed in exchange for a subordinate's compliance, i.e. funds for a subordinate's salary, are supplied by the corporation, not by the person in the authority position. Or, stated in another way, a leader in generalized exchange has earned the resources for extracting compliance from his subordinates by dint of his or her own effort, whereas a bureaucratic leaders earns only his position of leadership, while the resources for the compliance of his subordinates to his command come from another source.

Balanced *cum* Generalized Exchange

The crucial question to be asked, and this constitutes the heart of this essay, is what happens when these two types of authority – generalized and balanced – are empirically combined. *Prima facie*, combining these two would imply a contradiction. Generalized exchange and balanced exchange are polar opposites, as particularism and universalism are, and as functional diffuseness and functional specificity also are. How can such contradictory principles be combined in a given empirical system? Weber's answer to this question was clear and unambiguous: they cannot be. Bureaucracy, therefore, at least as an ideal, had to be defined in terms of concepts representing one end of the polar opposites – universalism and functional specificity, or balanced exchange, in our terminology. Intrusion of the other principles – particularism and functional diffuseness, or generalized exchange – is regarded as a danger to the bureaucratic system.[6] 'Nepotism rule', where closely related kin are not allowed employment in the same organization, for example, has been widely adopted by many bureaucracies in the West in order to prevent generalized exchange, which is likely to occur between individuals related by kinship employed in the same organization.

This incompatibility of generalized exchange with balanced exchange was assumed by Weber (Weber, 1946; 1947) to be a universal truth, and has been accepted by generations of Western social scientists (for example, Crozier, 1964, p. 107; Merton, 1968, pp. 249,252). I submit here that this assumption is wrong, and that the assumed incompatibility between generalized and balanced exchange is a culture-bound phenomenon. That is, in Western culture, and in many other cultures for that matter, introduction of generalized exchange in bureaucracy does tend to undermine the goal of the bureaucracy while promoting the personal interest of those who engage in generalized exchange in the bureaucracy. Thus Eisenstadt and Roniger (1984, pp. 185–200) discuss the USSR, Israel and the United States as examples of societies in which universalistic societal principles serve as 'countervailing forces to the development of patron–client relations (which is based on generalized exchange).' For Weber, however, this incompatibility, which, I suggest, is culture-specific, was elevated to the level of universal truth.

It is here that Japan enters as a crucial case in point to revise the Weberian model. For the Japanese case demonstrates that generalized and balanced exchange – or generalized exchange in bureaucracy – need not produce a contradictory situation or loss of efficiency.

Before I elaborate on the empirical case of Japan, let us examine conceptually the situation in which generalized exchange is embedded in bureaucracy. Assuming that a bureaucratic organization has its own goals and also that a group within it consisting of a superior and his or her subordinates engaged in generalized exchange has its own goals, when such a group is embedded in a bureaucratic organization, two alternative situations may be envisaged: one in which the two goals do not coincide, but in which the group in generalized exchange would try to promote its own goals at the expense of the goals of the bureaucracy; the other alternative is one in which the two goals coincide, in which the group engaged in generalized exchange identifies its goals with those of the bureaucracy. In this case there is no incompatibility and no contradiction. And this is quintessentially the Japanese case.

In the first of these two situations, as in the West, the strong emphasis on the ideology of individualism has led to the conception of each person having to look out for his or her own interests, to the Hobbesian conception of war of each against all other, and to the social Darwinism of cut-throat competition. In such an ideological environment, an individual is tempted or even motivated to use the organization for personal gain, for furthering one's own interest at the expense of the organization's goals. This fact necessitates elaboration, in the organization's rule book, of safeguards to be instituted in the organization in order to prevent individuals from taking advantage of his or her bureaucratic position for furthering personal goals. The 'nepotism rule', whereby a husband and wife are prohibited from employment in the same organization, is a manifestation of this concern.

In the second situation, where the individual is able to identify his personal goals with those of the organization for which he works, the afore-mentioned problem does not arise. In Japanese bureaucracy the tendency is overwhelmingly for individual goals and bureaucratic goals to coincide, such that the individual is motivated to use his or her personal resources for the good of the organization. How this happens and why this happens in Japan and not in other civilizations, is an important question. I am unable to provide an adequate answer, but I will try. One thing that can be said is that Japanese culture lacks the strong ideological emphasis on individualism of the sort that has developed in the West, one in which the interests and rights of the individual are considered foremost and in many (including legal) ways prior to those of the organization to which the individual belongs. In Japan, one does not find a strong ideological or legal basis which would mitigate against the individual from identifying his or her personal goals and interests with those of the organization. Instead, in Japan, one finds an alternative ideology emphasizing value orientation of the individual to the group.

To be sure, this notion of group orientation has been vastly overemphasized and exaggerated in the literature on Japan, as I have argued in a number of publications (for example, Befu, 1980a, 1980b). The received notion of Japanese groupism assumes blind loyalty of the members to the group goal. What I have argued above should amply demonstrate that what is called 'loyalty' turns out largely to be, in a closer analysis, a commitment made by members in exchange for rewards provided or promised by the group for the commitment. Hamaguchi, who has written recently a great deal on the Japanese group, has made similar interpretations (Hamaguchi 1981, p. 50).

Generalized Exchange in Japan

The question of course is: Where does this value orientation come from? While not an adequate answer, a partial answer is found in the nature of interpersonal relations in Japan, which emphasizes and, moreover, values generalized exchange between individuals. In this situation, mutual trust and bond between individuals in Japan, which may supersede kinship bonds, is the crux of this issue. Hamaguchi (1977) has labelled this *kanjin shugi*, which I translate as 'interpersonalism'. The basic building block of Japanese society, according to Hamaguchi, is not the individual, as is the case in Western civilization, but the relationship between individuals. Thus mutual trust based on generalized exchange of both instrumental and expressive resources, rather than on the individual's rights and interests, is the fundamental substance of society in Japan. I introduce this idea and data below as a suggestion to account for the development of different bureaucratic patterns in Japan and in the West.

Data set 1

In 1969–70, in collaboration with psychologists, Yasuyuki Kurita and Akihiro Nagata, I conducted research in Kyoto on interpersonal relations, in which we selected twenty 'exchange acts' – acts which are relatively common – and asked a random sample in Kyoto to evaluate the 'worth' of these twenty acts on a 5-point scale, O being the least and 5 being the greatest. Respondents were asked to do this twice, once on an instrumental scale (how useful is this act?) and once more on an expressive scale (how much intimacy or affection does this act express?). A list of the twenty exchange acts is reproduced in Appendix 1 at the end of this chapter. A high correlation was found between the instrumental and expressive evaluations of these acts, such that an act with a low instrumental score generally had a low expressive score, and an act with a high instrumental score tended to have a high expressive score. Also, as a whole, expressive scores were higher than instrumental scores. This was especially true for acts with high absolute expressive scores.

We also asked the same respondents to pick a person from their social life – among friends, at work, in the neighbourhood – and to evaluate this person, again, on the instrumental and expressive dimensions. The results corroborated those of the evaluation of exchange acts. This is, the higher the instrumental value a respondent attached to a person, the higher the expressive value he or she attached to the same person.

Now, exchange acts of a small instrumental or expressive value, such as greeting friends, are those which are carried out with individuals of slight acquaintance, whereas those of a high instrumental or expressive value, for example, loaning a large sum of money, are those which one would do only with a person with whom one has a close relationship. Acts of low scores, in other words, are generally done before acts of high scores are carried out.

What seems to be happening is that, in Japan, as people exchange instrumental values through an act, they simultaneously exchange expressive values of an even greater worth. As the relationship continues, they exchange acts of greater and greater instrumental and expressive values. In the United States, we have no data exactly like what I collected in Kyoto, but the following observation may be made. The relationship between instrumentality and expressivity does not seem to go hand in hand in the United States. People seem to confine instrumental relations, such as at work, by and large to an instrumental relationship, leaving expressivity pretty much out of the picture, though of course to some extent workers exchange pleasantries and other resources of an expressive nature.

If trust is to develop between individuals, it is likely to develop out of expressive relationship rather than out of instrumental relationship. In fact, trust probably does not develop in a purely instrumental relationship, which, precisely because of absence of trust, is characterized by legal documentation, such as a written contract, receipt, etc., to safeguard one's interest.

With instrumentality and expressivity tending to be simultaneously exchanged in Japan, society allows human relations where high instrumentality is involved, such as at work, to be coupled with high expressive relationships. The latter then, provides the basis for trust to develop among workers in a bureaucratic setting.

Data set 2

Another set of data, coming from studies conducted by Hamaguchi with middle management workers in Japan, supports this argument. In one study, conducted in 1976 (Hamaguchi 1980), Hamaguchi asked fourteen pairs of questions, each of which consisted on one statement emphasizing human relationship and the other emphasizing individualistic orientation. (See Appendix 2 at the end of this chapter for the list.) Hamaguchi asked 1,499 respondents from some twenty companies to choose one or other of the pairs. Excluding 'no answer' responses, 74.70 per cent of the respondents chose 'human relations' in eight or more pairs, i.e. in more than half of the pairs, indicating a tendency to value interpersonal, as against individualistic, orientation.

In order to analyse the nature of 'human relations', Hamaguchi (1982) asked 4,200 workers in about twenty companies in Japan to fill out a sentence completion test, 'in order to get along with others. . .' Data were categorized under several headings, among which the following five categories scored more than 10 per cent: empathy (28.8 per cent), mutual understanding (21.6 percent), self control and giving others chances (14.5 per cent), trust (10.5 per cent), and cooperation (10.2 per cent). These categories may be regarded as contents of resources exchanged in order to enhance expressivity in social life at work. The nature of generalized exchange, as mentioned above, is such that the longer it is maintained and the more often exchange of services is repeated between parties to an exchange relationship, the more valuable the resources being exchange become, and therefore the deeper the level of commitment between the two.

This contrast – coupling of the instrumental and the expressive in Japan and divorcing the two as much as possible in the West – should be analysed together with another observation, namely that, in Japan, workers tend to stay with an organization longer than in the United States, allowing the possibility of Japanese workers to develop stronger commitment to each other than those in the United States. To be sure, in Japan, workers in a large organization of several hundred workers or more are likely to be transferred from one department to another. Thus the exchange relationship does not continue in the same work unit for the duration of the worker's tenure in the organization. Nevertheless, his life in a given work unit often far exceeds an American's life in a similar work unit.

Control and Compliance in a Japanese Bureaucracy

So far the discussion of commitment and trust has not distinguished between egalitarian and hierarchical exchange. In both, one assumes the same process operates in developing commitment and trust. In Japanese bureaucracy, a superior and his or her subordinates are bound together in generalized exchange, and a strong commitment develops between them. Given this commitment of a generalized exchange nature between a leader and subordinates in a bureaucratic organization, subordinates are likely to manifest compliance in their leader, whether or not his demands are based strictly on regulations of the organization.

Data set 3

Hamaguchi (1977) analysed leadership quality in a questionnaire to the same sample of 1,499 managers as in the study cited above.

Ten of the twenty behaviour items in the questionnaire dealt with 'performance (or instrumental) functions' or 'goal achievement functions' of the leader, such as 'clearly state the target date', 'make sure all rules are observed', and 'being knowledgeable about equipment'. The other ten had to do with 'process maintenance (or expressive) functions'. Examples are 'trust your team member', 'when there is trouble in the team, seek the opinions of members', and 'try to understand the point of view of team members'.

Respondents were asked to pick the six most important items among the twenty for a leader. Of the respondents, 40.4 per cent picked four or more items of the 'process maintenance' type, whereas only 23.9 per cent picked four or more items of the 'performance maintenance' type, with 33.8 per cent picking an equal number of each type. Again, one finds an emphasis on human relations in Japanese leadership quality.

Data set 4

Another set of data comes from the National Character (*kokuminsei*) Surveys, which have been conducted every five years since 1953. It is instructive that in these surveys, in spite of vicissitudes of rapid economic and social changes affecting the attitudes of the Japanese in the past thirty years, sample populations have consistently adhered to the idea that a supervisor who is overly demanding at work but is willing to listen to personal problems and is concerned with the welfare of workers is preferred to one who is not so strict on the job, but who leaves the worker alone and does not involve himself with their personal matters. The former type of supervisor was preferred by at least 75 per cent of the samples in all surveys from 1953 to 1978 without showing any sign of decline (Tokei Suri Kenkyuzyo, 1979, p. 51). Here, then, one can see the Japanese preference for functionally diffuse, particularlistic relationship between a supervisor and his or her charges.

As another quality of leadership important in Japanese business management, Masumi Tsuda of Hitotsubashi University, who has written extensively on Japanese management practices, emphasizes the 'whole character' of the leader, as against emphasizing functional competence in a limited area of expertise. 'In its purest form', writes Tsuda, '[the leader] is a secular god.'

179

This idea, according to Tsuda, comes close to Weber's concept of *pietat* (Tsuda, 1977, p. 250), which is far from what Weber regarded as characteristic of those holding bureaucratic authority.

Ryushi Iwata of Musashi University, who also has written a great deal on the 'Japanese style' management, echoes Tsuda's observation when he includes among 'the conditions for commands to be obeyed' 'attractiveness of the personal character of the leader.' He goes on to claim that 'skills in human relationship are more important than technical expertise.' As for 'authority' as defined by Weber, or *kengen* in Japanese, use of the term itself is shunned by bureaucratic leaders in Japan. This fact indicates an absence of saliency of bureaucratically defined authority in the minds of Japanese leaders, as well as their preference for a personalistic approach to leadership.

As long as the leader is motivated, then, to help the organization achieve its goals, that is in so far as the leader identifies his or her goals with those of the organization, subordinates are ready and willing support. Now, this leader, too, is a subordinate to a higher level supervisor, to whom he is also bound by a trust relationship of a generalized exchange nature. Thus the dynamic obtaining between the lowest level and its immediately higher level is repeated up the hierarchy until the top level if reached.

The sort of commitment described here of a subordinate to the superior is often interpreted as 'group orientation' or 'loyalty to organization'. As an epiphenomenon, it does look like a group phenomenon, since the chain of commitment goes level by level from the lowest to the highest, encompassing the whole organization. Operationally, however, this should be seen as a cumulative consequence of binary commitments. This is not to deny that some individuals may espouse and proclaim loyalty to the organization as an entity distinct from the individual members making it up. To the extent that this is observable, there is genuine 'group orientation'. What is loosely called 'group orientation' in popular parlance, however, should be analytically separated into two parts: cumulative binary commitments and genuine orientation to the group. If this is done, I submit that a good deal of what has been called 'group orientation', 'group loyalty', etc., would be subsumed under the rubric of 'binary commitment', i.e. trust, confidence and loyalty between a supervisor and his or her subordinates, which have developed over a period through generalized exchange which has taken place between them, rather than an individual's commitment to some abstract notion of group.

It is through this binary commitment that a supervisor can make demands which are far in excess of the 'normal call of duty' for subordinates, for example, to ask them to work overtime on a rush job. A good illustration of this is the Ministry of Finance at the time of budget formulation. During this time, ministry bureaucrats do not go home for days because they must literally work around the clock to get the budget proposal in shape. Although this has in part become an established routine for the Finance Ministry bureaucrats, how willingly they do this is very much dependent on the personal leadership which supervisors manifest in generalized exchange. In order for a superior to be able to command the obedience and loyalty of subordinates, the superior must not only be technically competent in carrying out his or her own assigned tasks, but must also have won the confidence and trust of the subordinates. He or she would win this by engaging in generalized exchange with them, for example, by taking them out for drinks after work, bringing them home for a drink or a meal, listening to their children's education or in-law problems, serving as a go-between for their marraige, showing concern over illness of their family members, attending the funerals of their close relatives, being extra-generous in con-tributing to office parties, or not failing to attend parties sponsored by subordinates and contributing towards their expenses far more than their normal share. These activities are over and beyond the call of duty defined strictly in functionally specific terms. Yet, in Japan, a superior who does none of these is not likely to win the confidence of subordinates. Nor can he expect maximum efficiency from them or be able to extract their compliance in extraordinary situations.

A person in a supervisory position is expected to be generous in giving out his or her resources in generalized exchange. These resources by and large are his or her *personal* resources rather than those of the organization. Sometimes the organization does have a budgetary resource, such as an expense account, or some other resource over which the supervisor has discretionary control. Its use for his subordinates is, of course, an act of generalized exchange. However, more often, he or she must use personal funds and resources to be good to subordinates. Such 'giving' in generalized exchange is to be paid back in the subordinates' extra loyalty to the superior.

The fact that in Japan an individual in a bureaucracy tends to identify his or her goals with the organization's rather than take advantage of the bureaucratic position of authority for personal gain is well illustrated by the fewness of reported cases of corruption. Bribery is an act in which a government official receives unwarranted compensation for, in effect, impeding regular bureaucratic processes. It is an act which counters the goals of the organization. When a supervisor has 'trusted lieutenants', formed through generalized exchange, who are willing to carry out his or her orders whether or not they are strictly in adherence to bureaucratic rules, it is tempting for the supervisor to accept a bribe from an outsiders – since he or she is in a position to use the authority in order to carry out whatever task asked by the outside briber. For example, a government tax official may be asked by an executive in a private corporation to 'go easy' in checking the company's tax returns in compensation for a sum of money. Now, a lowest echelon clerk in a tax office cannot execute this because there are many checks along the way, and his 'leniency' is likely to be discovered by his supervisors. But a supervisory official, who makes the last check, is in a better position to do so if subordinates are willing to take his order to 'go easy' on a particular case. The subordinates are likely to follow the order if there has been a generalized exchange relationship established between them and the supervisor, as is generally the case in Japan. Thus a supervisory tax official is in an excellent position to amass a small fortune if he or she wishes to do so. Such cases, however, are exceedingly few; and the few cases of bribery do receive wide publicity in the media. But the paucity of these cases is a dramatic indication of the scrupulous honesty of tax bureaucrats in Japan.

According to Japanese government statistics, 431 arrests of government officials were made for bribery in 1983, of which 306 cases actually resulted in prosecution (Japan Ministry of Justice, Hōmu Sōgō Kenkyūjo, 1984, p. 39). Since the total number of central and local government employees in 1983 was a little over four million, 431 cases constitute roughly 1 per cent of 1 per cent of the total bureaucratic population. The honesty of Japanese officials, as glimpsed from these bribery figures, is remarkable. It is especially remarkable because of the very fact that the social setting in which generalized exchange is inextricably intertwined with balanced exchange is so temptingly conducive, as argued above, to the abuse of bureaucratic authority.

Summation

The purpose of this chapter, as stated at the beginning, is to revise Max Weber's social theory and to contribute towards the general theory of civilization by examining the Japanese case and proposing a theory which would account for its peculiarities, rather than dismissing them as exceptions or celebrating Japan's uniqueness. With this goal in mind, I examined Weber's theory of bureaucracy and suggested its possible culture-boundness. The culture-boundness of the theory comes from the ideology of individualism rooted in Western civilization, which tends to motivate members of a bureaucracy to use the organization for their personal gain. To combat this tendency, bureaucracy in the West has had to institute mechanisms to safeguard the bureaucracy's interests from being undermined by its members. Without realizing that this is a peculiarity of Western bureaucracy, Weber and generations of Western social scientists after him have propounded a theory of bureaucracy based on a 'legal–rational' principle with universalism and functional specificity, at the exclusion of a 'paternalistic' principle with particularism and functional diffuseness. In the terminology used here, they have defined bureaucracy in terms of balanced exchange, disallowing incursion of generalized exchange.

Realization that the effectiveness of a bureaucracy would not be undermined, but could rather be enhanced with generalized exchange, comes when we become aware of the possibility that culture can motivate its members, by and large, to identify their own goals and interests with those of bureaucracy, rather than pitting the individual's goals and interests against the organization's. Japan happens to be such a society.

Thus bureaucratic efficiency can be secured by two different means, only one of which Weber discusses, namely through rigorous elimination of generalized exchange. This means is necessary when the value system of a society is such that

183

individuals tends to view their rights and goals as prior to those of the organization to which they belong, as is the case in the West. The other means of insuring bureaucratic efficiency is actively to incorporate generalized exchange into bureaucracy. But this means is successful only when most members of the society do not regard self-interest as being prior to the organization's interests, but rather are able to consider bureaucratic interest and goals their own, as in the case with Japan.

It may be proposed that one major reason why, in many countries around the world such as in Latin America and South-East Asia, bribery and other forms of corruption are rampant (Bayley, 1966) is that in these countries, for whatever reasons, generalized exchange has not been rigorously eliminated from their bureaucratic structure *and*, against for whatever reasons, self-interest of members of the organization has remained foremost and taken precedence over organizational goals. The mistake of past theorizing has been to assume precedence of individual members' interests over bureaucratic goals as self-evident and inevitable. What the Japanese case proves is that this assumption derives from the culture-blindness of basing theory only on the experience of the Western civilization. It also demonstrates that, contrary to Weber's claim of the superiority of bureaucratic organization based purely upon impersonal rules over other forms of organization (Weber, 1946, p. 214), a bureaucracy which involves generalized exchange can function effectively in modern industrial society.

In the Japanese bureaucracy, which has incorporated generalized exchange, there is a constant danger, as indicated above, of personal loyalty of subordinates to their superior being misappropriated for the personal gain of the superior, again inimical to the goal of the organization which he or she is to serve. Japan solved this problem, by and large, by developing vertical binary commitments from the bottom of the organization to the top, on the one hand, and on the other hand by instilling a sense of commitment to the organization's goal – often called 'loyalty' – at a separate level. The latter, however, by itself, is a scaffold on sand. Without the firm ground of interpersonal commitment rooted in generalized exchange, it will readily collapse.

That this Japanese system is not perfect, that it does not always work as it should, is seen in cases of bribery. The most notorious recent case was the Lockheed scandal, in which the then prime minister Kakuei Tanaka used the authority of his office to execute the purchase of Lockheed planes by Japanese concerns in exchange for millions of dollars of bribery payment from Lockheed. This is a sober reminder that the Japanese system is faced with lurking risk, and that conflict between the goal of an organization and the personal gain of its members is an ever-present danger. There is good reason why Weber characterized bureaucracy in terms without generalized exchange. Yet, that a bureaucracy with such exchange can also work is an important sociological discovery.

A question arises as to which of the two patterns is more efficient. I do not believe there is a ready answer to it. Some might want to argue that the Japanese pattern is the more efficient of the two because it combines the efficiency of the legal–rational system as argued by Weber and the effectiveness of mutual trust and loyalty as implied in generalized exchange. Proof of this efficiency is seen, they may argue, in the current economic success of Japan. This argument, however, is premature. First, Japan's economic success is due to numerous factors, and isolating the extent of the contribution of the 'Japanese style' bureaucracy (or 'management style' as it is often called) out of myriad factors is well nigh impossible. Secondly, in comparing Japanese bureaucracy with other bureaucracies, we need objective measures which would allow comparison first in terms of efficiency and second in terms of organizational structure. But it is not easy to achieve consensus as to what 'efficiency' means, whether it refers to output in monetary terms, in product terms, or in some other terms. Also, the organizational structure of Japanese and Western bureaucracies, to be compared, must be of 'comparable' nature. But we do not know what 'comparable nature' means. In the absence of operational definitions of key concepts, we are not in a position to make a comparative statement as to the relative efficiency of bureaucracies in Japan and the West. To claim superiority of the Japanese or Western bureaucracy without operational definition and without an operational test is to fall into the trap of ethnocentrism, as have already fallen an army of *Nihonjinron* writers.

What we do know is that a system which combines generalized and balanced exchange, Western social theory notwithstanding, works, and for good reasons. Such a system is not an aberrant anomaly in ethnographical exotica. Instead it serves as an important case in point. Japan is not a 'unique' exception in a sociological zoo, but a civilization capable of making contributions to social theory.

Notes

1 The paper which forms the basis of this chapter was extensively revised from the one submitted for inclusion in a preceding volume resulting from the Third International Symposium on Japanese Civilization, which was held in March 1985 in Osaka and Otsu, Japan

   Part of the research on which this paper is based was supported by grants from the National Science Foundation, the National Endowment for the Humanities, and Stanford University, to which grateful acknowledgement is made.

2 This is emphatically not to say that every social action can be explained in terms of exchange of resources. There are certainly many areas of human behaviour which cannot be accounted for by exchange theory. This then implies the need to define the domain of social phenomena accountable by social exchange theory, beyond which exchange theory is not to be applied. This issue, important though it is, is not germane to the specific problem under consideration, namely, bureaucratic control as an exchange phenomenon, and thus will not be elaborated upon here.

3 In reality, there is another twist to this process of balance determination. This has to do with the actor's perception of how the receiver would evaluate the resource given and the receiver's perception of the giver's valuation of the same resource. In terms of social psychological theory, these variables are entered in the equation as follows. Let us say A and B are two parties in an exchange relationship and that X and Y are the resources possessed by A and B, respectively, and are to be exchanged between them:

   (1) A's valuation of X ....Xa
   (2) B's valuation of Y....................................... Yb
   (3) A's valuation of Y ....Ya
   (4) B's valuation of X...................................... Xb
   (5) A's assessment (guess) of B's valuation of X .... aXb
   (6) B's assessment (guess) of A's valuation of Y .... bYa
   (7) A's assessment (guess) of B's valuation of Y .... aYb
   (8) B's assessment (guess) of A's valuation of X .... bXa

In order for exchange to take place, possessor (A) of a resource (X) must think the value of his resource (X) is less than the value of the resource (Y) which another (B) has. Otherwise A has nothing to gain, that is, if the values of (X) and (Y) are equal; or A will lose, if the value of (X) is greater than the value of (Y) in his assessment. At the same time, A must believe that B is willing to exchange (Y) for (X), i.e. in A's assessment, B must think (X) has higher value than (Y). In equation, this relationship would be expressed as follows:

(9) $AxB > AyB$

Simultaneously, in order for exchange to take place, B must think that A has something to gain from the exchange, i.e.:

(10) $BxA < ByA$

But for the exchange to be more or less balanced, both A and B must believe that the gain through the exchange was roughly even. To put this more precisely, A's assessment of his (A's) own gain (yA − xA) must be roughly equal to his (A's) guess about B's assessment of his (B's) own gain (AxB − AyB), or:

(11) $yA - xA = AxB - AyB$;

and at the same time, B's assessment of his (B's) own gain (xB − yB) must be about the same as his guess about A's assessment of his (A's) own gain (ByA − BxA), or:

(12) $xB - yB = ByA - BxA$.

If (11) and (12) both obtain, then both A and B are satisfied that the exchange is equal from A's and B's perspectives. It is possible in a given exchange for (11) to be satisfied but not (12), such that one party is satisfied with exchange, but the other believes he or she received a short end of the deal.

The above is a social psychological exploration. This chapter is concerned with social institutions and cultural values, leaving out, for the sake of the argument, but not dismissing as irrelevant, psychological dimensions, which should be investigated in another context.

4 Weber does recognize control arising out of market monopoly, and is thus aware of remunerative 'control'; but he does not develop this notion since his primary concern is with power and authority.

5 Eisenstadt and Roniger (1984) have developed a generalized model of patron–client relationship, which, defined in terms of generalized exchange, closely matches the social system based on generalized exchange as outlined here. In fact, they use *dēzoku* and *oyabun-kobun* systems as Japanese examples of this model. (1984, pp. 145–50)

6 To Weber, in evolutionary terms, authority based on generalized exchange is an earlier form than the one based on balanced exchange. But this evolutionary question does not concern us here.

Appendix 1

Twenty common exchange acts used in the 1970 Kyoto Survey (listed in rank order of mean expressive values)

	Exchange Acts	Mean Scores Expressivity	Instrumentality
1	Giving personal loan	4.5	3.2
2	Serving as a guarantor	4.1	2.3
3	Giving seasonal gifts, e.g., *chugen* or *seibo*	4.0	2.4
4	Helping house-cleaning or moving	4.0	2.4
5	Giving a gift on a personal occasion, e.g., birthday or wedding	4.0	2.3
6	Giving someone a gift brought back from a trip	4.0	2.1
7	Sending a gift on a special business or professional occasion, e.g., starting a new job or a new business	3.8	2.6
8	Giving a person beneficial information	3.5	2.3
9	Giving a gift on mishap, i.e., accident or illness	3.5	2.3
10	Treating a person to a dinner	3.5	2.3
11	Taking a gift when visiting a person at home	3.3	2.1
12	Serving as confidant on family or work-related problems	3.2	2.4
13	Providing introduction to a doctor	3.0	2.1
14	Speaking up for a person being criticized	3.0	2.1
15	Willingly listening to complaints	3.0	2.1
16	Extending words of concern when misfortune		

	occurs, e.g., illness or accident	2.9	2.0
17	Informing a person of recent developments in one's own life, e.g., change of jobs or address	2.9	2.0
18	Sending New Year's greeting card	2.3	1.8
19	Taking the initiative in greeting a person	2.1	1.7
20	Willingly seeing a person who has come to visit	2.0	2.1

Appendix 2

Questionnaire items used by Hamaguchi to measure (a) contextualism and (b) individualism

1   (a) Since we owe what we are to others, we should try to get along with others and help each other.
(b) As much as possible we should not depend on others. Instead, we should develop a strong and independent self, do everything on the basis of our own judgment and take responsibility for our own action.

2   (a) As human beings, we should not forget the debt we owe those who help us and take care of us, as if they were our true kin; and we should strive to pay back this debt as much as possible.
(b) As a human being, it is important not to be bound, not to be interfered with, and to act as a free and independent individual.

3   (a) Knowing about one another's family situation to some extent helps smooth relationships at work.
(b) In terms of efficiency at work, we should not give special consideration to individuals' personal situations.

4   (a) It is better to consult others and get their opinion before you do anything.
(b) Nothing will go well unless you do it on the basis of your own judgment and with confidence.

5   (a) In any society, others would act towards you as you would act towards them.
    (b) In any society, unless you make explicit demands, you cannot get what you want.
6   (a) I tell everything truthfully to my best friends and to my spouse, even if what I say might incriminate against me.
    (b) I would never tell even my best friends or spouse what concerns my privacy.
7   (a) As the saying goes, 'travellers are companions; what you need in life is empathy/sympathy;' thus you can trust even a person you meet for the first time.
    (b) It is only human just to look out for oneself; you cannot always trust others.
8   (a) One should cultivate one's relationships with others. If you cannot be in intimate and trusting relations with others, there is no use living.
    (b) It is after all because we love ourselves that we try to get along with others.
9   (a) It is better to consult close friends and get their ideas before making decisions on your future.
    (b) You should decide your future on your own.
10 (a) If anything, I try to meet the demands of my group even if it means controlling my own desires to some extent.
    (b) Since satisfying my own desires is the most important thing, I try to decline any request from my group which would interfere with my desires.
11 (a) In life, you are not allowed to act as you please. At work, too, you should abide by customs and conventions.

References

Aruga, K. (1943), *Nihon kaoku seido to kosak seido*. Tokyo.

Bayley, D.H. (1966), 'The effects of corruption in a developing nation', *Western Political Quarterly*, 19, pp. 719–32.

Befu, H. (1980a), 'The group model of Japanese society and an alternative', *Rice University Studies*, 66 (1). pp. 169–87.

Befu, H. (1980b), 'The group model of Japanese society: a critique', *Social Analysis*, 5/6, pp. 29–43.

Crozier, M. (1964), *The Bureaucratic Phenomenon*. Chicago, University of Chicago Press.

Eisenstadt, S.N. and L. Roniger (1984), *Patrons, Clients and Friends – Interpersonal Relations and the Structure of Trust in Society.* Cambridge, Cambridge University Press.

Etzioni, A. (1961), *A Comparative Analysis of Complex Organization.* New York, Free Press.

Hamaguchi, E. (1977), *Kigyo ni Okeru Seikatsu Kachikan.* Osaka Daigaku, Ningen Kagakubu.

Hamaguchi, E. (1980), 'Nihonjin ni totte no Shishugi', *Gendai no Esprit*, 160, pp. 5–21.

Hamaguchi, E. (1981), 'Bunka no Jidai no Nihon-teki Soshiki', *Kikan Chuo Koron*, Spring Issue, pp. 106–19.

Hamaguchi, E. (1982), *Nihonjin no ningen moderu to 'aidagara'.* Osaka Daigaku, Ningen Kagakubu, 8, pp. 207–40.

Ito, D. (1980), *Gendai Nihon Kanryosei no Bunseki.* Tokyo, Daigaku Shuppanka.

Japan Ministry of Justice (1984), *Hanzai Hakusho.* Tokyo, Ministry of Finance Printing Bureau.

Merton, R. (1968), *Social Structure and Social Theory.* New York, Free Press.

Sahlins, M. (1965), 'On the sociology of primitive exchange' in M. Banton (ed.), *The Relevance of Models for Social Anthropology.* New York, Praeger, pp. 139–236.

Tokei Suri Kenkyuzyo (1979), *Nihonjin no Kokuminsei.* Tokyo, Shiseido.

Tsuda, M., *Nihon-teki keiei no ronri chuo keizaisha.*

Weber, M. (1946), *From Max Weber.* New York, Free Press.

Weber, M. (1948), *The Theory of Social and Economic Organization.* New York, Free Press.

9 Religious Conflict in a Japanese Town: Or Is It?[1]

M. Ashkenazi

Introduction

In its most recent history (i.e. since 1945), Japan appears to exhibit a society largely free of conflictual situations, or at least of overt conflict. It is well to remember that this has not been the case historically. However, at least in one area – religious issues – the level of conflict in Japan, historically as well as today, is lower than in most other countries. Though we do find examples of religious conflict, these pale in comparison with conflict in politics and economics in both duration and intensity.

In this chapter I shall examine one aspect of the low degree of religious conflict in Japan. I shall draw on historical sources for some of my argument, but most of the material deals with conflict resolution on the local level. Basically I am asking what mechanisms defuse, limit, or contain religious conflict in a variety of instances. I will focus on the local level both because it is there that we can see conflict avertion and resolution in operation, and because at the micro level it is possible to understand processes that operate and have operated on a larger scale within Japanese society.

Dimensions of religious conflict and its avoidance

Religious conflict, properly speaking, is conflict in which one of the sides at least is concerned with establishing the domination of a religious practice (ritual, ideology, or organization, i.e. church) in a society or group. In this chapter, for reasons that will become clear, 'religious conflict' will refer to those conflicts which concern or involve any aspect of religion. I contend, and I admit this is not original, that (a) in general we must see religious conflict in the light of social, political, economic, and other factors which are often concealed by or unrelated to the religious conflict itself and (b) that *conflict* in Japan must be seen as part of a spectrum of antagonistic positions, some of which are more, some less, extreme.

It is necessary to view conflict in Japan in three distinct dimensions. One is that of inter-religious conflict, in which one religious system, or some aspect of it, is imposed upon another. This has occurred in Japan, for example, the clash between the Yamato clan faiths centred on Ise and the northern clan faiths centred on Izumo; the early clash between Buddhism and the Japanese indigenous religion; and the rise of Shin Buddhism. The second dimension is that of conflicts between central government and local interests. Such was the case to some extent during the early history of the so-called New Religions, and during the early days of the Meiji Restoration. The third dimension is that of conflicts that occur between and within religious bodies on the local level. Such conflicts generally arise because of differing interests. Different interests subsume not only scarcity or resources and the need for choice (Lebra, 1976, p. xvii), but also difference of opinion on abstract, ideological, and even intellectual levels.

Unlike religion in Europe, for example, Japanese religion has not had any significant level of religious conflict. I shall look at some of the reasons for this in a contemporary context, to show how religions conflict is avoided in modern Japan. That is, the focus is on conflict *avoidance* and conflict *resolution*. I shall quote examples of religious conflicts, and of conflicts within the social framework of religion. My objective is to describe the mechanisms whereby potential conflict in the religious sphere is avoided, mitigated, muted, or resolved. The data derives largely from fieldwork in a Japanese town, including observation, local historical records, and interviews.

The Historical Dimension

A number of historical conflicts in Japan have been described as 'religious'. Violent conflicts include the *Ikko ikki* (lit. 'single-minded insurrection') of the Amidist sects which seized power in the fifteenth century in the Kaga and Noto provinces and held them for a century. Most notable is the Shimabara rebellion in 1637, which was inspired by Christians. Conflicts with religious backgrounds which involved less violence include the establishment of Nichiren's Hokke-shu, the suppression of the New Religions in the period following the arrival of the Black Ships, and, more significantly here, the separation of Buddhist and Shinto establishments (Hall, 1971) and the following 'shrine merger movement' in the early twentieth century (Fridell, 1973). The pre-nineteenth century conflicts are of no concern here, except for the fact that they illustrate on the national scale the principles I am dealing with: a broad range of conflictual issues, underlying them a range of economic and social sources for conflict, and a broad range of solutions.

The story of religious conflict in Japan since 1870 involves all three of the perspectives noted above. On the national and inter-religious level, Buddhist and Shinto establishments fought for control of shrines and temples, religious 'sects' such a Tenrikyo and the *Mukyokai*[2] movement fought for recognition from the government, and Protestant missionaries struggled for the right to propagate their faith (see, for example, the description of Townsend Harris's emphasis on the rights of missionaries to act in Japan in Statler, 1969).

The beginning of the Meiji era was also a time of vertical struggle between the mass of popular practices and beliefs and government policies. The effects of *shinbutsu-bunri* (the separation of Buddhism and Shinto) in 1873 were, among other things, a revitalization of repopularization of Buddhism, notwithstanding government attempts to denigrate it (Fridell, 1973; Hall, 1971; Sansom, 1973). Many Buddhist communities reaffirmed their commitment to Buddhism. The slightly later shrine merger movement of 1906–20 caused strong local reactions as communities attempted to defend their hamlet (*buraku*) shrines against attempts to merge them with village (*mura*) shrines.[3] The merger movement was initiated by the government and supported by many of the local priesthood. None the less, communities defended their shrines to the point of violence, and many re-established forbidden shrines after World War II.

In the more recent history of Japan (i.e. since 1946), religious conflicts have been muted, if noted at all. Sects such as, for example, Soka Gakkai have been militant in their activities, and have suffered consequent virulent attacks in the press and popular literature. Similarly, there have been instances of intra-religious conflict (e.g., the succession conflict in Shinshu Otani-ha) and conflicts at the level of national politics (e.g., the issue of visits to Yasukuni-jinja, which enshrines Imperial Army dead, by Japanese prime ministers).

The general picture, however, is one of relative calm. The few conflicts that do arise are resolved relatively easily, and rarely become major issues. Moreover, many of these conflicts are viewed with amusement and even contempt by many Japanese. 'Those are the fellows who quarrel so much', commented one acquaintance disparagingly when discussing an Otani-sect temple in Yuzawa.

Background: Yuzawa

The data presented here is concerned with religious conflicts on a local level. Both intra- and inter-religious conflicts will be looked at. National issues serve as a background against which local affairs are played out.

Yuzawa is a town of 18,000 residents in north-eastern Japan. It is considered by other residents of southern Akita prefecture to be relatively affluent, due largely to the presence, since the turn of the century, of a number of extremely successful saké breweries. The town has a number of wealthy families, some of them organized into *dozoku*.[4] There are a number of religious establishments: some forty public shrines, six Buddhist temples,[5] one Tenrikyo temple, and one church. The town has three major festivals, one of which, the *Daimyo Gyoretsu*, is the main ritual of the town's principal shrine, Atago-jinja. Festivals generally require great investment in resources: both finances and manpower. They are cohesive elements in the structure of the town and its individual neighbourhoods (cf., Akaike, 1976; Ashkenazi, 1987a; Bestor, 1985; Sadler, 1972). The *Daimyo Gyoretsu* is the focus of much community feeling, and, perhaps because of its complexity, is the arena for both conflict and cohesion with the community.

Data: The Conflicts

The cases presented here were gathered as part of fieldwork on festival and shrine practices in Japan. As will be seen, a variety of conflictual and semi- or quasi-conflictual situations have arisen over the past century in Yuzawa. These have led to a variety of solutions to the conflicts. It is in the spectrum of these responses that we find the available 'cultural inventory' that Japanese society uses for solving low-intensity conflicts. Some of the data is historical. My sources include written material from Yuzawa, as well as interviews with informants. For the purposes of this study both sets of data are of equal validity. Informants commenting on the doings of their ancestors illuminate not only the activities of those ancestors, but also the reactions of modern Japanese to situations of religious conflict: the objective of this chapter.

Shinbutsu-bunri and the *dozoku*

Shinbutsu-bunri ('separation of Buddhism and Shinto') is the name given to the government-inspired process of separating Buddhist temples and practices from Shinto ones. In some areas of Japan the process caused anguish and inspired acts of destruction and violence (Fridell, 1973). There is no evidence of that being the case in Yuzawa, though the separation of some shrines was a difficult one in practical and material terms. It must be recalled that the times were difficult and uncertain. The Meiji Restoration was, in the early 1870s, on its first shaky legs. Some of the Restoration wars were still to be fought.

The government-initiated separation of Buddhism and Shinto does not seem to have affected most families in Yuzawa to any great degree. Two families, however, the Ota and the Takahashi, appeared to be split by religious differences. I have no evidence of the state of the relationship between these two important (that is, wealthy) merchant families before *shunbutsu-bunri*. The Ota families were a *dozoku* of mainly landholding *ie*. The Takahashi were largely merchants, and, to the best of my knowlewdge did not have a formal *dozoku* organization, though it may be assumed that some of the characteristics of *dozoku* were present among them as well. The former became committed Shintoists, the latter Buddhists. This identification is a self-identification, and an uncommon one in Japan: '*Ware ware-wa Bukkyo: Ota-san Shinto-desu*' ('We are Buddhists, the Ota are Shintoists,') said one member of the Takahashi.

None-the-less, these two families cooperate in a number of matters. Notably, though it might be assumed this would be a source of conflict, the families also cooperate in ritual matters, such as running the town's festivals. The most significant realm of cooperation is, however, in marriage. Women of both surnames have been married into the other camp. Ota women who have married into Takahashi families lose their Shinto identity and perform the Buddhist rituals as required by their new families. This is of course expected. As Bachnik (1983) has noted, marriage into a Japanese family is a process of *recruitment*, with all the duties inherent in the term.

What is significant here, beyond the frame of the conscious (perhaps) choice of religious affiliation, is the fact that a situation which *could* have become conflictual, did not. Religious differences that were not conditioned, or did not include other points of issue, did not, in this case at least, develop into a situation of conflict. The solution, in effect, to a potentially dangerous state of conflict was avoided by compartmentalizing the issue, on the one hand, and by creating (or perhaps merely strengthening) ties of communal solidarity on the other. Under other circumstances in Japan where the same period *did* produce actual and sometimes violent conflicts, I could suggest that we look elsewhere for the cause: in the realms of politics, economics, etc. It would also be interesting to speculate on the genesis of this particular solution to potential conflict. It must be recalled that the period was one of great uncertainty in Japan, with pro- and anti-government forces both active, with a new and untried government in power, and with a great deal of popular unrest, part of it of a religious and even messianic nature. Were the Ota and Takahashi families betting on both sides simultaneously?

Such things are not unknown in Japanese history: many clans avoided total destruction during the Civil War period by having members fight on different sides. Or, perhaps, were the common interests greater than any possible disagreement over religion?

Shinbutsu-bunri and the priests

Far more significant than differences between laymen is the difference between priests. Buddhist and Shinto priests refer to one another in unflattering terms. However, as the following examples show, there is a considerable range of cooperation. Morioka (1975), pp. 6–8) accounts for the lack of conflict between Shinto and Buddhism by the fact that the functions of Japan's two major religions, Shinto and Buddhism, are complementary. The converse of this thesis, as Morioka himself notes, is that conflicts can occur where religious organizations are *not* complementary, i.e. within the same sect or group. Such cooperation or, more properly, co-tolerance does not imply affection, as the following examples show.

One Shinto priest has his family grave on the site of the local temple. This is the normal practice in Japan where Buddhist priests are largely responsible for mortuary rites, and where each temple has its attached graveyard. This particular priest is vehement in his disapproval of the Buddhist priesthood. None the less, he insures that the Buddhist priest performs memorial rituals for the dead over this shrine, as over all other shrines in the graveyard, at the appropriate times. Similarly, a Buddhist priest who is rather contemptuous of the Shinto priesthood is at pains to attend the main festivals of the town's shrine, and to perform proper obeisance there. To cite a more extreme case, on several occasions I have observed two priests, one Buddhist, the other Shinto, both of whom have expressed private doubts about the other's religious practices, alternating in the performance of rituals for the same shrine.

All the cases cited here have one thing in common. In each case, the proper performance of a ritual duty is a social obligation. The Shinto priest, whatever his beliefs (and to my knowledge they are deep and sincere), has a social role to play in the community. The same goes for the festival-going Buddhist priest. In the 'cooperative' ritual, both priests have an obligation to perform for the managers of the shrine who have hired them.

Social obligations overcome personal feelings, however deeply felt.

In other words, differences in religious themes and convictions are restrained because of community interests and the need to preserve, both outwardly and inwardly, a cooperative attitude. A priest, whatever his individual ideological convictions, who provoked conflict *on religious grounds alone*, would probably find himself in a situation where he lacked supporters, whatever the merits of his cause.

This can be illustrated on a national level from other data. The response of Japanese society to the exclusiveness of Soka Gakkai[6] is conditioned at least partly by the anti-communitarian nature of that group. That is, the very exclusivity of the Soka Gakkai movement and its refusal to participate in community ritual practices causes strains in the social fabric, and arouses a great deal of antagonism *notwithstanding* the fact that, ideologically, the sentiments it espouses are not radical in Japanese religious terms. In contrast, another group, Tenrikyo, though it espouses what is probably a more radical religious ideology, is able to cooperate successfully and avoid provoking conflicts on religious grounds within the community (Chinnery, 1971).

The *kensha* case

Those religious conflicts that are prominent, and in which a great deal of tension is created, are, paradoxically, conflicts in which purely *religious* issues may be absent. They are, at least in the Yuzawa case, intra- rather than inter-religious conflicts. This supports the converse of Morioka's argument: inter-religious conflict is limited by the cooperation between Shinto and Buddhism, but intra-religious conflict is not so constrained. On the contrary, as Lebra (1976) notes, the argument in intra-religious conflict is often over shared resources, a mainstay of conflict in any culture.

During the shrine consolidation period (1910–35), shrines were ranked according to a government-determined order. One of Yuzawa's oldest shrines was supported by a coalition of families in the centre and at the southern end of town, in which the Ota family were major partners. Another coalition was headed by the Ishii family at the northern end. These two coalitions competed for the right to have their shrine promoted to the official rank of *kensha*. Promotion to such a rank, an official government act, was dependent on a number of factors: size of shrine, number, affluence and social position of supporters, and ability to maintain a permanent priest. Only one shrine in a given area was likely to reach the coveted rank. The resource in Lebra's terms – prestige and official recognition in this case – was certainly limited.

The Ota coalitin won. Through a series of manoeuvres, which included some arm-twisting of fence-sitters (admit the southern coalition descendants) and some outright chicanery (say the northern alliance descendants), the southern shrine was awarded the coveted title. The other shrine was ranked lower in the official hierarchy, which affected its subsequent size and prestige, and its right to perform certain types of rituals and to enjoy certain privileges.

The Ishii have continued to support their own shrine. They and the residents of their neighbourhood exhibit a keen sense of pride in the neighbourhood, which is one of the most cohesive in Yuzawa. One measure of this is the great number of festival events that are carried out in their shrine. In addition, the Ishii and the residents of the neighbourhood contributed materially to the main shrine of the town, the one declared a *kensha*.

Somewhat later than the incident of the *kensha*, the brewers of Yuzawa found it necessary to consolidate their operations (the town had fourteen breweries by the 1930s). Not coincidentally, perhaps, the Ishii were allowed the opportunity to acquire a lion's share of the new company's stocks. The reasons, as best I can identify them, were economic: however, it seems probable (and at least one informant who is in the saké business confirms this) that had the Ishii *not* been the losers in an earlier conflict, the opportunity to secure such an advantage in the new firm without a struggle would not have been open to them.

The *yakkofuri*

The main festival of Atago-jinja includes a massive parade, the *Daimyo Gyoretsu*, of men dressed in Edo period costumes. Among the performers are a group called the *yakkofuri*. The *yakkofuri* are all residents of the Atago neighbourhood, the southernmost neighbourhood in town. The Atago neighbourhood borders on Fuppari, one of the five neighbourhoods that run the

Daimyo Gyoretsu in rotation every year. The same families have the traditional right to positions in the *yakkofuri*, and the managers of the group claim to be the direct descendants of men who held the position a century before under the Satake *daimyo* who ruled the town during the Edo period. The Atago neighbourhood has no managerial or other rights in the *Daimyo Gyoretsu*. This right is reserved for the five oldest neighbourhoods in town.

In the past few years, the *yakkafuri* have been demanding to be paid for their performance, which includes marching in the parade and dancing at set points along the route (cf. Ashkenazi, 1987a). The sum demanded is considerable: 300,000 yen (about US$1.3 at the rate of exchange at the time). The demand caused considerable controversy when it was first raised. On that occasion, disagreement was muted by a personal donation from the titular manager of the parade. The second year the solution was not so simple. The managers of the parade that year were the Maemori neighbourhood in the north end of town. Lengthy negotiations, including polite but icy exchanges, were unable to settle the problem. Eventually, however, the festival managers capitulated and the sum was paid.

Festivals and other social events in Japan include a number of sessions of self-criticism and analysis of the event. In these, the performance of groups running the event are examined, activities criticized, and grievances aired (cf. Ashkenazi, 1987b). In the discussions that followed the parade that year (managed by Maemori), some argued that the entire *yakkofuri* group from Atago be dismissed and another group appointed in its place to fulfill the same role. The motion failed, but the issue caused – and continues to cause – a great deal of resentment.

The following year's parade managers were from Yanagi, a mercantile neighbourhood in the centre of town. They were of a different sort. Their management style was much more relaxed and informal than that of Maemori's. They met the problem head on by agreeing to pay the *yakkofuri*'s demand from the outset *in principle*, and then bargaining them down from their original demand. This time the *yakkofuri* demands were met by a counter-offer, and the sides eventually agreed on a substantially lower sum.

The responses of these three neighbourhood management groups are significant, and they illustrate some of the principles

201

that are relevant to dispute settlement. Fuppari, the first neighbourhood, borders on Atago. It has few young men, and a generally small population. It relies for manpower on its larger neighbour – Atago – though this reliance is informal, since only five neighbourhoods have the traditional right to run the festival. Atago is not one of the five.

Maemori has claims, overt and covert, to primacy in terms of prestige in Yuzawa. It is the largest neighbourhood and one of the oldest. It has a famous shrine of its own, strong in its own traditions, and is the site of three major saké breweries. Atago, however, is moving hard on its heels. It is the fastest growing neighbourhood, the second largest in terms of size, and it has its own traditions. No less important is the presence of Atago-jinja, the town's main shrine within the borders of the neighbourhood. The former site of Atago-jinja is still preserved by the Atago neighbourhood as 'our' shrine. Thus Maemori's outrage at the demand is conditioned as well by the covert (and sometimes overt) rivalry between the two neighbourhoods, each occupying one end of the town.

Yanagi's case is different. The managing committee has a core consisting of a group of close friends. They are mainly the heirs-in-waiting of owners of local businesses. Their style of management is easier and more relaxed because of their closeness in age, tastes, and residence. They did not feel their prestige was threatened by the *yakkofuri* demands, nor were they dependent on Atago: their neighbourhood is relatively small and relatively well-off, with no particular claims to prestige or leadership in town. They could therefore choose the pragmatic course, of paying what appeared to them to be a reasonable price, while attempting (and succeeding) in minimizing the damage.

The position of the *yakkofuri* too is enlightening. The group is managed by two men who are the descendants of the local lord's chief body-servants. Each year these two men select men for the *yakkofuri* performance from among residents of the neighbourhood. To some degree, many of the neighbourhood residents are involved in the preparation, manning, or training of the *yakkofuri*, who are a source of pride for the neighbourhood. Their demand for payment was based overtly on the fact that they danced, not merely marched, and that they performed every year, whereas residents of other neighbourhoods manned the parade only once in five years.

Another motive surfaced privately, however. Only five neighbourhoods – the Go Cho – manage the festival. Atago, the second largest neighbourhood, and the site of Atago-jinja and the home of the *yakkofuri*, had no management rights: in other words, no recognition. This was a source of mild resentment against the other neighbourhoods. In a sense, the monetary demand was a claim for recognition and full participation, more than a demand for remuneration.

Discussion

I have presented the data above to demonstrate two main points: the relative lack of purely *religious* conflict in the ideological sense of the word, in Japan: and the variety of means available to contain and even eliminate conflict altogether. Also, I am more concerned with how conflicts are resolved or even avoided in the realm of religion, than with how they are generated.

'Religious' conflict in the Japanese case must be circumscribed by the understanding that such conflict is not strictly 'religious'. Motivations may be nationalistic, economic (the two *dozoku* mentioned were and are both competitors and cooperators in several fields), and sometimes political. Second, there are various devices for settling such low-key conflicts. It is not sufficient to claim that the Japanese ethos, or Japanese culture, requires some mystical 'harmony'. There are determinate reasons within the culture which reduce such conflict.

As can be seen, many different solutions are employed which, in aggregate, defuse conflict, channel it elsewhere, or mitigate it. Other mechanisms exist as well, as evidence from the literature. To cite but one example, *mura hachibu*[7] served not only as a punishment, but also to sanitize and contain the extension of possible conflict in the fragile environment of the hamlet (cf. Embree, 1939; Fukutake, 1967; Irokawa, 1975). Other devices used include forced mediation (R.J. Smith, 1983, p. 33), etc. It is notable that not all conflicts are terminated or hidden: some conflicts become overt, even violent. But at least those in the field of religion are, generally speaking, well-contained.

We ask therefore why the field of religion is special in the

Japanese case. That is, beyond the attempts to contain conflicts which are a general feature of modern Japanese society, *religious* conflicts appear to be particularly well-controlled or perhaps non-crucial. This is true in the historical dimension as well.

One possible explanation is to be found in the nature of Japanese religion. Though the Japanese are as committed religiously as any other people, the religious thrust is syncretic rather than exclusive. With some exceptions (i.e. the Shin sects), most Japanee practices and sects are willing and sometimes eager to accept external ideas and teachings. Religious commitment is a matter of private concern and public duty. Private religious practices are part of the autonomy of the household, and thus generally not a matter for public concern, provided the household in question fulfils its religious obligations in the public sphere, obligations which are largely as much social as religious. Therefore we often find an individual attending a public ritual he disagrees with, only to return home and perform a private ritual that fits his conception of how the thing must be done (as witnessed a number of times in Yuzawa).

The structure of organized religion in Japan is such that religious differences, particularly on the local level, do not lend themselves to conflict. One's co-worshippers are also one's neighbours, and conflict with them has major ramifications. Shinto shrine parishes are almost co-extensive with neighbour-hoods. The same is often true of Buddhist temples, though their parishes are also wider and membership lines cross-cut neigh-bourhood affiliations. Neighbourhood residents who are *ipso facto* also a Shinto congregation may or may not be members of the same Buddhist temple, and may be members of the same, or different, *koju* or *ujiko* groups[8] as well. Bailey (1960), and to a lesser degree Coser (1967), have noted that where there are cross-cutting social ties, conflict is less likely to appear, or tends to be confined and mitigated. This is at least one aspect of the Japanese religious case. In many of the cases cited above the social ties that reduce conflict are as salient as the differences that cause it. Where such cross-cutting ties are limited by other factors, and particularly where there are other reasons for conflict, the conflict tends to become stronger. This largely explains the differences between the Fuppari, Maemori, and Yanagi reactions to the *yakkofuri* demands.

An important mechanism for reducing conflict that comes into operation is one we can perhaps call compensation. The Japanese normative preference is to avoid providing clear-cut 'winners' and 'vanquished'. This does not of course imply that historically, such have not emerged in a number of struggles. Following Lebra (1976), however, we can see that the avoidance of clear-cut polarities in this realm is a 'cultural preference': something sought, at least publicly and normatively, even if not always achieved. This is accomplished by what amounts to an unexpressed promise of delayed reward. That is, even when conciliation fails, as it often does, continued membership of the group and participation in its ultimate goals implies that at some future date the loser will be given some additional benefit (cf., Plath, 1969, for the operation of this principle in the formulation and execution of group goals). The Ishii in the case cited above were the beneficiaries of such a mechanism.

Conclusion

We would do well to recall that in the field of violence, Japan has one of the most remarkable historical records. On the one hand, the country has been characterized by periods of excessive and endemic violence of massive proportions. On the other, it has had experience of length periods of great tranquility. We can ask two questions: Are the two extremes related? and why have we had evidence of little religious conflict?

The answer to the first question relates perhaps to one result of violence. Violent and overwhelming sanctions by rulers in Japan forced the evolution of means of avoiding, or at least containing, conflict to as great a degree as possible. The majority of the Japanese were commoners, largely powerless peasants; (in the Edo period the samurai numbered no more than 7 per cent of the population). Massive recourse to violent sanctions, the need to cooperate communally to make a living under harsh conditions, and strict limits on available resources, combined perhaps to force Japanese, at all levels, into evolving a culture in which conflict *must not* become overt, if at all possible. The penalties were too severe to be contemplated by most of the population except in the most dire circumstances. Moreover, the formally held ideology of the governing élite demanded at least the surface appearance of tranquility and conflict-free existence, whatever the reality.

The answer to the second question derives partly from the answer to the first, partly from factors inherent in non-Judaic religions (i.e. Christianity, Islam, and Judaism, who draw their basic precepts from the same source). The cultural preference is for non-overt conflict, and means are devised for securing this preference, which is also found in the area of religion. Moreover, many non-Judaic religions – in Japan all but the Shin sects – are non-exclusivist. There is no ideological commandment against dual membership. Most Japanese practise, and have practised, either a mixture of religions (Shinto, Buddhism and, more recently, Christianity), or have overtly belonged to synthesizing sects such as Ryobu Shinto.

Though conflicts have arisen and do arise in Japanese society, often even violent ones, the nature of Japanese religion is such that, barring some exceptions, the various forms for mediating conflict can operate fairly smoothly. There is no *religious* barrier to conflict, but Japanese religion is not, for a number of reasons discussed above, conducive to significant levels of conflict. Moreover, there are certain positive, cross-cutting factors which work to eliminate conflict in religion. Since religion is private as well as public, private and public practices can be different. *Public religious* practices, however, must conform to general public *social* conduct: they must avoid conflict as much as possible. Private practices, on the other hand, are indeed private, out of the public eye, and therefore are less of a potential source of conflict. Where we do find religious conflict is in areas where the mitigating factors do not operate fully. That is, for example, within the same religious group where there may be struggles for a particular resource. This struggle may not be mitigated by the factors enumerated above. Moreover, non-religious groups that are in conflict may create the appearance of religious conflict, in the sense used in this chapter, because communal groups in Japan are often ritual and festival communities as well. A conflict between two communities may well take on the *appearance* of religious conflict, because the religious emblems are used as rallying points. The severity of historical conflicts in the three dimensions outlined at the beginning of this chapter can be put into the same context. Inter-religious conflict is relatively mild, unless other extra-religious factors – for example, government nationalist policies – override the limiting factors. The same is true of religious conflict on the local-national dimension as well.

Notes

1 The paper on which this chapter is based was originally read in two slightly different versions at the Hebrew University Graduate Seminar on Japanese Society and at the Truman Institute Workshop on Conflict Resolution in Japan. I am grateful to my colleagues at these fora and to the students who attended the seminar for their comments on these earlier drafts. The final draft was edited for publication by Jeanne Jacob.

   I am grateful to two local Yuzawa historians for access to records of their respective family histories, elements of which appear in this chapter.

2 '*Mukyokai*' is the name of an indigenous Christian religious movement that flourished sporadically in Japan before World War II. It exerted an intellectual influence far beyond its size. It was the subject of persecution by the government before and during the war.

3 I purposely do not use the official terms for shrines of these classifications (i.e. *sonsha* and *gosha*) since the argument focuses precisely on these, government-inspired, definitions and their implications.

4 *Dozoku* are cooperative associations of traditional households – *ie* – in which a 'stem' or founder *ie* is tied ritually, and often economically and politically, to one or more 'branch' or cadet *ie*, each of which functions independently.

   There are several *dozoku* in Yuzawa, though not all have the same degree of cohesiveness, of extent, and of cooperation.

5 'Shrine' (Jap. *jinja*) is the designation for a structure used for Shinto rituals.

   'Temple' (Jap. *otera* or the suffix *-ji*) is the designation for a Buddhist temple, of whatever sect.

   Tenrikyo is one of the so-called 'New Religions' which engage in active proselytization in Japan. They have a main temple in Tenri City, and branch temples throughout the country. Their practice is a mixture of Shinto, Buddhism, and innovative elements.

6 Soka Gakkai is a proselytizing lay organization associated with the Nichiren sect of Buddhism. In common with many Nichiren organizations, it is exclusivist, demanding renunciation of all other religious affiliations by its members.

7   *Mura hachibu* (lit. 'village eight-parts') was a traditional sanction
    applied by villagers to members who had transgressed village norms
    to an unacceptable degree. It involved a complete boycott of the
    culprit's household, with the exception of burial and fire-fighting. In a
    society in which cooperation was a way of life and a prerequisite for
    survival, *mura hachibu* was a major threat.
8   Buddhist temples and Shinto shrines are organized differently in
    managerial and economic terms. Temples are supported by lay
    organizations called *danka*, whose members may be from different
    areas. The binding tie is the family graves. There is a division of
    labour – Buddhism in Japan being concerned largely with the
    afterlife, Shinto with the mundane. Graveyards in Japan are
    maintained by Buddhist temples (cf., Morioka, 1975, pp, 75–116.
       Koju and *ujiko* are types of voluntary religious associations, the
    first usually completely voluntary, the second often based on
    inherited position (cf., Davis, 1977, pp. 63–92).

References

Akaike, N. (1976), 'Festivals and neighborhood associations', *Japanese Journal of Religious Studies*, 3(2–3), pp. 127–74.

Ashkenazi, M. (1987a), 'The structure of the Daimyo Gyoretsu parade of Yuzawa-shi', *Asian Folklore Studies*, 46(1), pp. 35–54.

Ashkenazi, M. (1987b), 'A native model for Japanese quality circles' in T. Blumenthal (ed.), *Japanese Management at Home and Abroad*. Beersheva, Ben Gurion University Press.

Bachnik, J. (1983), 'Recruitment strategies for household succession: rethinking Japanese household succession', *Man*, 18, pp. 160-82.

Bailey, F.G. (1960), *Tribe, Caste, and Nation: A Study of Political Activity and Political Change in Highland Orissa*. Manchester, Manchester University Press.

Bestor, T. (1985), 'Tradition and Japanese organization: institutional development in a Tokyo neighbourhood', *Ethnology*, 24(2), pp. 121–36.

Chinnery, T. (1971), *Religious Conflict and Compromise in a Japanese Village*. Vancouver, University of British Columbia Publications in Anthropology.

Coser, L. (1967), *Continuities in the Study of Social Conflict*. New York, The Free Press.

Davis, W.B. (1977), *Towards Modernity: A Developmental Typology of Popular Religious Affiliation in Japan*. Ithaca, Cornell East Asia Papers.

Embree, J. (1939), *Suye Mura*. Chicago, University of Chicago Press.

Fridell, W. (1973), *Japanese Shrine Mergers 1906–1912*. Tokyo, Sophia University.

Fukutake, T. (1967), *Japanese Rural Society*. Ithaca, Cornell University Press.

Hall, J. (1971), *Japan from Prehistory to Modern Times*. Tokyo, Charles Tuttle.

Irokawa, D. (1975), 'The survival struggle of the Japanese community', *The Japan Interpreter*, 9(4), pp. 465–94.

Lebra, T.S. (1976), *Japanese Patterns of Behavior*. Honolulu, The University of Hawaii Press.

Morioka, K. (1975), *Religion in Changing Japanese Society*. Tokyo, University of Tokyo Press.

Plath, D. (1969), *The After Hours*. Berkeley, University of California Press.

Sansom, G. (1973), *Japan: A Short Cultural History* (revised edition). Tokyo, Tuttle.

Smith, R.J. (1983), *Japanese Society*. Cambridge, Cambridge University Press.

Statler, O. (1969), *Shimoda Story*. New York, Macmillan.

Part Four
CONCLUDING OBSERVATIONS

10 Four Models of Japanese Society and their Relevance to Conflict[1]

H. Befu

Introduction

In this chapter I will present four models of Japanese society in a summary form, since space limitation precludes anything but a brief discussion of the models. After each model is presented, how conflict can be treated in the framework of each model will be considered.

The four models will be labelled 'consensus model', 'stratification model', 'exchange model', and 'conflict model'.

Consensus Model

Of the four models, the consensus model, also known by such aliases as 'harmoney model' (Krauss, Rohlen and Steinhoff, 1984) and 'group model' (Befu, 1980, 1982; Mouer and Sugimoto, 1986, pp. 54–63), is by far the best-known and the most popular. It is embedded, nay enshrined, in the popular genre of *Nihonjinron*, a field which endeavours to define Japan's unique characteristics and identify the basis of Japan's claim of its 'uniqueness'.

While the idea of the Japanese being consensus-oriented has a long history in Japan, it was probably made well known to the West through such works as Nakane's *Japanese Society* (1970), Reischauer's *The Japanese* (1978) and Vogel's *Japan as Number One* (1979). Of late, this idea is widely invoked in the management circle as a key to understanding *the* Japanese management style, said to be responsible for the high productivity of Japanese industry (e.g. Abegglen, 1973; Gibney, 1982; Lee and Schwendiman, 1982a, 1982b; Masatsugu, 1982).

As the appellations indicate, this model emphasizes the ideology of harmony and consensus within the group to which the individual Japanese belongs. Cooperation among members and conformity to group norm are critical components of the group model. Open conflict and competition conversely are taboo. This is a small, face-to-face group in which relationship is particularistic and functionally diffuse. The Japanese concept of *amae* (emotional dependence upon one another), à la Doi (1973), is invoked by subscribers to the group model as the psychological underpinning of social processes. Trust is an important ingredient of the interpersonal relationship among members of the group. 'Familistic' is a proper characterization in that the psychological and social processes typifying the Japanese group are said to be derived from the family institution. These characteristics promote in-group loyalty and out-group prejudice and hostility.

Structurally this group is hierarchically organized, with a strong tie between leader and followers. The leader leads with benevolence and magnanimity, and supports and protects followers at all costs. It is in this sense *inter alia* that the Japanese group is often said to be 'paternalistic'. Followers in turn are expected to be loyal to the leader and to the group, sometimes even at the expense of self-interest. Lateral solidarity of group members is absent or, at best, weak.

As mentioned above, the Japanese style of management has been touted as a special application of the consensus model. Japanese specialists on Japan's business management have by and large endorsed this interpretation (Hazama, 1971; Iwata, 1977; Nishida, 1982; Tsuda, 1977). Among the major features of the group model as applied to business management are paternalistic or familistic ideology, permanent employment, seniority system, and enterprise unionism. The security of permanent employment is said to promote commitment and loyalty of workers to the company. The seniority system of reward is based on the assumption that the length of service to the company should in itself be an object of reward in an group-oriented organization. Enterprise unionism, too, is an expression of the fact that the company is an indivisible unit and that even a labour union should not have an organization which would cross-cut and split the unity that is the company.

One may regard the group model as a 'cultural' model in the sense that the model is predicated upon the exercise and observance of cultural values and norms and that it is best described with the aid of culturally specific or 'emic' concepts. For example, Nakane introduces the term *ba*. While translating it as 'frame', she says 'it is hard to find the exact English counterpart.' (Nakane, 1970, p. 1) The term *amae* is so culture-specific that it is widely used without translation in many English language writings on Japan. It is even used as a title of a book in English (Mitchell, 1976).

Why this model is so popular and no other model is anywhere nearly as widely accepted in Japan or abroad is a question deep in the realm of the sociology of knowledge. This model is at best a highly partial and inaccurate representation of the reality, as argued by a number of writers in recent years (Befu, 1980a, 1980b; Gendai Shakaigaku, 1980; Kawamura, 1982; Mouer and Sugimoto, 1986; Shukan Toyo Keizai, 1981). Conferences have been organized specifically to analyse the group model of Japanese society and special issues of journals have been issued to air views countering the group orientation thesis of Japanese society.

Yet the model's popularity has not dwindled one iota. Instead it is continually invoked in one guise or another to 'explain' Japanese behaviour. This is especially true in the management field. Accounting for this fact would require us to examine a larger context in which the group model is embedded, namely the whole genre of *Nihonjinron*, and the voluminous literature dealing with Japan's essential uniqueness. But we have no space here to delve into this fascinating topic. The reader is urged to examine other sources (Befu, 1983, 1984; Mouer and Sugimoto, 1986) for further elaboration of the issue.

Relevance to Conflict

It is not hard to see that, with its emphasis on harmony and consensus, conflict is assumed to be dysfunctional in the group model and is avoided at all cost. Mechanisms are created in Japan to minimize open expression of conflict, for example, by instituting the system of intermediary in dealing with potentially conflictual situations. One such situation is marriage negotiation. In arranging marriage between two families previously unknown to each other, i.e. between parties where trust and confidence have not developed, a go-between who knows and has the trust of both parties serves as an arranger. This system avoids any possible embarrassment, should the negotiation fail.

The system of *nemawashi*, or prior consultation, also helps to avert potential open conflict in a formal meeting. This is done by informally 'touching base' with all relevant parties beforehand, finding out their respective positions on the issue at hand, identifying areas of possible conflict, and working out compromise among them prior to the formal meeting. Thus when all parties meet at a formal meeting, positions of compromise already known to all are presented, and any possible conflict can be avoided. Emphasis placed on the distinction between *tatemae* and *honne* is also relevant here. The former has to do with the formal and public position one takes, as against *honne*, which is the privately held view of the individual. In a situation of potential conflict within a group which emphasizes harmony, cultural prescription requires that one state a *tatemae* position which is not likely to cause conflict, regardless of what one might think as *honne*.

Structurally, as Krauss, Rohlen and Steinhoff (1984) point out, conflict is often avoided in Japanese companies by frequent transfer of personnel from one unit to another, thus creating personal networks of trust and confidence throughout the company. This policy helps to avoid the development of sectionalism, wherein each unit in a company tends to become an independent group manifesting hostility and distrust to other units in the company. In a large organization, such as a ministry in the central government, this policy does not function too successfully, and factionalism tends to develop (Campbell, 1984). Factionalism in the Liberal Democratic Party is a good example of internal sectionalism, where sub-units of the Party become semi-autonomous in competing for resources within the Party, although to be sure, *vis-à-vis* other political parties, they act in unison, as seen in their practice of bloc voting in the Diet.

One simple way in which conformity to the group norm was enforced in the past in rural areas was to exercise village ostracism (*mura hachibu*) toward nonconformist families. In *mura hachibu*, the community would make a pact not to cooperate with transgressors, not to lend needed help in times of rice transplanting, harvesting, funerals, etc. In effect, the family was placed in sociological exile without physically being forced to move out of the community.

The consensus model assumes a unified moral community where a world view shared by all members of the community prevails. When this world view is not shared, conflict is likely to arise between those sharing the world view and those who share another. Peasant uprisings in the Tokugawa and modern periods often involved this sort of 'mismatch' in the world views of the peasants and of the political rulers or landlords, where the latter sometimes exploited the peasants while the peasants themselves espoused a paternalistic world view in which those in power and authority were mandated to look after the welfare of the ruled.

In the 1960s and 1970s, when environmental pollution by industry was rather rampant, causing not only damage to property but also injury to nearby residents, hue and cry were heard in the local community which demanded executives of the company polluting the local area to pay visits to the victims and apologize to them. The reason for the importance of this is that the act of apologizing is an open admission that company executives shared the same value system and world view as the victims and recognized what they had done was wrong, as the victims themselves saw the situation. Without this act of apologizing, the community would remain morally split between the residents who saw the polluting as wrong and the company executives, who are also residents of the community, but who would not share the same values and world view. Thus the community faced a moral crisis, which could be mended only by the executives admitting their wrong and apologizing for the company's wrong-doing.

To take a specific example, when Chisso Company was found guilty of polluting the offshore waters of Minamata with deadly mercury, and moreover, of concealing its knowledge of polluting the waters and of causing incurable injuries to local residents, the outrage of the community had a definite moral overtone. The residents saw a clear breach of moral commitment on the part of Chisso to act in good faith. As the only major industry in town, Chisso was, in the eyes of the locals, obliged to act morally and to help the community, as a feudal lord was obliged to rule his domain with benevolence. Instead, Chisso acted in bad faith, and consequently left a foul taste in everyone's mouth. Then, when the Chisso president went from one home to another of the victims who died of mercury poisoning to apologize to the family of the deceased, praying at the family altar where the victims were enshrined, he demonstrated his admission of guilt and his acknowledgement that he shared the same moral values as residents. This act, then, restored Minamata as a moral community.

Stratification Model

Mention of a stratification model is likely to remind one of the recent polls taken in Japan showing that the vast majority of Japanese – some 90 per cent – consider themselves middle class. On the face of this finding, it may seem that Japan is virtually a classless society: if everyone is middle class, then 'class' begins to lose meaning with reference to reality. A stratification model of Japanese society, then, may seem highly unrealistic. Krauss, Rohlen and Steinhoff (1984) take the accepted view of consensus theorists that class as such in Japan is not a very significant issue and that post-war Japan 'has produced surprisingly little class conflict in the traditional Marxian sense.' (1984, p. 388) One could probably say the same, however, with respect to the United States and other Western societies, that the traditional Marxian sense of class conflict is not a common sight.

The reason for this relative absence of class consciousness in Japan lies in the emphasis on the group, we are told. The primacy of group orientation, of commitment to the organization to which one belongs, mitigates against developing horizontal consciousness cutting across vertically structured groups. While this is a compelling argument, signs of stratified phenomena in Japan are not lacking. It may well be that such phenomena should not necessarily be called 'class phenomena'; none the less, stratification in a broad sense does have empirical reality in Japan, as Mouer and Sugimoto have argued in their attempt to interpret Japanese society from the stratification point of view (1986, pp. 273–374). While their model suffers from being in part a suggested conceptual scheme, rather than an empirically tested model, of how Japan may be viewed, it nevertheless does open up a new way of understanding Japan. Another important point not to be missed is that the model of social stratification proposed by Mouer and Sugimoto offers the possibility of cross-national comparison. In fact, as they point out, there is a great deal of similarity across industrial societies in the structure of stratification, in the patterns of distribution of rewards, whether in terms of wealth, income, occupation, education, information, or any other measure. Granting, of course, some definite differences among societies, similarities among societies which do not share cultural heritage, such as between Japan and Western societies, are still impressive.

Empirical phenomena indicating stratification, or ranking, defined here as uneven distribution of rewards, are numerous in Japan. All of the usual indices of stratification, such as income, education, power, authority, information, status, prestige, and occupation, can be brought to bear to demonstrate that these rewards are not evenly distributed throughout the population.

Japanese sociologists have worked for generations collecting data on social stratification and mobility employing these and other indices. The voluminous data collected in the numerous surveys and the extensive analyses of the data cannot even be summarized in this limited space. Suffice it to say that we do not lack evidence for stratification of Japanese society, defined objectively or subjectively.

Even the remark made above that most Japanese perceive themselves as being middle class can be interpreted as a tell-tale sign of class consciousness of a sort. To call oneself middle class is to deny oneself lower or upper class status, and is an evident sign of awareness of class distinction. That is, since we are here dealing with subjective assessment of class affiliation, one Japanese answering a survey questionnaire is not aware of what another is answering. As far as he or she is concerned, middle class attribution is meaningful because and only because the respondent is aware of lower class and upper class as categories to which some other Japanese belong. Thus, from the point of view of each Japanese, Japan is a class society.

Only when data are treated in aggregate do we find that most Japanese perceive themselves as belonging to a single class, namely middle class. In aggregate, then, one might say Japan is nearly a classless society. That observation, however, should not be confounded with the subjective perception of the Japanese as living in a class society.

Other evidence of existence of social strata in Japan may be briefly mentioned. While most labour unions in Japan are enterprise unions, some are not. Japan Teachers' Union and Japan Seamen's Union are notable exceptions to this rule. In both cases the unions manifest existence of a strong lateral bond among those who share the same occupation.

Also, according to the research carried out by Christena Turner in the late 1970s in various factories, workers do have a sense of belonging to an industrial workers' class, but this sense is not foremost in the minds of workers at all times. Instead, in certain contexts, such as at the time of union meetings or workers' demonstrations against the banks which own the establishment, their consciousness as workers and as part of the working class consisting of workers all over Japan is heightened. Rhetoric of working-class consciousness becomes the reigning mode of communication in such situations. In other situations their consciousness as industrial workers united by the sense of exploitation and oppression by capitalists is only remotely felt at best. To say that therefore their consciousness as workers with lateral ties to workers of other companies is false would be missing an important point. It is important to realize that how an individual conceptualizes his or her position in the world is situationally determined and that the respective world views a person holds in different situations are equally real and equally valid.

Structural inequal distribution, too, is evident in Japan. What has normally been referred to as 'dual economy', but one which Clark (1979, pp. 64–73) more appropriately calls 'industrial gradation', is an example here. From the top companies like Matsushita, Dentsu, Hitachi, etc., that is, those equivalent to the 'Fortune 500', through intermediate-size companies down to cottage industries of the sorts Wagatsuma and DeVos (1984; describe from Arakawa Ward in Tokyo, there is infinite gradation of industrial firms in terms of size, scale, capital investment, length of credit extension, wages, fringe benefits, prestige, and many other indices. As Clark points out, this industrial gradation parallels stratification in terms of other criteria. Thus workers in top companies tend to earn more than those in other companies, other things being equal. Those at the top tend to have received better education than those below, and so on.

Similarly, schools are graded in terms of their quality, prestige, facilities, etc. The ranking of schools may seem like a totally different kind of phenomenon from the ranking of social classes; none the less, parallelism between the two is inescapable. Those going to better schools end up earning more income, working at more prestigeous companies, etc.

At the college level, as is well known, Tokyo University is at the apex of the prestige hierarchy, followed by other former imperial universities and such 'vintage' private schools as Keio and Waseda. High schools, too, are ranked in each community from the best to the worst on the basis of how many graduates of these high schools enter top universities. Top high schools at the community level are also ranked nationally on the same basis. Even cram schools (*yobiko*), which train high school and post-high school students in taking entrance examination to college, are ranked according to the success ratio in sending their students to top colleges. If high schools are ranked by their ability to send students to prestige colleges, elementary schools, too, are ranked on the basis of their ability to send their graduates to prestige junior high schools, although in this case, districting and other constraints placed on students in public schools restrict free mobility on the basis of school prestige.

Speciality stores, restaurants and department stores are also ranked. This ranking plays an important role in gift-giving. Since stores wrap their merchandise with their own wrapping paper showing well-marked logo or insignia, the provenance of the gift is evident to anyone receiving it. A gift should be purchased at a store which carries high prestige, since this is the way to communicate the high esteem the giver accords the receiver. Giving a gift obtained at an unknown store, even if the contents are identical, would carry a negative connotation to the receiver. Thus even though one may be able to purchase an item more cheaply at a discount store, one should go to a pretige store and pay the full price, if one wishes to communicate the proper message to the receiver through the gift.

A last example of ranking is of urban centres. All cities in Japan are ranked like a 'tree'. At the apex is Tokyo, the seat of the national government, the pivot of economic activities, the locus of the most prestigious educational institutions, the centre of 'high culture' – such as music, art, theatre and fashion. Kyoto of course enjoyed this apical position for a thousand years until the political centre moved to Tokyo. Kyotoites would like to dispute Tokyo's claim as number one. Many of them still

221

wishfully think of themselves as better and more 'cultured', and look down on Tokyoites as erstwhile peasants and uncouth 'new comers' to the prestige game. In doing so, however, they are admitting, like anyone else in Japan, the firm existence of the fact of ranking of cities.

If Tokyo is the undisputed urban centre for all except some die-hard Kyotoites, each of the prefectural seats of government is the local centre – political, economic, educational, and cultural. Prefectural capitals are to prefectural hinterlands as Tokyo is to the rest of Japan. All other urban centres take a secondary place to the prefectural capital. These secondary cities, however, are then the 'stars' *vis-à-vis* their respective hinterlands.

As colleges are ranked nation-wide, so are cities. After Tokyo come a small number of major cities of national importance, such as Osaka, Kyoto, Kobe, Yokohama and Nagoya, which are of course all prefectural capitals. They are then followed by smaller prefectural capitals, located mostly in the Tokaido-Inland Sea corridor, with prefectural capitals away from areas of high density in terms of population, economic activities and historic events in the past thousand years taking the lowest positions on this totem pole or urban hierarchy.

Relevance to conflict

Given unequal distribution of rewards in the stratification model, conflict is likely to arise particularly when participants espouse the value of egalitarianism. Much of the world in the twentieth century has embraced egalitarian ideology in one form or another, in most cases enshrining the ideal in the constitution. The contradiction between the ideal of egalitarianism and the reality of inequal distribution of rewards, then, is a likely basis for conflict. In feudal Japan, inequality was assumed to be the reality of the social arrangement and an integral part of the world view, and peasants did not question the fact that they did not have the right to act on an equal basis with samurai, or to become a samurai. But now, with democracy reigning, the situation has radically changed, though this does not imply that centuries of feudal legacy is totally obliterated. In fact, I submit that one cultural reason why this contradiction is not so much an issue in Japan as it is in Western societies is that the feudal world view, predicated as it was on hierarchical structure and inequal distribution of rewards, unmitigated by egalitarian values, still to this day provides a generalized mood or disposition to accept authority relatively unquestioningly. The introduction of unmitigated egalitarianism as an ideology into Japan, it should be remembered, is a relatively recent thing, dating only since 1945, although, to be sure, from the Meiji period on, the concepts of democracy and people's rights have been introduced into Japan and debated by intellectuals. However, the impact of such exercise among intellectuals upon the masses was negligible until 1945.

Another source of conflict in the stratification model is of course Marxian. It is one derived from conflict of interest between those who own the means of production and those who do not, between industrial workers and capitalists. Krauss, Rohlen and Steinhoff argue that the classic form of Marxian class conflict does not exist in Japan, and they are probably right. However, the hundreds of Marxist scholars in Japan cannot all be wrong. At the very least, the Marxist rhetoric is adopted by Japanese workers when they make wage demands and when they fight what they consider to be the injustice of the management. Thus Marxism does play a part in industrial conflict, even though, admittedly, causes of industrial conflict in Japan may not be strictly in accordance with Marxist formula.

One other source of conflict, arising out of the combination of the group model and the stratification model, must be mentioned. This situation is found in enterprises with multiple unions, which orient workers both to the company and to industrial workers as a social class (Kawanishi, 1977). While a typical company would have one union, a small percentage of companies have multiple unions. Japan National Railways, as an extreme case, had more than ten unions. More typically, a company with multiple unions would have two unions. In such a case, one of the two has a leftist tendency, possibly with a leadership dominated by members of the Socialist, or even Communist Party, and tends to oppose management measures or make demands which the management does not wish to meet. The leadership of such a union has a strong identification with members of the working class, and a commitment to further the workers' cause and to promote their interests as workers. Members of this union are strongly committed to the values of the working class as a social stratum, whether they work for the

same or different companies. The other union is more conservative, or is oriented towards the establishment and cooperates with
the management. What one sees here is two opposing orientations of workers. Those espousing the group model, so to speak,
belong to the management-oriented union, while those embrac-
ing the stratification model belong to the leftist union. As a
result, the management has to negotiate with two or more unions
on every issue, which creates further conflict, this time between
the two unions, since the management tends to favour the
conservative union and to discriminate against the leftist union.

Social Exchange Model

In chapter 8 of this volume – a revision of Max Weber's theory of
bureaucracy – I presented an outline of social exchange theory in
some detail. To avoid redundancy, I will not repeat what I said
there. However, in the interest of symmetry, I will briefly go over
some of the elements of this theory as it applies to Japan.

Before I begin discussion of the model itself, it is necessary to
look at empirical facts to convince us of the appropriateness of
adopting a model based on exchange theory. The best place to
begin is in gift-giving (Befu, 1967, 1968). If one spends any
amount of time in Japan, one cannot avoid receiving gifts – from
friends, colleagues, stores, etc. In 1969–70, I conducted a survey
of households with regard to gifts they had given and received.
The sample was haphazard to say the least. I could not secure
anything like a statistically random sample, since the task
required meticulous record-keeping, and not everyone has the
propensity for this. I simply had to prevail on whoever was
willing to perform the task. Seventy-five housewives kept records
of all gifts, no matter how trivial or how large, including the date,
contents, value (estimated value in the case of a gift received),
relationship to the person who gave/received the gift, and the
occasion. Records were kept for a minimum of one month to a
maximum of twenty-four months.

An average household gave and/or received about twenty-five
gifts per month, based on the record. A certain amount of
unintentional omission (due to forgetting) was expected. The
recorder herself sometimes failed to remember to record. Also,

other members of the family did not always remember to report to the recorder the gift they gave or received. After accounting for these omissions, it might be assumed that an average household in Japan gives or receives a gift just about every day. Since the norm of reciprocity (Gouldner, 1960) governs gifting behaviour, though according to a complex set of rules which do not always call for direct and immediate return, all material gifting falls within the domain of social exchange.

Entirely apart from material gifts, the Japanese do favours of all kinds to one another. In fact the distinction between material gifts and non-material favours cannot be drawn clearly, as one is often exchanged for the other; sometimes a material gift is given simultaneously with a favour done; at other times the giving of the material gift is itself the favour to be done.

Thus, while gifting is a universal phenomenon, the significance of which was first elaborated upon in sociological terms by Mauss (1925), the prevalence and salience of gifting and reciprocal behaviour in Japan make the construction of a model of Japanese society using the concept of exchange particularly suitable.

Gouldner emphasizes the importance of the universal norm of reciprocity in human society. But this norm has to be expressed in a culturally specific way in each culture. Geertz once said people do not espouse 'religion' as some abstract concept; they believe in ghosts, fall in seance, speak in tongues, fear hell. By exactly the same token, we do not see people observing a universal human norm of reciprocity; instead we see them offering a glass of wine at a restaurant to a stranger sitting across the table, inviting to dinner a friend who invited you to dinner, etc.

The concept of the norm of reciprocity thus needs 'translating' into culturally specific forms. In Japan, this is expressed in such concepts as *giri* and *on*. *On* refers to the debt you have to anyone who has done something for you, notably your ancestors and mentors. The debts you have thus incurred must be returned. In a broad sense, *giri* is the value concept which prescribes this return, although in modern parlance, returning of *on* is not normally referred to as performing *giri*. *On* is a powerful concept which contains within it the imperative of return (*on-gaeshi*). Thus *on* immediately implies *on-gaeshi*. The two terms are paired in Japanese culture, as 'rights and obligations' and 'love and marriage' are in American culture. *Giri*, on the other hand,

225

refers to the norm of reciprocation in a broader context than the one in which the concept of *on* is applicable. As a normative value, however, it is as compelling as the concept of *on*. One who does 'not know *giri*' in Japan is relegated to a level somewhat below humanity.

The generalized norms of *on-gaeshi* and *giri*, however, are too broad in themselves to be useful in determining the specifics of reciprocation. The norms dictate that one must give and return; but they do not prescribe what specifically is to be given or returned. An elaborate set of rules govern the contents and manners of giving and returning. Etiquette books, of which there are many, generally have an extensive section on gifting, although none that I have seen is anywhere near complete.

To cite an example of specific rules for gifting, when a friend, relative or neighbour dies, one normally goes to the funeral, taking incense money (*koden*). As one leaves the funeral, a small token gift is given by the bereaved family to all attenders. Later, a return gift (*koden gaeshi*) for the incense money is delivered to all those who gave *koden* in a rough fraction of the amount of the incense money. Reciprocity does not end here. When death occurs in the family of an attender, one must attend the funeral, taking incense money of the same amount (adjusted for inflation, if years separate the two events). Of course the token gift is given and a return gift for the incense money would be delivered to complete the cycle. The protocol also requires that all these gifts be properly wrapped according to set rules. (Befu, 1976, 1984).

People, however, do not always act according to rules. In fact social rules are never set in such a way that they can be followed blindly. Rules have exceptions, and rules are guidelines. They are stated with latitude, forcing one to make decisions as to where in the range of acceptable behaviour one should stand. These considerations require one to develop a strategy of action to maximize the benefit accruing to the action. If, for example, one were to take incense money to a funeral, one must decide, perhaps in consultation with others who might be attending the funeral, what the appropriate amount would be – not so little as to offend the receiver and, moreover, to devalue one's social status, not so much as to appear arrogant, and also less than the amount to be given by a person who is one's senior in status, etc.

In the Japanese model of exchange, we must recognize three different kinds of agents engaged in exchange. The first is the normal, living member of society, and requires no elaboration. The second type is deceased ancestors and supernatural beings. It may strike one as being strange to enter into an exchange relationship with deceased ancestors, as the latter cannot take active part in exchange – at least in Western scientific thinking. However, Japanese ancestors play an important role in influencing the action of living descendants (Plath, 1964; Smith, 1974). The Japanese believe that ancestral expectations are to be taken seriously. If they are thwarted, ancestors can cause trouble. For example, ancestors may expect descendants to carry on the family business they started. The prospering family business is a resource given by ancestors, and descendants reciprocate for this gift, in the Japanese cultural context, by maintaining the business or, even better, by further expanding the business. If the family head does not heed ancestral wishes and neglects the family business, any illness which may strike a family member would be interpreted as an expression of ancestral wrath.

A third type of agent of exchange is a corporate body – as when the Japanese engage in exchange with the 'community' (*seken* or the 'society' (*shakai*). This notion is related to the concept of *on*. One owes to the community and the larger world for what one is. After all, without the external social world to help you in so many different ways, you would not have reached where you are. One then has the obligation to return this *on* to the world. When a person does some volunteer work, it is often justified as an act of returning his or her debt to the world. When a company announces some charitable contribution, it is often stated to be an act of returning to society (*shakai e no kangen*) what it owes to society for the profit it has made. Perhaps, as a special case of this, a corporate organization, such as a company, can also be an agent of exchange. It is in this special sense that the expression 'loyalty to one's company' should be understood, namely that a worker may feel debt or *on* to his or her company and show loyalty to the company as a way of returning the debt. This expression, however, is also used more indiscriminately in literature on the group model of Japanese society to refer to behaviours which are best characterized as dyadic exchange relationships, as discussed below.

It is important to realize that exchange is a means of communication. Gift-giving is a more obvious example in this respect, for the instrumental meaning of an exchange resource is more readily identifiable. It is the non-material meaning of an exchange resource which, from the social point of view, is more important. The giver of a resource intends to convey 'expressive' meaning – of love, affection, respect, appreciation, etc. – through the exchange act. In Japan in particular, expressive values of an act of exchange define the relationship between the two parties to exchange.

Exchange relationship begins between two individuals with the reciprocation of acts of relatively small instrumental and expressive values. Each completed exchange defines a level of expressive or emotional involvement and hence a certain level of trust between the two, and each previous act of exchange serves as a building block upon which to build a relationship affording exchange of resources of higher value and requiring greater trust. It works like a Guttman scale in this sense. When relationship is continuing and long-lasting, there is a chance for the relationship to be bonded with a strong tie. This is of course true anywhere, outside Japan as well as inside it. In the case of Japan, however, cultural norm endorses and encourages functionally diffuse and particularistic relationships, and recommends the building up of expressive debts and credits in relation to others, whereas in some other societies, such as in the West, functional diffuseness and particularism are discouraged from developing in spheres of life dominated by instrumentality, such as on-the-job or in-business relations, making it difficult, though not impossible, to develop affectively satisfying and trusting relationships. In a job or business situation where trust is needed or is helpful to have in achieving instrumental ends, the Japanese have an easier time accomplishing the goal. The reason is that trust is *inevitably* and *necessarily* built into the relationship because the resources being exchanged between individuals, at work or elsewhere, have both instrumental and expressive contents. In the United States, at work, instrumental exchange predominates, leaving out as irrelevant the expressive side of the deal, and one has to make an effort to build it into a work situation, with varying degrees of success.

This kind of 'instrumental-*cum*-expressive' relationship develops best in what one might call an 'intermediate organization', where face-to-face relationships govern the *modus vivendi*, rather than in a larger organization where contact on a personal basis is difficult to achieve. An intermediate organization may be a small shop, an informal group of students in school, a social club, or a section of a large company.

In this sense, the exchange model and the group model may seem quite alike. A major difference lies in the fact that the exchange model specifies social processes in terms of the exchange relationship obtaining in dyadic relationships. The group model at times recognizes dyadic relationship and specifies it, but this is not done systematically. Moreover, it recognizes the 'group' as having a hold on its members and dictating their behaviour. The exchange model basically sees the group structure as consisting of a series of dyadic exchange relationships, without, however, totally denying the place of the group as having a separate existence in the perception of participants. Thus a person can and does think of himself or herself as having a debt to the place of work and reciprocates by working extra hard, or rationalizes extra work in terms of paying back a 'debt' to the company. None the less, the notion of 'group' as used in the consensus model is largely an epiphenomenon, which in the exchange model can be translated into dyadic relationship. When this is done, it loses its mysteriousness and becomes empirically more comprehensible.

Relevance to conflict

In the framework of social exchange, conflict arises in a variety of ways. The most simple and obvious would be when giving is not reciprocated. This seldom happens, due to the strength of the norm of reciprocity as understood by the Japanese in terms of cultural concepts such as *on* and *giri*. But as the expression *on shirazu* (one who does not know what *on* is) indicates, there are those who neglect to repay their debts. The very existence of this negatively charged term is in itself a tell-tale sign of the problematic nature of reciprocity in Japan. A similar idea is expressed in the phrase *giri o wakimaenai* (not to know what *giri* is). To be characterized by these terms is the utmost shame, and every Japanese would go out of his or her way to avoid it.

One area in which non-return of favour becomes an issue, interestingly, is bribery (Befu, 1974). Bribery is of considerable interest to students of gift-giving, since it is a form of gift exchange, the only difference from other forms of gift exchange being its illegal nature. It is illegal to give a bribe as much as it is to receive one. Bribery seldom comes to light, since this crime, when committed perfectly, has no victims, no injured parties. One might possibly say that, ultimately, tax payers are the victims in the sense that the public servant involved in the bribery would not execute his or her charges as required and that the action of the public servant usually results in the misuse of public funds or reduced revenue to the government. For example, a tax officer, having received a bribe, would make sure the bribe-giver would pay less tax than was actually due.

Bribery does come to light from time to time, however. The most likely scenario for revelation of bribery involves a bribe-accepting public servant not delivering the goods. That is, after receiving a bribe and promising to do an illegal favour to the bribe-giver, the public servant simply does not do the favour. The public servant in such a case relies on the bribe-giver not reporting him to the authority, since reporting would reveal the bribe-giver's own crime. And this probably does happen more often than the Japanese government would care to know. But often the bribe-giver's anger gets the better of him and he reports the bribe-giving to the authority out of spite, resulting in the arrest and indictment of the public servant.

Conflict arises also when receipt of the gift is not properly acknowledged. When a gift is received or a favour done, the recipient is of course expected to thank the giver at the scene of receiving. It is equally important, however – and this is where foreigners in Japan often fail – to acknowledge and give thanks for the gift or the favour when the next contact – face-to-face, by phone, or by letter – is made. This makes especial sense when the resource given is a material gift. For in Japan a gift is normally not opened in front of the giver. Thus one can only give thanks for the gift, whatever it is, but not for the contents of the gift, which therefore has to be done at the time of the next contact. Failing to do this is likely to cause censure by the giver, who would remember the recipient as a person less than properly moral.

Conflict also occurs if a favour is reciprocated, but if the reciprocation is not commensurate to the favour received. As I indicated in the chapter on Weberian bureaucracy, calculation and estimation of the value of a received favour or gift is a rather complex socio-psychological process, in which one has to be rather sensitive to the whole context in which gifting takes place, as well as knowledgeable about the original giver. Japanese housewives have a rather uncanny knack of being able to guess the monetary value of merchandise given as a gift. Helmut Morsbach, a psychologist at the University of Glasgow, compared Japanese and European wives with respect to this ability, and found Japanese wives to be able to guess the value of merchandise much better than European wives. For the Japanese, this ability is necessary for social survival, for when a gift is received, a gift whose value is a function of the value of the gift received must be returned. The value must be roughly equal if the giver and the receiver are of roughly equal status. When the relationship is of unequal status, the person occupying the lower status generally gives a gift of lesser value than the one his or her superior would give. In this inequal relationship, giving a gift of equal value would bring about confict. Since it is generally the responsibility of the housewife to purchase gifts, even though she may not be the one who delivers it, she must develop an ability to guess the price of merchandise.

To avoid conflict, the return gift must not only be of appropriate value, it must also be of the right kind. For example, giving money as a gift to one's superior – except in the case of a funeral – is taboo. Transgression of this rule is likely to create animosity between the giver and the receiver.

Gifts – using the term in a generic sense referring to all exchange resources – generally have both instrumental and expressive components in varying degrees. While the value of a material resource is relatively easy to estimate, non-material, expressive resources are difficult to evaluate. If a doctor introduced to you by your friend cures a difficult illness your wife has had, the value of your friend's service in incalculable. A return favour of a 'comparable value' could range over a wide spectrum. There is no list anywhere of 'appropriate returns' of this sort of favour, in the way there are lists of appropriate 'return incense gift' (*koden gaeshi*). Only a long immersion in the culture and extended residence in the community would give one the needed intuition to know what is an appropriate return.

When a 'gift' is not reciprocated, or not reciprocated with resources of appropriate value, or resources of appropriate kind, a conflict would arise, the seriousness of which would depend on a number of factors, among which the degree of discrepancy between the actual and the expected and the extent to which the giver is or is not magnanimous are important. Whichever it is, resolution of the conflict would require an apology, perhaps through an intermediary, if it is serious and if the relationship between the two is slight. And the act of apology would – of course – have to be accompanied by a handsome gift.

An alternative to the restoration of the relationship through apology is to reduce the depth of the relationship or to terminate it altogether. The giver who suffered a loss may not extend favours any more to the same extent. In an extreme case, the giver may decide not to have anything to do with the 'debt forgetter' (*on shirazu*).

Conflict Model

In considering various models of Japanese society in which to examine the phenomenon of conflict, introducing a 'conflict model' seems somewhat strange. One reason for referring to 'conflict model' is that Krauss, Rohlen and Steinhoff (1984) and Mouer and Sugimoto (1986) have introduced the term in reference to conflict in Japan. These authors seem to suggest by this term the specific ways in which conflict manifests itself in Japan as opposed to in other societies.

Before reviewing these culture-specific patterns of conflict in Japan, we should note the extent to which conflict is widespread in Japan, so that we can appreciate the need for understanding the processes whereby conflict arises and is resolved or managed. An understanding of the extent of conflict in Japan would also point to the inadequacy of the consensus model.

As in most other countries, history in Japan is replete with wars and political intrigues. We do not need to chronicle the political history of Japan here. Suffice it to note the prevalence of military and political conflict throughout Japanese history; similarly for peasant uprisings, especially in the latter half of the Tokugawa period, when the political regime was experiencing financial crisis. With rising and severe taxes – which were often not reduced even in time of drought and crop failure, bringing about widespread famine – peasants often had to manage under the cruelty of exploitative landlords and *daimyos*. Peasant uprisings under the circumstance are a perfectly understandable outcome.

More recently, since the Meiji, we have seen rice-riots after World World I (with the attendant massacre of the outcast *burakumin*), the atrocities against Koreans in the aftermath of the Tokyo earthquake, massive exploitation of industrial workers, especially young women, legalized prostitution into which women were sold for a pittance, crackdown of the secret police and the military against liberals during World War II, labour disputes after World War II which culminated in the aborted general strike, the nation-wide student movement in 1960 against the security treaty with the United States in the late 1960s and again in the early 1970s, and citizens' and environmental movements in the 1970s. Each of these topics is a subject of voluminous studies. This 'laundry list', I hope, is sufficient to impress the reader that Japan is not in reality a harmonious society, even though harmony may be its motto, and that an understanding of the nature of conflict in Japan is urgently needed.

According to Krauss, Rohlen and Steinhoff, conflict results from incompatible goals and interests and inequal power, status and reward. In Japan, management of conflict takes on a special form, where informal and personal methods of resolution are sought either in a small group format or through a go-between. In the West, according to them, conflict management involves law, contract, arbitration, or unilateral decision by the highest authority. While this holds as a generalization, one immediately notes that Japanese society also has formal, institutionalized means of conflict management, such as law and courts, and that in the West, too, informal means of conflict resolution are often utilized. Thus, the difference at this level is a matter of degree, and not a qualitative one. Indeed, use of the courts in Japan is increasing in areas of conflict where they were seldom used in the past. Marital conflict and inheritance disputes are two areas of the family institution where the courts are more and more called up to resolve problems. Arbitration, too, is a common means of conflict resolution in contemporary Japan, particularly in labour disputes. Is this a case of 'convergence'? Is Japan becoming more and more like 'any other modern society'? A limited convergence has to be admitted, obviously. However, whether the present level of convergence will lead to full convergence, whether all modern societies would share similarities in their institutional arrangements, whether, in short, the past trend is an accurate indication of the future direction, no one can say.

The question, however, is to be answered in part in terms of levels of abstraction. At a higher level of abstraction, one can observe, for example, the operation of a court system in Japan. When glossed thus, Japan and the United States share this institution, and the fact becomes evidence for convergence. However, taking a closer look at another level, one finds that the Japanese court system is very different from that in the United States, and is influenced by Japan's historical heritage and its value system. At this level, then, convergence is not a reality. Japan's cultural heritage is very much alive, making modern Japan a different case from the West.

Turning now to Mouer and Sugimoto, after enumerating various types of conflict in Japan from its historical past to the present, they list three elements of conflict in Japan (Mouer and Sugimoto, 1986, p. 68):

1 'Many incidents represent the long culmination of tensions and that open conflict seldom resolved the issues involved.'
2 'Many of the conflicts revealed a very clear sense of self-interest on the part of those initiating the protest. . . .'
3 'Most conflicts were brought to a head by the use of power. Solutions through consultative mechanisms are few, although third parties often became involved in mediation. Authorities tend to use power to resolve the conflict.'

The first two seem rather obvious, or at least not at all surprising. The third element, on the other hand, is somewhat surprising in the light of much discussion in the volume on conflict in Japan edited by Krauss, Rohlen and Steinhoff. No doubt, conflict has often been 'resolved' through brute force. This was particularly true in the pre-1945 period. In the post-war period, too, witness the way the special tactical squad dealt with demonstrating students in the late 1960s and early 1970s, or the ways in which the grounds of the Narita airport were cleared of protestors. Without denying these highly charged cases, which tend to attract the attention of the public, it is important to be aware that the vast majority of conflict – whether domestic or public, whether criminal or civil – are so mundane that they go unnoticed by all except the few who are immediately involved.

Some conflict situations are so chronic one may speak of 'routinization of conflict', possible in Japan, I might add, only when the severity of conflict is relatively mild. (In the United States, however, one sees routinization of violence in the New York subway.) One example is the opposition between the ruling Liberal Democratic Party and opposition parties in the Diet, where they engage in shouting matches, bad-mouthing each other when an opposite number is making a speech. The 'spring offensive' may also be regarded as a case of routinization of conflict, in which labour interests gather their forces in an effort to make demands of better labour conditions on management.

Conclusion

This chapter has presented four models of Japanese society. This is not to imply that there are four and only four models to characterize Japanese society. In fact, there could be any number of models. Among the models I did not present, but which are quite relevant for Japan, is one which is based on symbolic interactionism. This model has a great potential in Japan, especially as developed by Irving Goffmann in a series of publications (1961, 1963, 1964, 1971, 1974). Though Goffman's works are translated into Japanese and are well known there, no one has seriously tried to apply the approach of symbolic interactionism to interpersonal relations in Japan. When this is done, we would be able to conceptualize theoretically face-to-face conflict and how it is managed in Japan. As impression management is an art, so is conflict management. Goffman's vivid and powerful analysis of how an American manages stigma (1964) gives much thought to how a Japanese person, armed with the cultural concepts of *tatemae/honne* ('front or facade'/'inner intention') and *omote/ura* ('front'/'back'), might handle face-to-face conflict. While Lebra (1984) and Nyekawa (1984) both discuss how face-to-face conflict is handled in Japan, their analyses are embedded in the Japanese cultural context, and are not done in the general theoretical framework.

235

These models of Japanese society are not competing and contending, but are complementary. They each fit into different 'niches', and help explain different phenomena. As such, a catholic attitude toward various models is the most profitable approach, rather than to insist on one and only one model at the exclusion of all others. Neither Marx nor Freud, powerful though their theories are, can account for every observable phenomenon in this world. Insistence on one approach at the expense of all others may seem parsimonious; but its consequence is simply disastrous. It results in leaving most of the world unexplained. This is the problem with the all-pervasive group model of Japanese society. It is not entirely false. But it leaves so much unaccounted for. In an attempt to account for the unaccountable, the group model theorists stretch the application of the model beyond justification, for example, in invoking groupism for events which can best be characterized in terms of social exchange, as suggested above. Among the phenomena which the group model has difficulty explaining is conflict, for conflict smacks of disharmony, absence of consensus. Thus, this is an area where other models can be more useful than the group model.

In sum, this has been an exercise in model-building and in the application of models to conflict. What we learn from this exercise is that the appropriateness of a particular model depends on the issue at hand. Any attempt to exclude models other than one's favourite is likely to bring about conflict.

Notes

1 Research for the paper on which this chapter is based was supported by the National Endowment for the Humanities, a Fulbright Fellowship, and Stanford University.

References

Abegglen, J.C. (1973), *Management and Worker: The Japanese Solution*. Tokyo, Kodansha International.

Befu, H. (1967), 'Gift-giving and social reciprocity in Japan: an exploratory statement', *France-Asie/Asia*, 188, p. 161–77.

Befu, H. (1968), 'Gift-giving in a modernizing Japan', *Monumenta Nipponica*, 23(3/4), pp. 445–56.

Befu, H. (1974), 'Bribery in Japan: when law tangles with culture' in E. Lenz and R. Riley (eds.), *The Self and the System*. UCLA, Western Humanities Center, pp. 87–93.

Befu, H. (1976), 'Shako' in *Koza Hikaku Bunka*. Kenkyusha, vol. 4, pp. 271–305.

Befu, H. (1980a), 'The group model of Japanese society and an alternative', *Rice University Studies*, 66(1), pp. 169–87.

Befu, H. (1980b), 'A critique of the group model of Japanese society', *Social Analysis*, 5/6, pp. 29–43.

Befu, H. (1983), 'Japan's internationalization and Nihon bunkaron' in H. Mannari and H. Befu (eds.), *The Challenge of Japan's Internationalization: Organization and Culture*. Tokyo, Kodansha International, pp. 232–66.

Befu, H. (1984a), 'Bunka-teki gainen toshiteno "zoto" no kosatsu' in M. Ito and Y. Kurita (eds.), *Nihonjin no Zoto*. Tokyo, Minerva Shobo, pp. 18–44.

Befu, H. (1984b), 'Civilization and culture: Japan in search of identity', *Senri Ethnological Studies*, 16, pp. 59–76.

Campbell, J.C. (1984), 'Policy conflict and its resolution within the government system' in E. Krauss, T.P. Rohlen and P. Steinhoff (eds.), *Conflict in Japan*. Honolulu, University of Hawaii Press, pp. 294–334.

Clark, R. (1979), *The Japanese Company*. New Haven, Yale University Press.

Doi, T. (1973), *Anatomy of Dependence*. Berkeley, University of California Press.

Gouldner, A.W. (1960), 'The norm of reciprocity', *American Sociological Review*, 25, pp. 161–78.

Gendai Shakaigaku (1980), Nihon shakairon, 7(1), pp. 1–87.

Gibney, F. (1982), *Miracle by Design*. New York, Time Books.

Goffman, I. (1961), *Encounters*. New York, Bobbs-Merrill.

Goffman, I. (1964), *Stigma*. Englewood Cliffs, Prentice-Hall.

Goffman, I. (1971), *Relations in Public*. New York, Harper.

Goffman, I. (1974), *Frame Analysis*. Cambridge, Mass., Harvard University Press.

Hazama, H. (1971), *Nihon-Teki Keiei*. Tokyo, Nihon Keizai Shinbunsha.

Iwata, R. (1977), *Nihonteki Keiei no Hensei Genri*. Tokyo, Bunshindo.

Kawamura, N. (1982), *Nihon Bunkaron no Shuhen*. Tokyo, Ningen no Kagakusha.

Kawanishi, H. (1977), *Shosuha Rodo Kumiai Undoron*. Tokyo, Kaien Shobo.

Krauss, E.S., T.P. Rohlen and P.G. Steinhoff (1984), 'Conflict and its resolution in post-war Japan' in *idem* (eds.), *Conflict in Japan*. Honolulu, University of Hawaii Press, pp. 377–97.

Lebra, T.S. (1984), 'Nonconfrontational strategies for management of interpersonal conflicts' in E.S. Krauss, T.P. Rohlen and P.G. Steinhoff (eds.), *Conflict in Japan*. Honolulu, University of Hawaii Press, pp. 41–60.

Lee, S.M. and C. Schwendiman (1982a), *idem* (eds.), *Japanese Management: Cultural and Environmental Considerations*. New York, Praeger.

Lee, S.M. and J. Schwendiman (1982b), *idem* (eds.), *Management by Japanese Systems*. New York, Praeger.

Lee, S. and C. Schwendiman (1982c), *The Modern Samurai Society: Duty and Dependence in Contemporary Japan*. American Management Associations.

Mitchell, D.D. (1976), *Amaeru: The Expression of Reciprocal Dependency Needs in Japanese Politics and Laws*. Boulder, Colo., Westview Press.

Mouer, R.E. and Y. Sugimoto (1986), *Images of Japanese Society: A Study in the Social Construction of Reality*. London, Kegan Paul International.

Nakane, C. (1970), *Japanese Society*. Berkeley, University of California Press.

Nishida, K. (1982), *Nihon Shakai to Nihon-teki Keiei*. Tokyo, Bunshindo.

Niyekawa, A.M. (1984), 'Analysis of conflict in a television home drama' in E. Krauss, T.P. Rohlen and P.G. Steinhoff (eds.), *Conflict in Japan*. Honolulu, University of Hawaii Press, pp. 61–84.

Plath, D.W. (1964), 'Where the family of god is the family', *American Anthropologist*, 66(2), pp. 300–17.

Shukan Toyo Keizai (1981), 'Nihon Tokushuseiron no Kento', Summer, 57.

Smith, R.J. (1974), *Ancester Worship in Contemporary Japan*. Stanford, Stanford University Press.

Tsuda, M. (1977), *Nihon-teki Keiei no Ronri*. Tokyo, Chuo Keizaisha.

Wagatsuma, H. and G.A. DeVos (1984), *Heritage of Endurance*. Berkeley, University of California Press.